Unruly Practices

Unruly Practices:
Power, Discourse, and Gender in Contemporary Social Theory

Nancy Fraser

University of Minnesota Press, Minneapolis

Published by the University of Minnesota Press
2037 University Avenue Southeast, Minneapolis MN 55414.
Printed in the United States of America on acid-free paper
Second printing, 1991

Chapter 2 appeared in *Ethics,* vol. 96, no. 1 (October 1985), © The
University of Chicago Press. Reprinted with permission.

An earlier version of Chapter 8 appeared as ''Talking about Needs:
Interpretive Contests and Political Conflicts in Welfare-State Societies''
in *Ethics,* vol. 99, no. 2 (January 1989), © The University of Chicago
Press. Portions of that version are reprinted here with permission.

The remaining chapters were originally published as follows:
Chap. 1 *Praxis International,* vol. 1, no. 3 (October 1981) 272–87;
Chap. 3 *Salmagundi,* no. 61 (Fall 1983) 55–70;
Chap. 4 *New German Critique,* no. 33 (Fall 1984) 127–54;
Chap. 5: *Praxis International,* vol. 8, no. 3 (October 1988) 257–72;
Chap. 6: *New German Critique,* no. 35 (Spring/Summer 1985) 97–131;
Chap. 7: *Hypatia: A Journal of Feminist Philosophy,* vol. 2, no. 1
(Winter 1987) 103–21.

Library of Congress Cataloging-in-Publication Data

Fraser, Nancy.
    Unruly practices : power, discourse, and gender in contemporary
social theory / Nancy Fraser.
       p.   cm.
    Includes index.
    ISBN 0-8166-1777-5
    ISBN 0-8166-1778-3 (pbk.)
    1. Sociology—Philosophy.   2. Radicalism.   3. Feminism.
I. Title.
HM24.F732   1989
301'.01—dc20   89-32093
                                                             CIP

The University of Minnesota
is an equal-opportunity
educator and employer.

Contents

Acknowledgments

I feel very fortunate to have enjoyed many forms and sources of support during the long and often difficult process of working on this book. It is a pleasure to acknowledge them here.

I received generous financial support from four institutions. The University of Georgia Research Foundation funded a research trip to France in 1982; without this support, I could not have written Chapter 4 of this book. The Stanford Humanities Center provided a Mellon Fellowship in 1984–85, giving me the great gift of a year away from the ordinary cares of academic life. I am grateful to Ian Watt and to Mort Sosna for creating a congenial and stimulating environment in which my interdisciplinary interests flourished. The Mary Ingraham Bunting Institute of Radcliffe College awarded me a Bunting Fellowship in 1987–88, another precious gift of time and space in which to think and write. I am especially pleased to thank Ann Bookman and Elizabeth McKinsey for their work in sustaining this unique institution, a research and study center for women. Finally, Northwestern University gave me supplementary financial support during both fellowship years, a quarter of paid leave in 1983, and the occasional odd course reduction when the going got tough. I am grateful to former Dean of Arts and Sciences Rudolph Weingartner and to Associate Dean Robert Sekuler for these much appreciated forms of support.

At each of these institutions, I relied on the professional skills and personal warmth of secretarial staff. It is a pleasure to thank Lucile Epperson, Dee Marquez, Marina Rosiene, and Audrey Thiel for their help in giving material embodiment to wispy thoughts.

In addition to formal institutions, I have also relied on the support of informal networks and communities. I enjoyed many hours of fruitful and stimulating discussion at meetings of the Society for Women in Philosophy (especially midwestern SWIP), the Radical Philosophy Association, and the social theory group of the Center for Psychosocial Studies. I learned much also from women's studies discussion groups at Northwestern University.

It is more difficult to identify the many individual colleagues whose general interest, stimulating conversation and concrete suggestions have played such a large part in the making of this book. I have tried where possible to acknowledge specific intellectual debts in the footnotes to each chapter. Some people, however, deserve special mention here.

Sandra Bartky, Jerry Graff, Tom McCarthy, Linda Nicholson, and Judy Wittner have been my intellectual companions, as well as my good friends, for many years. I have relied here, as elsewhere, on their willingness to indulge my heterodox inclinations and on their good sense in restraining my wilder flights of fancy.

I owe a debt of gratitude of another kind to colleagues whose long-term encouragement and interest in my work have been sustaining and inspiring. Here, I would like to thank Jonathan Arac, Seyla Benhabib, Hubert L. Dreyfus, Jürgen Habermas, David Hoy, Alison Jaggar, Martin Jay, Richard Rorty, Terry Winant, and Iris Young.

To other friends and colleagues I owe thanks for a kind of support that defies the distinction between the intellectual and the personal. Here, I must single out Barbara Brenzel, Arlene Kaplan Daniels, Jean E. Friedman, Maria Herrera, Paul Mattick, Susan Reverby, Robert Roth, Antonia Soulez, Sue Weinberg, and Karl Werckmeister. And I must add a special word of thanks for the privilege of having known my dear and deeply missed friend Barbara Rosenblum.

Next, I want to express my gratitude to Terry Cochran of the University of Minnesota Press. He had the vision to believe there was a book where I could scarcely imagine one. I am also grateful for the superb copyediting of Mary Caraway. And I very much appreciate the support and patience of John Thompson of Polity Press.

Finally, I wish to thank my parents, Ed and Freida Shapiro, to whom this book is dedicated. Over the years, they have unfailingly found room in their home and their hearts for a sometimes wayward and often difficult daughter. It is to them that I owe whatever political passion and intellectual seriousness I have managed to infuse into this book.

Unruly Practices

Introduction
Apologia for Academic Radicals

It is fashionable nowadays to decry efforts to combine activism and academia. Neoconservatives tell us that to practice critique while employed by an educational institution is a betrayal of professional standards. Conversely, some independent left-wing intellectuals insist that to join the professoriat is to betray the imperative of critique. Finally, many activists outside the academy doubt the commitment and reliability of academics who claim to be their allies and comrades in struggle.

No one who has tried to be a politically critical academic in the United States can simply dismiss such complaints without residue. The distortions of bad faith notwithstanding, each of these charges points to a strand in the knot of genuine tensions and contradictions that are endemic to our situation. Radicals in academia *do* find themselves subject to competing pressures and counterpressures. We *do* internalize several distinct and mutually incompatible sets of expectations. And we *do* experience identity conflicts as we try simultaneously to wear several different hats. However, we should not rush to join in the chorus of left-wing professor bashing. The real contradictions of our lives notwithstanding, the radical academic is not an oxymoron.

The essays collected here were *not* written with the specific intention of prov-

I thank Seyla Benhabib, Barbara Brenzel, Paul Mattick, Tom McCarthy, Susan Reverby, Robert Roth, and Judy Wittner for helpful comments and suggestions. I gratefully acknowledge the generous fellowship support of The Mary Ingraham Bunting Institute, Radcliffe College.

ing that thesis. They were, rather, occasional interventions in various political-and social-theoretical debates of the 1980s. Nevertheless, it seems to me now that this collection can credibly be read as a contribution to ongoing arguments about the social role and political function of intellectuals. It is also the record of one socialist-feminist's and former New Left activist's struggle to *be* a politically committed, critical intellectual within the academy.

In one essay, I cite Marx's definition of critique as "the self-clarification of the struggles and wishes of the age." This definition can stand as an epigraph for the entire volume. It intertwines three ideas about the relationship between critical theory and political practice: first, it valorizes historically specific, conjunctural struggles as the agenda setters for critical theory; second, it posits social movements as the subjects of critique; and third, it implies that it is in the crucible of political practice that critical theories meet the ultimate test of viability.

Something like this nexus of ideas provides the existential and political underpinnings of this volume. At the same time, the political and intellectual history of a generation lends it a distinctive physiognomy. The struggles and wishes of *our* age have found expression in movements for social justice ranging from civil rights, welfare rights, and anti-imperialism, to environmentalism, feminism, and gay and lesbian liberation. Moreover, as the radical impulses informing these movements have been simultaneously disseminated and attenuated, numerous veterans and well-wishers of such struggles have found their way into the academy. These scholars are working to recover and to extend the intellectual heritages of American radicalism, brutally severed and suppressed by McCarthyism. As a result, even despite the decline of mass activity and the rise of an unfavorable broader *Zeitgeist,* we are seeing the emergence of a vital academic left counterculture. One consequence is a veritable explosion of new theoretical paradigms for political and cultural critique, paradigms ranging from variants of Western Marxism, Foucauldian new historicism, and the theory of participatory democracy, to deconstruction, postmodernism, and the many varieties of feminist theory.

The essays in this book grew out of this specific generational history. Accordingly, they are bifocal in nature, responding simultaneously to political conditions and to intellectual developments. Whatever the subject under discussion, I have always kept one eye on theoretical debates and the other on actual or possible political practices. In other words, I have tried to keep simultaneously in view the distinct standpoints of the theorist and of the political agent, not to reduce one to the other. For example, as a partisan of, and participant in, the feminist movement, I have insisted on holding new theoretical paradigms accountable to the demands of political practice; at the same time, as a critical social theorist, I have tried to assess the viability of alternative forms of practice in light of the results of theoretical reflection.

This double aim is reflected in the character and style of my writing. These essays are abstract and theoretical, yet they evince an accent of urgency that bespeaks engagement. On the one hand, I write as a social theorist trained as a philosopher and influenced by recent developments in literary theory, feminist theory, and cultural studies. On the other hand, I write as a democratic socialist and a feminist. In general, I have tried to perform the difficult but not impossible trick of straddling the ground between a scholarly profession and a social movement. Consequently, even the most unabashedly theoretical pieces are responses to problems generated in, and solvable only through, political practice; and even the most ostensibly impersonal essays grew out of existential dilemmas and personal/political conflicts.

The first three chapters—the essays on Foucault—are a case in point. What attracted me to Foucault was his focus on "power/knowledge." This was a compelling subject for a newly certified Ph.D. with a political past who was struggling to establish herself as a "professional philosopher." Indeed, I read in Foucault a theoretical reflection of my own divided consciousness: on the one hand, I observed a new kind of institutional critique of academic business as usual; on the other, I discerned a voice and a stance that exemplified an alternative intellectual practice. This was an irresistible combination for someone who had once protested the war research of the "New Mandarins" and tried to lure workers to study groups on Marxist political economy but who was now having to grade students and to publish or perish.

It was the great works of Foucault's middle period that I found most compelling. Here was an approach to "the politics of truth" that simultaneously contributed to and extended more familiar theoretical and political paradigms. *Discipline and Punish,* for example, proposed new ways to understand what the Marxist tradition cast as "the formation of the professional-managerial class," "the increasing social division of manual and intellectual labor," and "the spread of Taylorism." By tracking these processes beyond the boundaries of the official economy,[1] Foucault also recast what Weberians and Critical Theorists have understood as "societal rationalization" and "bureaucratization."

Many of Foucault's great themes recur throughout the essays in this volume. I return again and again to the problem of the politics of knowledge, especially to the relation of intellectuals and of expertise to social movements and to the state. Indeed, it is a focus on the problem of expertise in relation to the institutionalization of "social services" that links the papers on Foucault in Part 1 of this book with those on "the politics of need interpretation" in Part 3.

However, even as I have taken up Foucault's thematic focus, I have been puzzled by his self-positioning. What, the activist in me has repeatedly wondered, were the sources of his engagement? What was his practical intent, his political commitment? On the one hand, his account of the "capillary" character of modern power seems to multiply possible sites of political struggle and to valorize the proliferation of new social movements; it thereby gives theoretical support to New Left critiques of economism and to an expanded sense of what counts as "political." On the other hand, it is harder to know what to make of Foucault's extreme reticence on normative and programmatic matters, his reluctance to consider how all these various struggles might be coordinated and what sort of change they might accomplish, and his much-discussed archaeological "coldness."

Puzzled by these and related lacunae in Foucault's work, I have tried in the three essays that make up Part 1 to dope out the normative political orientation of his writings. I have looked for standards of critique, for the sketch of an alternative, for a rhetoric of resistance that could promote the struggles and wishes of contemporary social movements. In short, I have tried to understand and to evaluate Foucault's analysis of "disciplinary power/knowledge" from the standpoint of the exigencies of political practice.

A related set of preoccupations informs the essays constituting Part 2 of this volume. Here the focus shifts from the "specific intellectual" to the "universal intellectual," from the social scientist to the philosopher and the all-purpose critic of culture. Consequently, the problem of "power/knowledge" shifts to the construction and deconstruction of elite traditions; and the politics of knowledge takes the form of struggles over where to draw the line between "the philosophical" and "the political," "politics" and "culture," "the public" and "the private."

In Chapter 4, "The French Derrideans," I cast a political-theoretical eye on the phenomenon of deconstruction. The context for this essay was the flowering in the United States of this astonishingly energetic new movement of literary criticism. Given my political history, I was fascinated by the figure of the intellectual as deconstructor, an academic virtuoso whose rhetoric was leftist but whose practice verged on esoteric formalism. And, once again, I was puzzled by the sources of contemporary critical vitality. Why did deconstructionists see critiques of the metaphysics of presence as *political* acts? Why did they think that to undo binary oppositions in high culture literary texts was to contribute to social transformation? How did they square their insistence on the unity of the "closure of the West" with their opposition to historically specific inequalities and oppressions?

On leave in Paris, I sought answers in the more explicitly and self-consciously political writings of a group of French deconstructionist philosophers. I was surprised to learn that for them the critical intellectual bore a striking resemblance to the transcendental philosopher. On the one hand, they privileged the archaeologist of the conditions for the possibility of "the political" over the participant in political struggles. On the other hand, they hoped to extract an ethos of political engagement directly from their philosophy without having to make a "detour" through empirical sociology or normative political theory. In general, they wanted "the political" without "politics," and so they spared themselves the effort of trying to connect their theoretical reflections with the struggles and wishes of the age.

"The French Derrideans" bares some of the dilemmas inherent in this "pure" deconstructionist *Weltanschauung*. It does not, however, tell against more limited and selective uses of deconstruction as a technique of *Ideologie-kritik* for political ends such as feminism. Nevertheless, the essay seems to me to have acquired some timely new resonances in the wake of revelations about the political pasts of Martin Heidegger and Paul de Man. The problem of "the po-litical" and "the philosophical" is central to controversies surrounding these writers; and in *their* postwar writings, too, one finds an attitude of disdain for the "merely ontic" character of politics, history, and society. But of course the dif-ference is that in Heidegger and de Man this attitude has subterranean roots in unmastered histories of fascist involvement.

One response to the tortured relations of some European intellectuals with politics is to celebrate the down-to-earth, reformist ethos of American pragma-tism. This is the tack taken by Richard Rorty, the subject of Chapter 5, "Soli-darity or Singularity?" Rorty figures here as a major influence on my intellectual development, since it was his brilliant immanent critique of the analytic tradition, in *Philosophy and the Mirror of Nature,* that created a space in American phi-losophy in which former New Leftists could "go continental."

As my essay makes clear, my response to Rorty's later work is deeply divided. On the one hand, my own holism, historicism, and antiessentialism find a con-genial echo in his pragmatism. One could hardly ask for a more elegantly artic-ulated distrust of the universalist pretensions of traditional philosophy—nor for a more thoroughgoing insistence on the priority of practice, on the contingent, his-torically conditioned character of subjectivities and rationalities, and on the de-cisive importance of vocabulary choice for the framing of political issues. This certainly looks like an approach that is "user-friendly," open to the potentially transformative voices and aspirations of subordinated social groups. On the other hand, I am considerably less impressed by Rorty's political views: the knee-jerk anti-Marxist one-liners, the smug celebratory references to the glories of "the rich North Atlantic bourgeois democracies," and the cozy assurances that radical metaphilosophical critique does not threaten politics as usual. I am profoundly out of sympathy with the voice that professes loyalty to "postmodernist bour-geois liberalism," and I am not won over when it repackages itself as "social democracy."

Entertaining such a divided response, I could not help but wonder: What is the relation between Rorty's philosophy and his politics? How can such critical metaphilosophical views sit so comfortably with such complacent political atti-tudes? Is there some deep connection between pragmatism and "bourgeois liberalism"? Or is their conjunction in Rorty merely fortuitous? Can a democratic-socialist-feminist accept Rorty's metaphilosophy while rejecting his politics? Or, in embracing the one, will she be led ineluctably to the other?

In "Solidarity or Singularity?" I try to settle accounts with Richard Rorty. I take a close, hard look at his dichotomization of "public" and "private" intellectuals. I argue against a division of cultural labor that allows for the atheoretical practice of liberal social workers and engineers, on the one hand, and for the apolitical theory of radical ironists and aesthetes, on the other hand, but that has no place for the radical political theory of critical intellectuals with ties to oppositional movements. My aim in this essay is to rescue the possibility of another pragmatism—a democratic-socialist-feminist pragmatism—with another understanding of the relation between theory and practice.

Several recurrent themes run through the essays I have just been discussing. One is an insistence that you can't get a politics straight out of epistemology, even when the epistemology is a radical antiepistemology like historicism, pragmatism, or deconstruction. On the contrary, I argue repeatedly that politics requires a genre of critical theorizing that blends normative argument and empirical sociocultural analysis in a "diagnosis of the times." In this, I am affirming a fairly classical left view found in Marx and in Frankfurt school Critical Theory. At the same time, I am opposing a tendency in some sections of the academic Left to engage in what can only appear as esoteric forms of discourse unless and until connections to practice are elaborated, indeed mediated, through sociopolitical analysis.

However, this is not to endorse a traditional, narrow definition of "the political." A second and closely related recurrent theme in these essays is precisely the broadening of that designation to encompass issues classically viewed as "cultural, " "private," "economic," "domestic," and "personal." Interestingly, this question about the limits of the political is precisely a *political* question. In addition, it furnishes an excellent example of the process by which practical exigencies give rise to theoretical problems. This issue was put on the critical-theoretical agenda by New Left, feminist, and gay and lesbian liberation movements fighting to legitimate heretofore marginalized struggles over things like sexuality, medicine, education, and housework. In this respect, these movements have followed in the tradition of working-class and socialist movements, which fought to make "economic" issues "political."

My own approach in this volume is to defend the broader conception of politics. On the other hand, I have also wanted to specify more directly than many left academics the ways in which cultural critique is political. I have elaborated a quasi-Gramscian view, in which struggles over cultural meanings and social identities are struggles for cultural hegemony, that is, for the power to construct authoritative definitions of social situations and legitimate interpretations of social needs. *Pace* some left critics of the academic Left, such struggles can and do occur in universities as well as in extra-academic public spheres. In both cases, their political bite comes from their links, however mediated, to the oppositional movements whose needs and identities—indeed, whose struggles and wishes— are at stake.

This question of links between left academics and social movements is another major theme of this volume. It emerges most concretely and explicitly in the essays in Part 3. There, I put my own involvement as a feminist at the center, and I write from amid the struggles and wishes currently swirling about gender. In my case these struggles and wishes have roots in painful experiences of sexism in the New Left, in the academy, in fact in all spheres of cultural and social life. But they are also informed by countervailing, empowering experiences—of consciousness-raising, sisterhood, and participation in the creation of feminist theory. Because they are enlivened by a personal stake, the essays in this section bear a special intensity. They represent the coming together of a radical academic's individual needs with the historical needs of a political movement. Thus, these essays are exercises in *situated* theorizing. In addition, they are *interventions*. They function to dispel the myth that all critical intellectuals are similarly placed with respect to the levers of social power, on the one hand, and to the movements that oppose them, on the other.

Chapter 6, "What's Critical about Critical Theory?" is a case in point. Here, I cast a feminist eye on the social theory of Jürgen Habermas. This theory attracted my notice for two reasons. First, Habermas is the heir to the tradition of Frankfurt school Critical Theory; his work, therefore, had a prima facie claim on the attention of a former New Leftist once directly touched by the thought of Herbert Marcuse. Second, Habermas's social theory is the most ambitious recent attempt to do for the capitalist societies of the late twentieth century what Marx's *Capital* tried to do for those of the late ninteenth. It aims to identify the structural dynamics, the crisis tendencies, and the forms of conflict characteristic of these societies. Moreover, the theory is elaborated with the "practical intent" of promoting emancipatory social transformation. It seeks to clarify the situation and prospects of social movements whose practice might contribute to such a transformation. Thus, critical intellectuals with ties to social movements have no choice but to engage it.

My essay assesses the empirical and political adequacy of Habermas's theory from the perspective of feminist theory and practice. Thus, I have taken *political* issues—as opposed to metatheoretical issues about, say, "totality" or "foundationalism"—as my point of departure.[2] Consequently, I have elected not to affect a stance of supposed archimedean neutrality but rather to speak out of a sociologically specific, explicitly gendered, and practically engaged situation. In so doing, I am taking seriously Habermas's professed "practical intent" of clarifying "the emancipatory potential" of contemporary struggles. Likewise, I am taking seriously his professed support for the cause of women's liberation. My general strategy is to hold him to his word by measuring the success of his theory in terms of its ability to contribute to "the self-clarification of the struggles and wishes" of contemporary women.

Sadly, the results are less than satisfactory. It turns out that Habermas's work, like that of many male leftists, remains relatively untouched by the enormous recent outpouring of creativity in feminist theory. As a result, his social theory reproduces androcentric bias at the level of its basic categorial framework. It pre-supposes rather than challenges dualistic, ideological ways of counterposing "family" and "economy," "private sphere" and "public sphere," "symbolic reproduction" and "material reproduction," "system" and "lifeworld." These dichotomies make it difficult to see, much less to analyze, some important dimensions of male dominance in late capitalist societies. For example, they occult forms of domestic gender oppression that are not only "normative" but also "systemic" and "economic." Likewise, the dichotomies occult forms of gender inequality in the official economy and the state that are not only "systemic" but also "symbolic" and "normative." One result is that Habermas's theory mis-construes some empirical features of late capitalist societies. Another is that, politically speaking, it fails to do justice to the struggles and wishes of contemporary women.

Yet even despite all these problems Habermas's social theory remains extremely important. Given the scope of its ambitions and its general political seriousness, it contains scores of positive and negative lessons for socialist-feminist critical theorists. One of these lessons is that apparent indifference to gender often masks implicit masculinist bias. Another is that ideology loves dichotomies. It follows that critical theorists need to problematize gender-associated binary oppositions lest their theories succumb to the disease they aim to diagnose.

The last two essays in this volume represent my attempts to put these and other lessons to work in the making of socialist-feminist critical theory. Here, I have tried to put my money where my mouth is—that is, to bring to bear in constructive social theorizing the fruits of my critical work on Foucault, deconstruction, Rorty, and Habermas. In general, I have sought to develop an approach that integrates the useful dimensions of each of these critical paradigms while avoiding their respective weaknesses.

The approach elaborated in these last two essays is intended as an alternative to "dual systems theory," which was a type of socialist-feminist theory, popular in the late 1970s and early 1980s, that posited the existence of two "systems" of oppression—namely, capitalism and patriarchy—and then tried to understand how they were related. Dual systems theory was one of the first feminist efforts to avoid "single variable" models by theorizing the intersection of gender with class (and, in some cases, with race). But despite this laudable aim, it soon reached an impasse: having begun by supposing the fundamental distinctness of capitalism and patriarchy, class and gender, it was never clear how to put them back together again.

Some socialist-feminists have responded to this impasse by proposing to re-place dual systems theory with "single system theory," a theory in which class and gender, capitalism and patriarchy would be internally integrated from the very beginning through analysis couched in a single set of categories.[3] Although this represents an improvement over dual systems theory, it is not the route I have taken. Like Foucault and Habermas, I have wanted to avoid objectivistic, func-tionalist models that purport to show how "systems reproduce themselves." These models screen out "dysfunctional" actions that resist, contest and disrupt dominant social practices. In addition, they neglect the self-interpretations of so-cial agents. More generally, functionalist approaches slight the entire active side of social processes, the ways in which even the most routinized practice of social agents involves the making and unmaking of social reality. Unfortunately, "single system theory" remains implicitly functionalist, and so for all these rea-sons I decided to eschew it. I have tried instead to devise an approach capable of representing human agency, social conflict and the construction and deconstruc-tion of cultural meanings.

Chapter 7, "Women, Welfare, and the Politics of Need Interpretation" repre-sents one effort in this direction. It follows Habermas in taking on the method-ological task of relating structural and interpretive approaches to the study of so-cial life. But it combines this with the feminist *political* task of disclosing the existence and character of some specifically late capitalist forms of male domi-nance. Sometimes (somewhat misleadingly) called "public patriarchy," these forms of male dominance arise in the wake of greater state regulation of the econ-omy. They are characteristically found, among other places, in social-welfare programs.

The essay analyzes the continuation and exacerbation of sexism "by other means" in the U.S. social-welfare system. It shows that this system is currently divided into two gender-linked subsystems: an implicitly "masculine" social in-surance subsystem tied to "primary" labor force participation and geared to (white male) "breadwinners"; and an implicitly "feminine" relief subsystem tied to household income and geared to homemaker-mothers and their "de-fective" (i.e., female-headed) families. Premised as they are on the (counter-factual) assumption of "separate spheres," the two subsystems differ markedly in the degree of autonomy, rights, and presumption of desert they accord bene-ficiaries, as well as in their funding base, mode of administration, and character and level of benefits. In other words, they are separate and unequal.

The account presented in this chapter is simultaneously structural and inter-pretive. It treats what are usually seen as "economic" phenomena as "institu-tionalized patterns of interpretation." The point is that social-welfare programs provide more than material aid: they also provide clients, and the public at large, with a tacit but powerful interpretive map of normative, differentially valued gender roles and gendered needs. Thus, my analysis shows how social-welfare practices encode sexist and androcentric interpretations of women's needs, interpretations erected on the basis of ideological, gender-linked dichotomies like "domestic" versus "economic," "home" versus "work," "mother" versus "breadwinner," "primary" versus "secondary" labor.

Although these sexist need interpretations are powerful and institutionally sanctioned, they do not go uncontested. In Chapter 8, the last essay in this collection, I broaden the focus of inquiry to take in the whole arena of conflict over needs in late capitalist societies. Here, interpretations embedded in the practices of the social state represent only one of several major kinds of discourses about needs. They intermingle, often polemically, with competing interpretations associated with oppositional social movements, social science experts, and neoconservatives, respectively. Likewise, state-based actors represent only one of several kinds of agents engaged in interpreting people's needs. They interact, often conflictually, with social-welfare clients, professional knowledge producers, movement activists, trade unionists, party politicians and others.

"Struggle over Needs" theorizes this "politics of need interpretation." It represents my most ambitious effort to date to develop a socialist-feminist critical theory. By analyzing contests among rival discourses about needs, I draw a map of late capitalist social structure and political culture. I link the politicization of needs to shifts in the boundaries separating "political," "economic," and "domestic" spheres of life. I also show how needs politics is implicated in the constitution of oppositional social identities, on the one hand, and in professional class formation, on the other. In addition, I identify three major kinds of "needs talk" in welfare state societies: "oppositional" discourses, "reprivatization" discourses, and "expert" discourses. Finally, in a series of examples I chart two countervailing social tendencies: one is the tendency for the politics of need interpretation to devolve into the administration of need satisfactions; the other is the countertendency that runs from administration to resistance and potentially back to politics.

In "Struggle over Needs," I have put discourse at the center for several reasons. First, by focusing on "the politics of interpretation," I have tried to provide an alternative to standard theories about needs that look only at the distribution of satisfactions. Second, by applying ideas from literary studies to the domain of social and political theory, I have tried to bridge the divide between culture and society, the humanities and the social sciences. Third, by insisting on a plurality of agents and discourses, I have tried to develop an alternative to currently fashionable discourse theories that suppose a single, monolithic "symbolic order."

I have assumed throughout that there are multiple axes of power in late capitalist societies. Thus, I have tried to allow both for crosscutting lines of stratification and for complex processes of group formation. Likewise, I have assumed there are a number of different "publics" in which groups and individuals act.

Thus, I have tried to avoid oversimplistic, dichotomous conceptions of public and private. Finally, I have advanced a general theoretical account of late capitalist political culture. Thus, I have tried to provide the sort of big diagnostic picture necessary to orient political practice while at the same time respecting historical specificity, societal differentiation, and cultural multiplicity. I have tried, in short, to develop a new type of socialist-feminist critical theory that overcomes the limitations of the currently available alternatives.

Above all else, "Struggle over Needs" aims to contribute to "the self-clarification of the struggles and wishes of the age." It identifies some problems progressive movements face in multi-sided struggles with needs "experts" in and around the social state. Here, I pay special attention to the institutional fabrication and operation of expertise. I examine needs discourses developed in universities, think tanks, professional associations, and social-service organizations. I analyze these as *bridge* discourses, which mediate the relations between social movements and the state. I show how expert discourses play this mediating role by translating the politicized needs claimed by oppositional movements into potential objects of state administration.

Thus, in this last essay, I provide yet another take on the problem of the social role and political function of intellectuals. And so I come full circle to the issues with which I began. What light does this discussion shed on the situation of academic radicals?

We, too, I think, occupy a mediating position. Accordingly, we, too, are in the business of building bridges. In relation to our academic disciplines, we function as the oppositional wing of an expert public. In relation to extra-academic social movements, on the other hand, we function as the expert wing of an oppositional public. In addition, many of us also relate to still other publics. As teachers, we try to foster an emergent pedagogical counterculture. As faculty advisers, we try to provide guidance and legitimacy to radical student groups on our campuses. Finally, as critical public intellectuals, we try to inject our perspectives into whatever cultural or political public spheres we have access to. The point is that we function in several distinct institutionalized publics. Necessarily, then, we speak in several voices. Insofar as we find ourselves talking both to experts and to activists, we are situated *between* movements and professions.

One way to think about this "between" is as a point where oppositional discourses and expert discourses intersect. One thing, then, that critical intellectuals do—apart from speaking to movements, on the one hand, and to experts, on the other hand—is to find ways to knit their disparate discourses together. In other words, we are engaged in creating bridge discourses and in opening new hybrid publics and arenas of struggle.

The essays I have been introducing here illustrate the varieties of this engagement. In some of them, I have written with my activist voice in the forefront. Here, I typically address an expert public as a quasi outsider, intruding a sensibility and an agenda that originate elsewhere. This is the case in "What's Critical about Critical Theory?" where I make a feminist foray into the masculine heartland of Critical Theory. Another example is "Solidarity or Singularity?" where I intrude a socialist-feminist perspective into debates about pragmatism and liberalism.

In other essays, my expert voice takes the lead. Here, I address theoretical reflections to an oppositional public already committed to my political cause. This is the case in "Women, Welfare, and the Politics of Need Interpretation": drawing on occupational skills acquired as a result of the social division of labor, I show how existing social-welfare programs perpetuate the subordination of women. And, in response, I propose a theoretically informed but practice-oriented way of thinking about social-welfare to feminist scholars and activists.

In contrast, still other essays in this collection are aimed neither at expert nor at activist audiences per se but, rather, at a more loosely defined public presumed to contain both experts and activists. This is the case in "Foucault's Body Language" and in "The French Derrideans," where I assume the general perspective of a left intellectual in order to examine new historicism and deconstruction, respectively, as cultural phenomena.

Finally, there are some hybrid cases, essays aimed simultaneously at several different audiences, in which my expert and activist voices get roughly equal billing. These essays are the most self-conscious exercises in bridge building in this collection. Here, I am knitting disparate discourses together in order to help create a new, larger, amalgamated public. This is the case in "Struggle over Needs," where I am trying to amalgamate several different scholarly publics — social and political theory, women's studies and feminist theory, literary theory and cultural studies — together with a broad oppositional public composed of participants in a wide range of social movements. In this essay, I am addressing different messages to different groups simultaneously. For example, I am encouraging literary scholars to study discourse in social-institutional context. In addition, I am prodding social and political theorists to integrate gender into their analytical frameworks. At the same time, I am proposing to feminist theorists a way of treating gender as one axis of inequality among others. Finally, I am suggesting that activists and participants in *all* oppositional social movements think through their relations to the state.

Of course, the creation of bridge discourses and hybrid publics is always a tricky affair. It is understandable that some radicals find that the risks outweigh the benefits. I realize that some feminists, for example, will question my willingness to speak to and about men in many of these essays. I do not wish to minimize the difficulties of this sort of practice. By definition, any bridge discourse is, at the least, a two-way street. Thus, it is always relevant to ask, What is getting lost or altered in the process? How is the movement's impact on the profession refracted through the profession's impact on the movement? What are the countervailing costs and benefits of trying to join them?

Still, I would insist that these are better treated as conjunctural, strategic questions than as matters of principle — and that, in principle, there is no alternative to bridge building. No single oppressed group can possibly win significant structural change on its own, nor can any be trusted to look out for the interests of the others. Moreover, social transformation requires struggle in the sense of engagement with one's opponents. In academic arenas this means challenging ideological distortions built into mainstream perspectives and, insofar as possible, compelling their adherents to respond. This is not an alternative to building counterinstitutions within the academy but, rather, an additional, concurrent, and vitally necessary task. It is one of the aims of the essays that follow.

Notes

1. For my use of the expression 'the official economy', see Chapter 6, n. 13.

2. In general, I am not persuaded that poststructuralist suspicions of "totality," certainly well-founded when it comes to ahistorical philosophical "metanarratives," tell against attempts to devise "big" empirical theories about historically specific social formations. Rather, I assume a big diagnostic picture is both epistemically possible and politically useful. Likewise, I do not believe that Habermas's first-order, substantive social theory is undermined by his attempts, unnecessary and unsuccessful, to ground it in "quasi-transcendental" metatheories of "social evolution" and "universal pragmatics." I assume instead that it is possible to disentangle the two levels of analysis and to evaluate them separately. In sum, I believe that if Habermas's social theory turns out to be untenable, this will be neither because it is big, nor because it has been saddled with an indefensible foundationalist metainterpretation, but rather because it is empirically and/or politically inadequate. For a discussion of the relation between "metanarrative" and "big empirical narrative," see Nancy Fraser and Linda Nicholson, "Social Criticism without Philosophy: An Encounter between Feminism and Postmodernism," *Theory, Culture, and Society* 5, nos. 2–3 (June 1988): 373–94.

3. For the debate over dual systems theory, see the essays in *Women and Revolution: A Discussion of the Unhappy Marriage of Marxism and Feminism,* ed. Lydia Sargent (Boston, 1981). For the proposal for a single system theory based on the concept of the gender division of labor, see the essay in that volume by Iris Young, "Beyond the Unhappy Marriage: A Critique of the Dual Systems Theory."

Part 1

Powers, Norms,
and Vocabularies of Contestation

Chapter 1
Foucault on Modern Power:
Empirical Insights and Normative Confusions

Until his untimely death in 1984, Michel Foucault had been theorizing about and practicing a new form of politically engaged reflection on the emergence and nature of modern societies. This reflection, which Foucault called "genealogy," has produced some extremely valuable results. It has opened up new areas of inquiry and problematized new dimensions of modernity; as a result, it has made it possible to broach political problems in fruitful new ways. But Foucault's work is also beset by difficulties. It raises a number of important philosophical questions that it is not, in itself, equipped to answer. This paper aims to survey the principal strengths and shortcomings of Foucault's work and to provide a balanced assessment of it.

Most generally, it is my thesis that Foucault's most valuable accomplishment consists of a rich empirical account of the early stages in the emergence of some distinctively modern modalities of power. This account yields important insights into the nature of modern power, and these insights, in turn, bear political sig-

---

This paper was originally written in 1980–81, before Michel Foucault's death. I cast it in the present and future tenses on the assumptions that my dialogue with him would be ongoing and that his thinking on the subjects discussed would continue to develop. Now that these assumptions no longer hold, I have had to reconsider the question of tense. I have proceeded as follows: in instances where the present or future tense seemed to me jarringly inappropriate, I have substituted the past tense; in instances where the present tense seemed to suggest, entirely rightly, the continuing relevance of Foucault's work, I have left it unchanged.

nificance—they suffice to rule out some rather widespread political orientations as inadequate to the complexities of power in modern societies.

For example, Foucault's account establishes that modern power is "productive" rather than prohibitive. This suffices to rule out those types of liberationist politics that presuppose that power is essentially repressive. Similarly, Foucault's account demonstrates that modern power is "capillary," that it operates at the lowest extremities of the social body in everyday social practices. This suffices to rule out state-centered and economistic political praxes, since these praxes presuppose that power resides solely in the state or economy. Finally, Foucault's genealogy of modern power establishes that power touches people's lives more fundamentally through their social practices than through their beliefs. This, in turn, suffices to rule out political orientations aimed primarily at the demystification of ideologically distorted belief systems.

This is not to suggest that the sole importance of Foucault's account of the nature and emergence of modern forms of power is the negative one of ruling out inadequate political orientations. More positively, it is that Foucault enables us to understand power very broadly, and yet very finely, as anchored in the multiplicity of what he calls "micropractices," the social practices that constitute everyday life in modern societies. This positive conception of power has the general but unmistakable implication of a call for a "politics of everyday life."

These, in general, are what I take to be Foucault's principal accomplishments and contributions to the understanding of modern societies. They were made possible, it seems, by Foucault's use of his unique genealogical method of social and historical description. This method involves, among other things, the suspension of the standard modern liberal normative framework, which distinguishes between the legitimate and illegitimate exercise of power. Foucault brackets those notions, and the questions they give rise to, and concentrates instead upon the actual ways in which power operates.

As I have said, Foucault's suspension of the problematic of legitimacy has unquestionably been fruitful. It is what enables him to look at the phenomenon of power in interesting new ways and, thereby, to bring to light important new dimensions of modern societies. But, at the same time, it has given, or is likely to give, rise to some grave difficulties. For example, it has been or may be supposed that Foucault has given us a value-neutral account of modern power. Or, alternatively, since this does not square with the obvious politically engaged character of his writing, that he has educed some other normative framework as an alternative to the suspended one; or, since none is readily apparent, that he has found a way to do politically engaged critique without the use of any normative framework; or, more generally, that he has disposed altogether of the need for any normative framework to guide political practice.

Clearly, a number of these suppositions are mutually incompatible. Yet Foucault's work seems simultaneously to invite all of them. He tends to assume that his account of modern power is both politically engaged and normatively neutral. At the same time, he is unclear as to whether he suspends all normative notions or only the liberal norms of legitimacy and illegitimacy. To make matters worse, Foucault sometimes appears not to have suspended the liberal norms after all but, rather, to be presupposing them.

These, then, are what I take to be the most serious difficulties in Foucault's work. They appear to stand in a rather curious relationship to the strengths I have mentioned; it seems that the very methodological strategies that make possible the empirically and politically valuable description of power are intimately tied to the normative ambiguities.

In what follows, I propose to explore these issues systematically. First, I shall outline Foucault's genealogical method, including his suspension of the liberal normative framework of legitimacy. Next, I shall give an account of Foucault's historical insights concerning the nature and origin of modern power that the genealogical method has made possible. After that, I shall briefly discuss the valuable political implications of the view of modern power that emerges. And, finally, in the fourth and last section of the paper, I shall discuss the difficulties pertaining to the normative dimensions of Foucault's work.

1. The Genealogical Method and the Bracketing of the Problematic of Legitimacy

Following Nietzsche, Foucault calls the form of his reflection on the nature and development of modern power "genealogy."[1] What he means by this can best be approximated negatively at first, in contrast to a number of other approaches to the study of cultural and historical phenomena. Genealogy represents a break, for example, with semiology and structuralism, which analyze culture in terms of systems of signs.[2] Instead, it seeks to conceive culture as practices. Furthermore, genealogy is not to be confused with hermeneutics, which Foucault understands (no doubt anachronistically) as the search for deep hidden meanings beneath language, for the signified behind the signifier. Genealogy takes it as axiomatic that everything is interpretation all the way down,[3] or, to put it less figuratively, that cultural practices are instituted historically and are therefore contingent, ungrounded except in terms of other, prior, contingent, historically instituted practices. Foucault also claims that genealogy is opposed to critique of ideology. Again, his understanding of that enterprise is somewhat crude; he means that genealogy does not concern itself with evaluating the contents of science or systems of knowledge — or, for that matter, with systems of beliefs at all. Rather, it is concerned with the processes, procedures, and apparatuses whereby truth, knowledge, belief are produced, with what Foucault calls the "politics of the discursive regime."[4] Moreover, Foucault contends that genealogy must be distinguished from history of ideas. It does not seek to chronicle the continuous development of discursive content or practices. On the contrary, it is oriented to discontinuities. Like Thomas Kuhn, Foucault assumes the existence of a plurality of incommensurable discursive regimes that succeed one another historically. He also assumes that each of these regimes is supported by its own correlated matrix of practices. Each includes its own distinctive objects of inquiry; its own criteria of well-formedness for statements admitted to candidacy for truth and falsity; its own procedures for generating, storing, and arranging data; its own institutional sanctions and matrices.[5]

It is the whole nexus of such objects, criteria, practices, procedures, institutions, apparatuses, and operations that Foucault means to designate by his term 'power/knowledge regime'. This term thus covers in a single concept everything that falls under the two distinct Kuhnian concepts of paradigm and disciplinary matrix. But, unlike Kuhn, Foucault gives this complex an explicitly political character. Both the use of the term 'power' and that of the term 'regime' convey this political coloration.

Foucault claims that the functioning of discursive regimes essentially involves forms of social constraint. Such constraints and the manner of their application vary, of course, along with the regime. Typically, however, they include such phenomena as the valorization of some statement forms and the concomitant devaluation of others; the institutional licensing of some persons as authorized to offer authoritative knowledge claims and the concomitant exclusion of others; procedures for the extraction of information from and about persons involving various forms of coercion; and the proliferation of discourses oriented to objects of inquiry that are, at the same time, targets for the application of social policy.[6] Their obvious heterogeneity notwithstanding, all of these are instances of the ways in which social constraint, or in Foucault's terms "power," circulates in and through the production of discourses in societies.

What Foucault is interested in when he claims to be studying the genealogy of power/knowledge regimes should now be clear: he concerns himself with the holistic and historically relative study of the formation and functioning of incommensurable networks of social practices involving the mutual interrelationship of constraint and discourse.

Foucauldian genealogy is obviously a unique and original approach to culture. It groups together phenomena that are usually kept separate and separates phenomena that are usually grouped together. It does this by adhering, or professing to adhere, to a number of methodological strategies that can be likened to bracketings.[7]

'Bracketing', of course, is not Foucault's term; given its association with the phenomenological tradition to which he is so hostile, he would doubtless reject it. Nevertheless, the term is suggestive of the sort of studied suspension of standard categories and problematics that he practices. It should already be apparent, for example, that Foucault's approach to the study of power/knowledge regimes suspends the categories truth/falsity or truth/ideology. It suspends, that is, the problematic of epistemic justification. Foucault simply does not take up the question of whether the various regimes he studies provide knowledge that is in any sense true or warranted or adequate or undistorted. Instead of assessing epistemic contents, he describes knowledge production procedures, practices, apparatuses and institutions.[8]

This bracketing of the problematic of epistemic justification is susceptible to a variety of construals. It can be seen as strictly heuristic and provisional and, therefore, as leaving open the questions whether such justification is possible and, if so, in what it consists. Alternatively, it can be seen less minimally as a substantive, principled commitment to some version of epistemological cultural relativism. The textual evidence is contradictory, although the preponderance surely lies with the second, substantive, construal.

Be that as it may, Foucault's views on epistemic justification are not my primary concern here. More to the point is another sort of bracketing, one that pertains to the problematic of *normative* justification. Foucault claims to suspend such justification in his study of power/knowledge regimes. He says he does not take up the question of whether or not the various constraint-laden practices, institutions, procedures, and apparatuses he studies are legitimate or not: he refrains from problematizing the normative validity of power/knowledge regimes.[9]

A number of very important questions arise concerning the nature and extent of Foucault's bracketing of the normative. What exactly is its intended scope? Does Foucault intend to suspend one particular normative framework only, namely, the framework of modern liberal political theory, whose central categories are those of right, limit, sovereignty, contract, and oppression? This framework distinguishes between, on the one hand, the legitimate exercise of sovereign power, which stays within the limits defined by rights, and, on the other, the illegitimate exercise of such power, which transgresses those limits, violates rights, and is thus oppressive.[10] When Foucault excludes the use of the concepts legitimacy and illegitimacy from genealogy, does he mean to exclude only these liberal norms? Or, alternatively, is Foucault's bracketing of the normative rather broader? Does he intend to suspend not only the liberal framework but every normative framework whatsoever? Does he mean he will bracket the problematic of normative justification *simpliciter*? In either case, how do Foucault's proclaimed intentions square with his actual practice of genealogy? Whatever he claims to be doing, does his work in fact suspend all political norms or only the liberal ones?

Furthermore, whatever the scope of bracketing, what is its character? Is Foucault's bracketing of the normative merely a methodological strategy, a temporary heuristic aimed at making it possible to see the phenomena in fresh new ways? If so, then it would leave open the possibility of some subsequent normative assessment of power/knowledge regimes. Or, alternatively, does Foucault's bracketing of the normative represent a substantive, principled commitment to ethical cultural relativism, to the impossibility of normative justification across power/knowledge regimes?

These questions have enormous importance for the interpretation and assessment of Foucault's work. But the answers, by and large, do not lie ready to hand in his writings. To begin to untangle them, it will be necessary to look more closely at the actual concrete use he makes of his genealogical method.

2. The Genealogy of Modern Power

Foucault's empirical study of modern societies focuses on the question of the nature and emergence of distinctively modern forms of power. It is his thesis that modernity consists, at least in part, in the development and operation of a radically new regime of power/knowledge. This regime comprises procedures, practices, objects of inquiry, institutional sites and, above all, forms of social and political constraint that differ markedly from those of previous regimes.

Modern power is unlike earlier powers, according to Foucault, in that it is local, continuous, productive, capillary, and exhaustive. This is so, in part, as a consequence of the circumstances in which it arose. Foucault claims that the modern power/knowledge regime was not imposed from the top down but developed only gradually in local, piecemeal fashion largely in what he calls "disciplinary institutions," beginning in the late eighteenth century. A variety of "microtechniques" were perfected by obscure doctors, wardens, and schoolmasters in obscure hospitals, prisons, and schools, far removed from the great power centers of the *ancien régime*. Only later were these techniques and practices taken up and integrated into what Foucault calls "global or macrostrategies of domination."[11]

The disciplinary institutions were among the first to face the problems of organization, management, surveillance, and control of large numbers of persons. They were the first, that is, to face the problems that would eventually become the constitutive problems of modern government. Hence, the tactics and techniques they pioneered are, in Foucault's view, definitive of modern power.

Foucault describes a variety of new disciplinary microtactics and practices. The one for which he is best known is *le regard* or "the gaze." The gaze was a technique of power/knowledge that enabled administrators to manage their institutional populations by creating and exploiting a new kind of visibility. Administrators organized these populations so that they could be seen, known, surveilled, and thus controlled. The new visibility was of two kinds, according to Foucault: synoptic and individualizing.

Synoptic visibility was premised on architectural and organizational innovations that made possible an intelligible overview of the population and of the relations among its elements. It is exemplified in the design of prisons after Bentham's Panopticon (rings of backlit cells encircling a central observation tower), in the separation of hospital patients according to their diseases, and in the arrangement of students in a classroom space articulated expressly to reflect their rank and ability.

Individualizing visibility, on the other hand, aimed at exhaustive, detailed observation of individuals, their habits and histories. Foucault claims that this visibility succeeded in constituting the individual for the first time as a "case," simultaneously a new object of inquiry and a new target of power.[12]

Both kinds of gaze, synoptic and individualizing, were micropractices linking new processes of production of new knowledges to new kinds of power. They combined scientific observation of populations and individuals, and hence a new "science of man, " with surveillance. This link depended upon the asymmetrical character of the gaze; it was unidirectional—the scientist or warden could see the inmate but not vice versa. This is most striking in the case of the Panopticon. Because the unidirectionality of visibility denied the inmates knowledge of when and whether they were actually being watched, it made them internalize the gaze and in effect surveil themselves.[13] Less overtly, the forms of scientific observation in other institutions objectified their targets and pried relentlessly into every aspect of their experience.

Foucault would not, however, have us conclude that the objectifying behavioral sciences have a monopoly on the use of the gaze as a microtechnique of modern power/knowledge. He demonstrates the similar functioning of what he calls the "hermeneutics of the psyche." Practices like psychoanalysis, which constitute the individual as speaking subject rather than as behavioral object, also involve an asymmetrical, unidirectional visibility, or perhaps one should say audibility. The producer of the discourse is defined as incapable of deciphering it and is dependent upon a silent hermeneutic authority.[14] Here, too, there is a distinctive use of coercion to obtain knowledge and of knowledge to coerce.

The importance for Foucault of micropractices such as the gaze far transcends their place in the history of early disciplinary institutions. As I noted earlier, they were among the first responses to the problems of population management that later came to define modern government. They were eventually integrated into global political strategies and orientations, but even in their early disciplinary form they evince a number of the hallmarks of a distinctively modern power.

Because they cause power to operate continuously, disciplinary tactics anticipate later developments in the genealogy of modern power. Panoptical surveillance is, in this respect, very different from premodern power mechanisms. The latter operated discontinuously and intermittently and required the presence of an agent to apply force. Modern power, as first developed in disciplinary micropractices, on the other hand, requires no such presence; it replaces violence and force of arms with the "gentler" constraint of uninterrupted visibility. Modern power, then, is distinctive in that it keeps a low profile. It has no need of the spectacular displays characteristic of the exercise of power in the *ancien régime*. It is lower in cost both economically, since it requires less labor power, and socially, since it is less easily targeted for resistance. Yet it is more efficacious. Given its connection with the social sciences, modern power is capable, according to Foucault, of an exhaustive analysis of its objects, indeed of the entire social body. It is neither ignorant nor blind, nor does it strike hit or miss, as did earlier regimes. As a result of its superior hold on detail, it is more penetrating than earlier forms of power. It gets hold of its objects at the deepest level—in their gestures, habits, bodies, and desires. Premodern power, on the other hand, could strike only superficially and from afar. Moreover, modern power, as first developed in disciplinary micropractices, is not essentially situated in some central persons or institutions such as king, sovereign, ruling class, state, or army. Rather, it is everywhere. As the description of panoptical self-surveillance demonstrated, it is even in the targets themselves, in their bodies, gestures, desires, and habits. In other words, as Foucault often says, modern power is capillary. It does not emanate from some central source but circulates throughout the entire social body down to even the tiniest and apparently most trivial extremities.[15]

Taken in combination, these characteristics define the operation of modern power as what Foucault calls "self-amplifying." In this respect also it is unlike the power of the *ancien régime*. The latter operated with, so to speak, a fixed amount of force at its disposal. It expended that force via what Foucault calls "deduction" (*prélèvement*); it simply counterposed itself to the opposing forces and sought to eliminate or minimize them. Modern power, on the other hand, continually augments and increases its own force in the course of its exercise. It does this not by negating opposing forces but rather by utilizing them, by linking them up as transfer points within its own circuitry.[16] Hence, the panoptical mechanism takes up the inmate within the disciplinary economy and makes her surveil herself. It aims not at suppressing her but rather at retooling her. It seeks to produce what Foucault calls "docile and useful bodies."[17] Borrowing Marx's terminology, it may be said that whereas premodern power functioned as a system geared to simple reproduction, modern power is oriented to expanded reproduction.

Foucault's description of the disciplinary origins of modern power is extremely rich and concrete. He produced less in the way of a detailed account of the processes whereby the local, piecemeal microtechniques were integrated into global macrostrategies. The fullest account of that is the one found in volume 1 of his *History of Sexuality*. There, Foucault discusses the modern macrostrategy of "bio-power." Bio-power concerns the management of the production and reproduction of life in modern societies. It is oriented to such new objects of power/knowledge as population, health, urban life, and sexuality. It objectifies these as resources to be administered, cultivated, and controlled. It uses new quantitative social science techniques to count, analyze, predict, and prescribe. It also makes use of widely circulating nonquantitative discourses about sexuality, whose origins Foucault traces to the self-interpretation and self-affirmation of the nineteenth-century middle classes.[18]

In his Tanner Lectures of 1979, Foucault linked his work on bio-power to the problematic of political rationality.[19] Indeed, his treatment of the development and use of social science as an instrument of population resource management and social control is clearly related to more familiar treatments of modernization as a process of rationalization. But there is one striking and very important difference. Whereas for other writers the concepts of rationality and rationalization have a two-sided normative character, in Foucault's usage they do not. In the thought of Jürgen Habermas, for example, rationalization involves a contrast between instrumentalization—which is a one-sided, partial, and insufficient rationalization—and a fuller practical, political rationality. It therefore carries with it a normative standard for critiquing modern societies. Foucault's discussion of political rationality in the Tanner Lectures, on the other hand, contains no such contrast and no positive normative pole. Rationality for him is either a neutral phenomenon or (more often) an instrument of domination *tout court*.[20]

3. The Political Implications of Genealogy

Foucault's picture of a distinctively modern power that functions at the capillary level via a plurality of everyday micropractices yields a number of significant political implications. Some of these are strategic and some are normative.

Consider that Foucault's analysis entails that modern power touches individuals through the various forms of constraint constitutive of their social practices rather than primarily through the distortion of their beliefs. Foucault dramatizes this point by claiming that power is in our bodies, not in our heads. Put less paradoxically, he means that practices are more fundamental than belief systems when it comes to understanding the hold that power has on us.

It follows from this view that the analysis and critique of such practices take priority over the analysis and critique of ideology. Foucault's insight thus tends to rule out at least one rather crude version of ideology critique as strategically inadequate to the social reality of modern power. It rules out, that is, the view that given the appropriate objective material conditions, the only or main thing that stands in the way of social change is people's ideologically distorted perception of their needs and interests. When stated thus baldly, it is questionable whether anyone actually holds this view. Still, Foucault's vivid reminder of the priority of practices is a useful corrective to the potential one-sidedness of even more sophisticated versions of the politics of ideology critique.[21]

A second strategic implication of Foucault's insight into the capillary character of modern power concerns the inadequacy of state-centered and economistic political orientations. Such orientations assume that power emanates from one or the other or both of these central points in society. But Foucault's description of the polymorphous, continuous circulation of power through micropractices belies this assumption. It shows, rather, that power is everywhere and in everyone; it shows that power is as present in the most apparently trivial details and relations of everyday life as it is in corporate suites, industrial assembly lines, parliamentary chambers, and military installations. Foucault's view, therefore, rules out state-centered and/or economistic political orientations. It rules out, that is, the view that the seizure and transformation of state and/or economic power would be sufficient to dismantle or transform the modern power regime.[22]

These two strategic political implications of Foucault's empirical work can be combined and stated more positively. In revealing the capillary character of modern power and thereby ruling out crude ideology critique, statism, and economism, Foucault can be understood as in effect ruling *in* what is often called a "politics of everyday life." For if power is instantiated in mundane social practices and relations, then efforts to dismantle or transform the regime must address those practices and relations.

This is probably the single most important feature of Foucault's thought. He provides the empirical and conceptual basis for treating such phenomena as sexuality, the family, schools, psychiatry, medicine, social science, and the like as *political* phenomena. This sanctions the treatment of problems in these areas as *political* problems. It thereby widens the arena within which people may collectively confront, understand, and seek to change the character of their lives. There is no question that a new move to widen the boundaries of the political arena has been underway in the West since the 1960s. Foucault has clearly been influenced by it and has, in turn, helped to buttress it empirically and conceptually.

In the foregoing considerations of political strategy, it has been taken for granted that the modern power regime is undesirable and in need of dismantling and transformation. But that assumption pertains essentially to the normative political implications of Foucault's genealogical description. It is these that require thematization now.

I have noted several times that in Foucault's account modern power is not applied to individuals by the state or sovereign in a top-down fashion. Rather, it circulates everywhere, even through the tiniest capillaries of the social body. It follows from this, claims Foucault, that the classical liberal normative contrast between legitimate and illegitimate power is not adequate to the nature of modern power. The liberal framework understands power as emanating from the sovereign and imposing itself upon the subjects. It tries to define a power-free zone of rights, the penetration of which is illegitimate. Illegitimate power is understood as oppression, itself understood as the transgression of a limit.

But if power is everywhere and does not emanate from one source or in one direction, then this liberal framework will not apply. Furthermore, given its inapplicability, Foucault claims that the proliferation of discourse governed by this liberal framework may itself function as part of the capillary deployment of modern power. This discourse may function, in other words, to mask the actual character of modern power and thus to conceal domination.[23]

It is clear that with this last charge Foucault has crossed the line between conceptual and substantive normative analysis. In using the term 'domination' at the same time that he is ruling out the liberal normative framework, it appears that he is presupposing some alternative framework. (I will discuss the question as to what that might be in the next section of this paper.) However, if correct, Foucault's empirical thesis that modern power is capillary does not by itself dictate the adoption of any particular normative framework. At most, it undercuts one traditional basis of the liberal one.

A similar situation arises with respect to the normative political implications of Foucault's insight into the productive and self-amplifying character of modern power, his insight into its orientation to what I called "expanded reproduction." This insight belies what Foucault calls "the repressive hypothesis." That hypothesis assumes that power functions essentially negatively, through such operations as interdiction, censorship, and denial. Power, in this view, just says no. It says no to what are defined as illicit desires, needs, acts, and speech. But if Foucault is right, modern power is equally involved in *producing* all these things. His empirical account rules out the repressive hypothesis and the liberationist political orientation it supports. That orientation, which is now rather widespread in the West, aims at liberating what power represses. It makes "illicit" speech, desires, and acts into expressions of political revolt. Not only does Foucault reject it as inadequate to the true nature of modern power, but once again he suggests that it is a feature of the deployment of modern power to proliferate liberationist discourse, once again to mask the actual functioning of domination.[24]

In ruling out the repressive hypothesis, Foucault is ruling out the radical normative framework, which substitutes the contrast "repression versus liberation" for the liberal contrast "legitimacy versus illegitimacy." He has linked both of these frameworks to the functioning of what he identifies as domination. It appears, therefore, that Foucault must be presupposing some alternative normative framework of his own. What might this be?

4. Unanswered Questions concerning the Normative Dimensions of Foucault's Genealogy

It is my thesis that despite his important contributions to the study of modern societies, Foucault's work ends up, in effect, inviting questions that it is structurally unequipped to answer. A brief recap of my line of argument to this point will clarify what I mean by this allegation.

I have claimed that Foucault adopts at least the minimal heuristic principle that power regimes be broached and described as neutral phenomena, that they not, for example, be interrogated immediately from the liberal standpoint as to their legitimacy or illegitimacy. I have also claimed that the use of this methodological strategy permits him to give a perspicuous account of the emergence of the modern power regime, an account that in turn brought to light some neglected features of the operation of power in modern life. Furthermore, I have argued that Foucault's account of modern power constitutes good grounds for rejecting some fairly widespread strategic and normative political orientations and for adopting instead the standpoint of a "politics of everyday life."

At the same time, I have left open the question of the nature and extent of Foucault's bracketing of the problematic of normative justification of power/ knowledge regimes. I have noted some indications that his description of modern power is in fact not normatively neutral, but I have not systematically pursued these. I now wish to reopen these questions by looking more closely at the politically engaged character of Foucault's work.

Let me begin by noting that Foucault's writings abound with such phrases as 'the age of bio-power', 'the disciplinary society', 'the carceral archipelago' — phrases rife, that is, with ominous overtones. I must also note that Foucault does not shrink from frequent use of such terms as 'domination', 'subjugation', and 'subjection' in describing the modern power/knowledge regime. Accordingly, the main outlines of his description can be tellingly restated as follows: In the early modern period, closed disciplinary institutions like prisons perfected a variety of mechanisms for the fabrication and subjugation of individuals as epistemic objects and as targets of power. These techniques aimed at the retooling of deviants as docile and useful bodies to be reinserted in the social machine. Later, these techniques were exported beyond the confines of their institutional birthplaces and were made the basis for global strategies of domination aimed at the total administration of life. Various discourses that have seemed to oppose this regime have, in fact, supported it, in part by masking its true character.

Put this way, it is clear that Foucault's account of power in modern societies is anything but neutral and unengaged. How, then, did he get from the suspension of the question of the legitimacy of modern power to this engaged critique of bio-power? This is the problem I want to address.

A number of possible explanations come to mind. First, one might read Foucault's critique as politically engaged yet somehow still normatively neutral. One might, that is, interpret his bracketing of the normative as covering *all* political norms, not just the liberal ones. In a variety of interviews, Foucault himself adopts this interpretation. He claims he has approached power strategically and militarily, not normatively. He says he has substituted the perspective of war, with its contrast between struggle and submission, for that of right, with its contrast between legitimacy and illegitimacy.[25] In this interpretation, Foucault's use of the terms 'domination', 'subjugation', and 'subjection' would be normatively neutral: these terms would simply be descriptive of the strategic alignments and modes of operation of the various opposing forces in the modern world.

Such an interpretation is open to a number of questions, however. It is usually the case that strategic military analyses identify the various opposing sides in the struggle. They are capable of specifying who is dominating or subjugating whom and who is resisting or submitting to whom. This Foucault does not do. Indeed, he rejects it as a possibility. He claims that it is misleading to think of power as a property that could be possessed by some persons or classes and not by others; power is better conceived as a complex, shifting field of relations in which everyone is an element.[26]

This claim does not square, strictly speaking, with the fact that Foucault seems at times to link bio-power with class domination and to implicitly accept (at least elements of) the attendant Marxian economic interpretation. Nor does it square with his tendency to identify such capillary agents as social scientists, technologists of behavior, and hermeneutists of the psyche with the "forces of domination."

But whether or not he does or can identify the forces of domination and those they dominate, the claim that his normative-sounding terminology is not normative but, rather, military runs into a second difficulty: the military usage of 'domination', 'struggle', and 'submission' cannot, in and of itself, explain or justify anyone's preference for, or commitment to, one side as opposed to the other. Foucault calls in no uncertain terms for resistance to domination. But why? Why is struggle preferable to submission? Why ought domination to be resisted? Only with the introduction of normative notions of some kind could Foucault begin to answer such questions. Only with the introduction of normative notions could he begin to tell us what is wrong with the modern power/knowledge regime and why we ought to oppose it.

It seems, then, that the assumption that Foucault's critique is engaged but non-normative creates serious difficulties for him. It would perhaps be better to assume that he has not bracketed every normative framework but only the liberal one, the one based on legitimacy. In that case, it becomes essential to discover what alternative normative framework he is presupposing. Could the language of domination, subjugation, struggle, and resistance be interpreted as the skeleton of some alternative framework?

Although this is certainly a theoretical possibility, I am unable to develop it concretely. I find no clues in Foucault's writings as to what his alternative norms might be. I see no hints as to how concretely to interpret 'domination', 'subjugation', 'subjection', and so forth in some completely new "postliberal" fashion. This is not to deny that these terms acquire rich new empirical content from Foucault's descriptions of disciplinary power; 'domination', for example, comes to include *dressage,* which involves the use of nonviolent yet physical force for the production of "normal," conforming, skilled individuals. But such important new meaning accretions and extensions are not in and of themselves tantamount to the elaboration of an entirely new normative framework. They do not, in other words, suffice to tell us precisely what is wrong with discipline in terms wholly independent of the liberal norms. On the contrary, their normative force seems to depend upon tacit appeal to the notions of rights, limits, and the like.

I suggested earlier that Foucault sometimes seems to presuppose that macro-strategies of global domination such as bio-power are connected with class domination and that the Marxian account of the latter is basically right. Could it be, then, that he is presupposing the Marxian normative framework? It is characteristic of that framework, at least on one widely accepted reading, that it does not fully suspend all liberal norms. Rather, it presupposes at least some of them in its critique of capitalist social and productive relations. For example, Marx demonstrates that although the contractual exchange of labor power for wages purports to be symmetrical and free, in fact it is asymmetrical and coercive. He is not, therefore, fully suspending the bourgeois norms of reciprocity and freedom. Perhaps Foucault could be read in similar fashion. Perhaps he is not fully suspending but is rather presupposing the very liberal norms he criticizes. His description of such disciplinary microtechniques as the gaze, for example, would then have the force of a demonstration that modern social science, however much it purports to be neutral and power-free, in fact also involves asymmetry and coercion.

This reading of Foucault's work is one I am sure he would have rejected. Yet it gains some plausibility if one considers the disciplinary, or carceral, society described in *Discipline and Punish*. If one asks what exactly is wrong with that society, Kantian notions leap immediately to mind. When confronted with the treatment of persons solely as means that are causally manipulated by various institutions, one cannot help but appeal to such concepts as the violation of dignity and autonomy. But again, these Kantian notions are clearly related to the liberal norms of legitimacy and illegitimacy defined in terms of limits and rights.

Given that no other normative framework is apparent in Foucault's writings, it is not unreasonable to assume that the liberal framework has not been fully suspended. But if this is so, Foucault is caught in an outright contradiction, for he, even more than Marx, tends to treat that framework as simply an instrument of domination.

The point is not simply that Foucault contradicts himself. Rather, it is that he does so in part because he misunderstands, at least when it comes to his *own* situation, the way that norms function in social description. He assumes that he can purge all traces of liberalism from his account of modern power simply by forswearing explicit reference to the tip-of-the-iceberg notions of legitimacy and illegitimacy. He assumes, in other words, that these norms can be neatly isolated and excised from the larger cultural and linguistic matrix in which they are situated. He fails to appreciate the degree to which the normative is embedded in and infused throughout the whole of language at *every* level and the degree to which, despite himself, his own critique has to make use of modes of description, interpretation, and judgment formed within the modern Western normative tradition.[77]

It seems, then, that none of the readings offered here leaves Foucault entirely free of difficulties. Whether we take him as suspending every normative framework, or only the liberal one, or even as keeping that one, he is plagued with unanswered and perhaps unanswerable questions. Because he fails to conceive and pursue any single consistent normative strategy, he ends up with a curious amalgam of amoral militaristic description, Marxian jargon, and Kantian morality. Its many valuable empirical aspects notwithstanding, I can only conclude that Foucault's work is normatively confused.

I believe that the roots of the confusion can be traced to some conceptual ambiguities in Foucault's notion of power. That concept is itself an admixture of neutrality and engagement. Take, for example, his claim that power is productive, not repressive. Throughout this paper I have supposed that this was an empirical claim about the self-amplifying nature of a distinctively modern power. But, in what is clearly an equivocation, Foucault simultaneously treats productivity as a conceptual feature of *all* power as such. He claims that not just the modern regime but every power regime creates, molds, and sustains a distinctive set of cultural practices, including those oriented to the production of truth. Every regime creates, molds, and sustains a distinctive form of life as a positive phenomenon. No regime simply negates. Foucault also makes the converse claim that no positive form of life can subsist without power. Power-free cultures, social practices, and knowledges are in principle impossible. It follows, in his view, that one cannot object to a form of life simply on the ground that it is power-laden. Power is productive, ineliminable, and therefore normatively neutral.[28]

How is this view to be assessed? It seems to me to boil down to a conjunction of three rather innocuous statements: (1) social practices are necessarily norm-governed, (2) practice-governing norms are simultaneously constraining and enabling, and (3) such norms enable only insofar as they constrain. Together, these three statements imply that one cannot have social practices without constraints and that, hence, the mere fact that it constrains cannot be held against any particular practice. This view is a familiar one in twentieth-century philosophy. It is implied, for example, in Habermas's account of the way in which the successful performance of any speech act presupposes norms of truth, comprehensibility, truthfulness, and appropriateness. Such norms make communication possible, but only by devaluing and ruling out some possible and actual utterances: they *enable* us to speak precisely insofar as they *constrain* us.

If this is what Foucault's thesis of the general productivity and ineliminability of power means, then power is a normatively neutral phenomenon indeed. But does this interpretation accord with Foucault's usage? In some respects, yes. He does include under the power/knowledge umbrella such phenomena as criteria of well-formedness for knowledge claims, criteria that simultaneously valorize some statement forms and devalue others; and he also includes social or institutional licensing of knowledge claimants, licensing that simultaneously entitles some speakers to make certain kinds of specialized knowledge claims and excludes others from so doing. If these are the sorts of things meant by power, then the thesis that power is productive, ineliminable, and therefore normatively neutral is unobjectionable.

But Foucault's power/knowledge regimes also include phenomena of other sorts. They include forms of overt and covert coercion in the extraction of knowledge from and about persons and also in the targeting of objects, including persons, for the application of policy in more subtle ways. These phenomena are far less innocuous and far more menacing. That *they* are in principle ineliminable is not immediately apparent. So if *they* are what is meant by power, then the claim that power is productive, ineliminable, and therefore normatively neutral is highly questionable.

I noted earlier that Foucault's notion of a power/knowledge regime covered a highly heterogeneous collection of phenomena. Now it appears that the difficulties concerning the normative dimension of his work stem at least in part from that heterogeneity. The problem is that Foucault calls too many different sorts of things power and simply leaves it at that. Granted, all cultural practices involve constraints—but these constraints are of a variety of different kinds and thus demand a variety of different normative responses. Granted, there can be no social practices without power—but it doesn't follow that all forms of power are normatively equivalent nor that any social practices are as good as any other. Indeed, it is essential to Foucault's own project that he be able to distinguish better from worse sets of practices and forms of constraint. But this requires greater normative resources than he possesses.

The point can also be put this way: Foucault writes as though he were oblivious to the existence of the whole body of Weberian social theory with its careful distinctions between such notions as authority, force, violence, domination, and legitimation. Phenomena that are capable of being distinguished through such concepts are simply lumped together under his catchall concept of power.[29] As a consequence, the potential for a broad range of normative nuances is surrendered, and the result is a certain normative one-dimensionality.

I mentioned earlier that though Foucault's genealogy of modern power was related to the study of modernization as rationalization, there was one very important difference. This difference was Foucault's lack of any bipolar normative contrast comparable to, say, Jürgen Habermas's contrast between a partial and one-sided instrumental rationality, on the one hand, and a fuller practical, political rationality, on the other hand. The consequences of this lack are now more fully apparent. Because Foucault has no basis for distinguishing, for example, forms of power that involve domination from those that do not, he appears to endorse a one-sided, wholesale rejection of modernity as such. Furthermore, he appears to do so without any conception of what is to replace it.

In fact, Foucault vacillates between two equally inadequate stances. On the one hand, he adopts a concept of power that permits him no condemnation of any objectionable features of modern societies. But at the same time, and on the other hand, his rhetoric betrays the conviction that modern societies are utterly without redeeming features. Clearly, what Foucault needs, and needs desperately, are normative criteria for distinguishing acceptable from unacceptable forms of power. As it stands now, the unquestionably original and valuable dimensions of his work stand in danger of being misunderstood for lack of an adequate normative perspective.

Notes

1. Foucault adopted the term 'genealogy' only relatively recently, in connection with his later writings; see, especially, "Nietzsche, Genealogy, History," in *Language, Counter-Memory, Practice: Selected Essays and Interviews,* ed. Donald F. Bouchard, trans. Bouchard and Sherry Simon (Ithaca, N.Y., 1977). Earlier he called his approach 'archaeology'; see, especially, *The Archaeology of Knowledge,* trans. A. M. Sheridan Smith (New York, 1972). For an explanation of the shift, see "Truth and Power," in *Power/Knowledge: Selected Interviews and Other Writings, 1972–1977,* ed. Colin Gordon, trans. Gordon et al. (New York, 1980).

2. Foucault, "Truth and Power." 114.

3. Foucault, "Nietzsche, Freud, Marx," in *Nietzsche* (Paris, 1967), 183–200.

4. Foucault, "Truth and Power." 118.

5. Ibid., 112–13, 131, 133.

6. Foucault, "The Discourse on Language," trans. Rupert Swyer, in *The Archaeology of Knowledge,* 216–38; "Nietzsche, Genealogy, History," 51 ff; and *Discipline and Punish: The Birth of the Prison,* trans. Alan Sheridan (New York, 1979), 17–19, 101–2, 170–73, 192.

7. That Foucault's project could be understood in terms of the concept of bracketing was first suggested to me by Hubert L. Dreyfus and Paul Rabinow. They discuss what I call below the bracketing of the problematic of epistemic justification (although they do not address what I call the bracketing of the problematic of normative justification), in *Michel Foucault: Beyond Structuralism and Hermeneutics* (Chicago, 1982).

8. Foucault, "Truth and Power," 113, and *Discipline and Punish,* 184–85.

9. Foucault, "The History of Sexuality," in *Power/Knowledge,* 184, and "Two Lectures," in *Power/Knowledge, 93, 95.*

10. Foucault, "Two Lectures," 91–92.

11. Foucault, "The Eye of Power," in *Power/Knowledge,* 158–59, and "Prison Talk," in *Power/Knowledge,* 38.

12. Foucault, "The Eye of Power," 146–65, and *Discipline and Punish,* 191–94, 201–9, 252.

13. Foucault, *Discipline and Punish,* 202–3.

14. Foucault, *The History of Sexuality, Volume I: An Introduction,* trans. Robert Hurley (New York, 1978). 61–62.

15. Foucault, "Power and Strategies," in *Power/Knowledge,* 142; "Truth and Power," 119, 125; "The Eye of Power," 151–52; "Two Lectures," 104–5; and *Discipline and Punish,* 201–9.

16. Foucault. "The Eye of Power," 160; *The History of Sexuality,* 139; and *Discipline and Punish,* 170.

17. Foucault, *Discipline and Punish,* 136–38.

18. Foucault, *The History of Sexuality,* 24–26, 122–27, 139–45.

19. Foucault, "Each and Every One: A Criticism of Political Rationality," Tanner Lectures, Stanford University, October 1979 (transcribed from tapes by Shari Popen).

20. Ibid.

21. Foucault, "Truth and Power," 118, 132–33.

22. Foucault, "Truth and Power," 122; "Body/Power," in *Power/Knowledge,* 60; and "Two Lectures," 89.

23. Foucault, "Two Lectures," 95–96.

24. Foucault, "Power and Strategies," 139–41; *The History of Sexuality,* 5–13; "Truth and Power," 119; and "Body/Power," 59.

25. Foucault, "Two Lectures," 90–92.

26. Foucault, "Two Lectures," and "Power and Strategies," 142.

27. This formulation combines points suggested to me by Richard Rorty and Albrecht Wellmer.

28. Foucault, *Discipline and Punish,* 27; "Power and Strategies," 141–42; "Two Lectures," 93; and "Truth and Power," 131–33.

29. I am indebted to Andrew Arato for this point.

Chapter 2
Michel Foucault: A "Young Conservative"?

In a recent discussion of postmodernism, Jürgen Habermas referred to Michel Foucault as a "Young Conservative."[1] This epithet was an allusion to the "conservative revolutionaries" of interwar Weimar Germany, a group of radical, antimodernist intellectuals whose numbers included Martin Heidegger, Ernst Jünger, Carl Schmitt, and Hans Freyer. To call Foucault a "Young Conservative," then, was to accuse him of elaborating what Habermas calls a "total critique of modernity." Such a critique, according to Habermas, is both theoretically paradoxical and politically suspect. It is theoretically paradoxical because it cannot help but surreptitiously presuppose some of the very modern categories and attitudes it claims to have surpassed. And it is politically suspect because it aims less at a dialectical resolution of the problems of modern societies than at a radical rejection of modernity as such. In sum, it is Habermas's contention that although Foucault's critique of contemporary culture and society purports to be postmodern, it is at best modern and at worst antimodern.[2]

As Habermas sees it, then, the issue between him and Foucault concerns their respective stances vis-à-vis modernity. Habermas locates his own stance in the tradition of dialectical social criticism that runs from Marx to the Frankfurt school. This tradition analyzes modernization as a two-sided historical process and insists that although Enlightenment rationality dissolved premodern forms of domination and unfreedom, it gave rise to new and insidious forms of its own. The important thing about this tradition, from Habermas's point of view, and the thing that sets it apart from the rival tradition in which he locates Foucault is that it does not reject *in toto* the modern ideals and aspirations whose two-sided actualization it criticizes. Instead, it seeks to preserve and extend both the "emancipatory impulse" behind the Enlightenment and that movement's real success in overcoming premodern forms of domination—even while it criticizes the bad features of modern societies.

This, however, claims Habermas, is not the stance of Foucault. Foucault belongs rather to a tradition of rejectionist criticism of modernity, one which includes Nietzsche, Heidegger, and the French poststructuralists. These writers, unlike the dialecticians with whom Habermas identifies, aspire to a total break with the Enlightenment. In their zeal to be as radical as possible, they "totalize" critique so that it turns against itself. Not content to criticize the contradiction between modern norm and modern reality, they criticize even the constitutive norms of modernity, rejecting the very commitments to truth, rationality, and freedom that alone make critique possible.

What are we to make of this highly charged attack on the most political of the French poststructuralists by the leading exponent of German Critical Theory?

On the one hand, Habermas's criticism of Foucault directs our attention to some very important questions: Where does Foucault stand vis-à-vis the political ideals of the Enlightenment? Does he reject the project of examining the background practices and institutions that structure the possibilities of social life in order to bring them under the conscious, collective control of human beings? Does he reject the conception of freedom as autonomy that that project appears to presuppose? Does he aspire to a total break with the long-standing Western tradition of emancipation via rational reflection?

But, on the other hand, even as Habermas's criticism directs our attention to such questions, it tends not to solicit the sort of inquiry that is needed to answer them. In fact, Habermas's formulation is too tendentious to permit a fair adjudication of the issues. It overlooks the possibility that the target of Foucault's critique may not be modernity *simpliciter* but, rather, only one particular component of it: namely, a system of practice and discourse that Foucault calls "humanism." Moreover, it begs an important question by assuming that one cannot reject humanism without also rejecting modernity. Finally, it jumps the gun with the alarmist supposition that if Foucault rejects a "universalistic" or foundationalistic metainterpretation of humanist concepts and values, then he must be rejecting these concepts and values entirely.

All told, then, Habermas raises the ante too precipitously and forecloses the possibility of posing to Foucault a more nuanced and analytically precise set of questions: Assuming that Foucault's target is indeed "humanism," then what exactly is it, and what is its relation to modernity more broadly conceived? Does Foucault really mean to reject humanism, and if so, then on what grounds? Does he reject it, for example, on strictly conceptual and philosophical grounds? Is the problem that the humanist vocabulary is still mired in a superseded Cartesian metaphysic? Or, rather, does Foucault reject humanism on strategic grounds? In other words, does he contend that though a humanist political stance may once have had emancipatory force when it was a matter of opposing the premodern forms of domination of the *ancien régime,* this is no longer the case? Does he thus think, strategically, that appeals to humanist values in the present conjuncture must fail to discourage—indeed, must promote—new, quintessentially modern forms of domination? Or, finally, does Foucault reject humanism on normative grounds? Does he hold that the humanist project is intrinsically undesirable? Is humanism, in his view, simply a formula for domination *tout court?*

If Habermas is to be faulted for failing to ask such questions, then Foucault must be faulted for failing to answer them. In fact, his position is highly ambiguous: on the one hand, he never directly pronounces in favor of rejectionism as an alternative to dialectical social criticism; but, on the other hand, his writings abound with rhetorical devices that convey rejectionist attitudes. Moreover, given his general reluctance to spell out the theoretical presuppositions informing his work, it is not surprising that Foucault fails to distinguish among the various sorts of rejectionism I've just outlined. On the contrary, he tends to conflate conceptual, strategic, and normative arguments against humanism.

These ambiguities have given rise to an interesting divergence among Foucault's interpreters, one that bears directly on the controversy sparked by Habermas. Because Foucault's texts contain stretches of philosophical, historical, and political reasoning that are susceptible to various rejectionist interpretations and because the conceptual, strategic, and normative dimensions of these are not adequately distinguished, interpreters have tended to seize on one or another of these elements as the key to the whole. David Hoy, for example, has interpreted Foucault as, in my terms, a merely conceptual or philosophical rejectionist of humanism;[3] other readers have taken or are likely to take him to be, again in my terms, a merely strategic rejectionist of humanism; and Hubert L. Dreyfus and Paul Rabinow have put the strongest construction of all on Foucault, reading him as, in my terms, a substantive, normative rejectionist of humanist values.[4] These, I believe, are the major, prototypical interpretations of Foucault now extant. Only by closely examining them can we hope to get to the bottom of the "Young Conservative" controversy.

In what follows, I shall consider each of these three interpretations of Foucault. I shall not be directly concerned, however, with the question, Who has got Foucault right? I believe that Foucault does not really have a single consistent position and that there is some textual evidence in favor of each reading; moreover, I do not wish here to debate where I think the balance of such evidence lies. My primary concern will be the substantive issues between Foucault and Habermas. I shall try to formulate these issues more precisely and persuasively than I think Habermas has done and to begin adjudicating them. My focus, then, will be the following problem: Which, if any, of the various sorts of rejectionism that can be attributed to Foucault are desirable and defensible alternatives to the sort of dialectical social criticism Habermas envisions?

1

One influential reading of Foucault is premised on the assumption that—*pace* Habermas—to reject a foundationalistic or universalistic metaphilosophical interpretation of the humanist ideals of modernity is not necessarily to reject modernity altogether. In this reading, a version of which has been expounded by David Hoy, Foucault is a merely philosophical rejectionist: he rejects only a certain philosophical framework, not necessarily the values and forms of life that that framework has served to underpin and legitimate.[5] Furthermore, this reading holds that such a position is defensible; Foucault is perfectly consistent in repudiating the Cartesian vocabulary in which humanist ideals have been articulated while retaining something like the substance of the ideals themselves.

Those who read Foucault in this way follow Dreyfus and Rabinow in seeing him as a Heideggerian of sorts, allegedly completing and concretizing Heidegger's program for the dismantling of Cartesianism.[6] Heidegger argued that the subject and object that modern philosophy (including political philosophy) took for necessary, universal, and ahistorical fundaments were actually contingent, historically situated products of the modern interpretation of the meaning of Being.[7] As such, they pertained only to one "epoch" in the "history of Being" (i.e., Western civilization), an epoch that had exhausted its possibilities and was ending. That these Cartesian interpretations of Being were contingent and derivative was evident in view of their relativity to and dependence on a prior, enabling background that remained necessarily "unthought" by them. For a variety of logical, historical, and quasi-political reasons, Heidegger thought that this background could be evoked only indirectly and metaphorically via words like *Lichtung* ("clearing").

Foucault is seen, accordingly, as continuing and concretizing Heidegger's delimitation of Cartesianism by spelling out what Heidegger might have or should have meant by the background, or *Lichtung*. The background is the historically specific system of norm-governed social practices (at first called the "episteme," later the "power/knowledge regime") that defines and produces each epoch's distinctive subjects and objects of knowledge and power. A new kind of historiography (first called "archaeology," later "genealogy") can chart the emergence and disappearance of such systems of practice and describe their specific functioning. Such historiography can illuminate the transitory character of any given episteme or power/knowledge regime, including, and especially, the modern humanist one. It can function as a kind of *Kulturkritik,* dereifying contemporary practices and objects, robbing them of their traditional ahistorical, foundationalistic legitimations, lending them an appearance of arbitrariness and even nastiness, and suggesting their potential openness to change. It can demonstrate, for example, that the Cartesian concepts of subjectivity and objectivity that have served to legitimate humanist values are "fictions" and that these fictions and the values correlated with them have in turn served to legitimate practices that, denuded of their aura of legitimacy, take on an unsavory appearance.

In this reading, Foucault follows Heidegger in singling out a constellation both call "humanism" as a target for genealogical critique and delimitation. Heidegger argued that in the development of modern Western culture since Descartes, a complex and disastrous complicity has been elaborated between the subjectivity and the objectivity that humanism simplistically opposes to each other.[8] On the one hand, modern mathematical science and machine technology have objectified everything that is (the first taking as real only what can be fitted into a preestablished research ground plan; the second treating everything as "standing reserve," or resources to be mobilized within a technological grid). But on the other hand, and at the same time, the "age of anthropology" has created a realm of subjectivities; it has given rise to such entities as "representations," "values," "cultural expressions," "life objectivations," "aesthetic and religious experience," the mind that thinks the research plan and its objects, and the will that wills the mobilization of standing reserve. This objectification and this subjectification, says Heidegger, are two sides of the same coin. Humanists are at best naive and at worst complicit in thinking they can solve the problems of modern culture by asserting the dominance of the subject side over the object side. Ontologically, the two are exactly on the same (non-"primordial" and "forgetful") level; ethically—the very notion of ethics is part of the problem. But, says Heidegger, none of this is meant to sponsor the glorification of the inhumane; it is aimed, rather, at finding a higher sense of the dignity of "man" than that envisioned by humanism.[9]

Those who emphasize Heidegger's influence stress Foucault's account of the modern discursive formation of humanism. Humanism, claims Foucault, is a political and scientific praxis oriented to a distinctive object known as "Man."[10] Man came into existence only in the late eighteenth or early nineteenth century, with the emergence of a new power/knowledge regime. Within and by means of the social practices that regime comprises, Man was and is constituted as the epistemic object of the new "human sciences" and also instituted as the subject who is the target and instrument of a new kind of normalizing power. Both as epistemic object and as subject of power, Man is a strange, unstable, two-sided entity, or "doublet." He consists in an impossible symbiosis of two opposing poles, one objective, the other subjective. Each of these poles seeks to exclude the other but, in so doing, manages only to solicit and enhance it, since each in fact requires the other. Humanism, then, is the contradictory, ceaseless, self-defeating project of resolving this Man problem.

In *The Order of Things,* Foucault provides a grid for the varieties of modern humanism by identifying three forms of the Man doublet. First, there is the transcendental/empirical double, in which Man both constitutes the world of empirical objects and is constituted himself, an empirical object like any other in the world. Second, there is the cogito/unthought double, in which Man is both determined by forces unknown to him and aware that he is so determined; he is thus charged with the task of thinking his own unthought and thereby freeing himself. Finally, there is the return-and-retreat-of-the-origin double, in which Man is both the originary opening from which history unfolds and an object with a history that antedates him.

Each of these three doubles contains a subject pole that suggests the autonomy, rationality, and infinite value of Man. As the one who transcendentally constitutes the world, Man is a meaning giver and lawmaker. As thinker of his own unthought, he becomes self-transparent, unalienated, and free. And as enabling horizon of history, he is its measure and destiny. But no sooner does this subject pole endow Man with this privilege and value than it defines the opposing object pole that denies them. As empirical object, Man is subject to prediction and control. Unknown to himself, he is determined by alien forces. And as a being with a history that antedates him, he is encumbered with a density not properly his own.

The humanist political project, then, is that of solving the Man problem. It is the project of making the subject pole triumph over the object pole, of achieving autonomy by mastering the other in history, in society, in oneself, of making substance into subject. Foucault's claim, both in *The Order of Things* and throughout his subsequent writings, is that this project, premised as it is on the "subjected sovereignty" of Man, is self-defeating, self-contradictory, and can lead in practice only to domination. Only a completely new configuration—a posthumanist one that no longer produces this bizarre Man doublet but, rather, some completely different object—offers a way out.

The reading of Foucault as a merely philosophical rejectionist takes the writings after *The Order of Things* as working out the social implications of the philosophical critique of humanism. *Discipline and Punish* is seen as chronicling the fabrication of the object side of Man; the first volume of *The History of Sexuality* and shorter pieces like "Truth and Subjectivity" chronicle the fabrication of the subject side.[11] Whereas a humanist might be expected to criticize the objectification of Man in the name of subjectivity, Foucault's work on sexuality putatively shows that subjectivity is every bit as problematic as objectivity. Indeed, the complicity and symmetry of the two poles is dramatically revealed in two other works, *Pierre Rivière* and *Herculine Barbin.*[12] In each of these books, Foucault juxtaposes the first-person subjective discourse of an individual (in the first, a nineteenth-century French parricide; in the second, a nineteenth-century French hermaphrodite) to the contemporary objective medical and legal discourses about him or her. Although he never explicitly clarified his intentions in these books, it seems safe to assume that Foucault's aim is not the humanist one of vindicating the subjective discourse over against the objective one. On the contrary, it must be the antihumanist aim of placing the two on a par, of showing that they depend on and require each other, that they are generated together within, and are illustrative of, the discursive formation of modern humanism.

When Foucault's works are read in this way, it is possible to treat his rejection of humanism as merely conceptual or philosophical. Just as Heidegger's delimitation of humanism was intended to enhance rather than to undermine human dignity, so Foucault's critique, *pace* Habermas, is not an attack on the notions of freedom and reason per se. It is rather a rejection of one contingent, superseded philosophical idiom or discursive formation in which those values have lately found their expression. What is novel and important in Foucault's social criticism, in this reading, is not its implied normative content—*that,* for all practical purposes, is "humanistic" in some looser sense. The novelty is rather the scrapping of the classical modern philosophical underpinnings of that content. Foucault has succeeded in producing a species of *Kulturkritik* that does not rely on—indeed, that explicitly repudiates—the subject-object framework in all of its familiar guises. He rejects the notion of progress—not only in its self-congratulatory Whiggish form but also in the more critical and sophisticated form in which it appears in Marxism and some versions of German Critical Theory. Thus, he produces genuine indictments of objectionable aspects of modern culture without presupposing a Hegelian teleology and a unitary subject of history. Similarly, he rejects the distinction between "real" and "administered" needs or interests, where the former are presumed to be grounded in something more than a contingent, historical power/knowledge regime or background of social practices. He is able, consequently, to condemn objectionable practices without presupposing the notion of autonomous subjectivity. Thus, David Hoy treats Foucault's explicitly political works—*Discipline and Punish* and the first volume of *The History of Sexuality*—as demonstrations of the dispensability of these anachronistic and questionable notions.[13] Foucault has shown that one does not need humanism in order to criticize prisons, social science, pseudoprograms for sexual liberation, and the like; that humanism is not the last word in critical social and historical writing; that there is life—and critique—after Cartesianism. One need not fear that in giving up the paradoxical and aporetic subject-object framework, one is giving up also and necessarily the possibility of engaged political reflection.

This reading of Foucault as a merely philosophical rejectionist is attractive. It suggests the possibility of combining something like Heidegger's and Foucault's postmodernism in philosophy with something like Habermas's modernism in politics. It thereby holds out the appealing promise that one can have one's cake and eat it, too. One gives up the foundationalistic metainterpretation of humanist values: the view that such values are grounded in the nature of something (Man, the subject) independent of, and more enduring than, historically changing regimes of social practices. One gives up as well the idiom in which humanist values have had their classical modern expression: the terms 'autonomy', 'subjectivity', and 'self-determination' lose their privilege. But one does not give up the substantial critical core of humanism. What Habermas would call its "emancipatory force" remains. One simply uses other rhetorical devices and strategies to do essentially the same critical work that the humanist tried to do—namely, to identify and condemn those forms of modern discourse and practice that, under the guise of promoting freedom, extend domination.

Aside from the question of the fidelity of this reading, is the project it attributes to Foucault a defensible and desirable one? I take it that a merely philosophical rejection of humanism is defensible and desirable in principle. It is very much on the current political-philosophical agenda, as can be seen from a wide variety of recent work: for example, analytic accounts of the concept of autonomy by John Rawls and Gerald Dworkin;[14] antifoundationalist reconstructions of liberalism by Richard Rorty and Michael Walzer;[15] antihumanist versions of Marxism inspired by Louis Althusser;[16] and deconstructive reconceptualizations of "the political" by French philosophers influenced by Derrida.[17] Even portions of Habermas's work can be seen as a (moderate) version of this project: his "communicative" reconstruction of Kantian ethics, for example, is an attempt to divest the humanist notion of autonomy of some of its Cartesian trappings (its "monologism" and its ahistorical formalism) while preserving its efficacy as an instrument of social criticism; his distinction between evolution and history is an attempt to disencumber humanism of the Hegelian presupposition of a metaconstitutive subject of history; and his "linguistic turn" is an attempt to detach humanism from the standpoint of the philosophy of consciousness.

But to endorse in principle the general program of de-Cartesianizing and de-Hegelianizing humanism is not yet to resolve a great many very important and difficult problems. It is only to begin to spell out the tasks and standards in terms of which a Foucauldian merely philosophical rejection of humanism is to be evaluated. Among these tasks and standards, I believe, is the adequacy of what Foucault has to say in response to the following sort of metaethical question: Supposing one abandons a foundationalist grounding of humanist values, then to what sort of nonfoundationalist justification can such values lay claim? This, however, is a question Foucault has never squarely faced; rather, he has tried to displace it by insinuating that values neither can have nor require any justification. And yet he has not provided compelling reasons for embracing that extreme metaethical position.

This puts Foucault in the paradoxical position of being unable to account for or justify the sorts of normative political judgments he makes all the time—for example, that "discipline" is a bad thing. Moreover, it raises the question as to whether the values implicit in his unabashedly value-laden descriptions of social reality would, if rendered explicit, constitute a coherent and consistent first-order normative outlook. That question is especially pressing, since Foucault has never, despite repeated insinuations, successfully argued that a coherent first-order normative outlook is dispensable in social criticism (see Chapter 1 of this volume).

But the problems that arise when we read Foucault as propounding a merely philosophical rejection of humanism run still deeper. Even if we absolve him of the onus of producing an acceptable moral theory, we may still question whether he has produced a satisfactory nonhumanist political rhetoric, one that does indeed do, and do better, the critical work that humanist rhetoric sought to do. We may question, for example, whether Foucault's rhetoric really does the job of distinguishing better from worse regimes of social practices; whether it really does the job of identifying forms of domination (or whether it overlooks some and/or misrecognizes others); whether it really does the job of distinguishing fruitful from unfruitful, acceptable from unacceptable forms of resistance to domination; and finally, whether it really does the job of suggesting not simply that change is possible but also what sort of change is desirable (see Chapter 3 of this volume). These, I take it, are among the principal tasks of social criticism, and they are tasks with respect to which Foucault's social criticism might well be judged deficient.

It is worth recalling that the reading of Foucault as a merely philosophical rejectionist of humanism included the claim that he had succeeded in producing a species of *Kulturkritik* without relying on Cartesian underpinnings. But that claim now seems open to question. We should conclude, then, that however laudable the general project, Foucault's version of merely philosophical rejectionism, or the version that has been attributed to him by readers like David Hoy, is incomplete and hence unsatisfactory. It tends, as a result, to invite the assumption that in Foucault's work one is dealing with a rejectionism of a stronger sort.

2

A second reading of Foucault holds that in addition to rejecting humanism on philosophical grounds, he also rejects it on strategic grounds. This reading offers a correspondent understanding of Foucault's position: it contends that he sees humanism as a political rhetoric and practice that developed at the beginning of the modern era in order to oppose what were essentially premodern forms of domination and oppression. Its targets were things like monarchical absolutism, the use of torture to extort confessions from criminals, and spectacular, cruel public executions. In opposition to such practices, humanism sought to limit assaults on people's bodies; it proclaimed a new respect for inwardness, personhood, humanity, and rights. However, the result was not the abolition of domination but, rather, the replacement of premodern forms of domination with new, quintessentially modern ones. The new concern for 'humaneness' fed into the development of a powerful battery of social science technologies that massively transformed and vastly extended the scope and penetration of social control. The astonishing growth and near-ubiquitous spread of these techniques amounted to a revolution in the very nature of power in modern culture. The operation of power was so thoroughly transformed as to render humanism irrelevant and *dépassé*. The democratic safeguards forged in the struggle against premodern despotism have no force against the new modes of domination. Talk of rights and the inviolability of the person is of no use when the enemy is not the despot but the psychiatric social worker. Indeed, such talk and associated reform practice only make things worse. Humanism, then, must be rejected on strategic as well as philosophical grounds. In the current situation, it is devoid of emancipatory force.

This reading gives great weight to the argument of *Discipline and Punish*. There, Foucault chronicles the emergence of the "norm" and its replacement of the "law" as the primary instrument of modern social control. This change came about, he claims, as a result of the development of a new power/knowledge regime that produced a new subject and object of knowledge and a new target of power, namely, Man. Whereas an earlier regime had produced a knowledge of overt actions (crimes or sins) and a power whose target was bodies, the new regime sought to know and to discipline character, or the "soul." This new power/ knowledge object was a deeper one: it was the sensibility or personality that underlay overt actions, the self or set of dispositions that was the ground or cause of those actions. Its very temporality was different; it persisted well beyond the more ephemeral actions that were its mere outward expressions. Hence, the knowledge of this object had a fundamentally different structure, and the production of such knowledge employed fundamentally different techniques. Along with Man, the "human sciences" were born. These sciences investigated the laws governing the formation, perseverance, and alteration of sensibility. They produced character typologies and classifications of "souls." They constituted individuals as "cases" and treated their overt actions as manifest signs of latent realities. Such signs had to be deciphered so that the particular "nature" of the individual in question could be determined — then his or her acts could be explained by that nature. Furthermore, once the laws governing a particular nature were known, prescriptions for altering it could be devised. Selves could be reprogrammed, old habits dismantled, and new ones inculcated in their place. Moreover, individualizing knowledges were complemented by synoptical ones. Statistical methods for surveying and assessing masses of population were developed. Statistical norms were formulated that made it possible to locate individuals on a commensurating scale. From the standpoint of social control, the relevant categories ceased to be the old-fashioned juridical ones of guilt and innocence. Instead, they became the social science ones of normalcy and deviancy. Henceforth, the world came to be populated less by malefactors than by "deviants," "perverts," and "delinquents."

Discipline and Punish thus describes the emergence and character of a new, distinctively modern form of power: normalizing-disciplinary power. It is the sort of power more appropriate to the bureaucratic welfare state than to the despotic regimes opposed by humanism. It is a power that operates quietly and unspectacularly but, for all that, continuously, penetratingly, and ubiquitously. It has no easily identifiable center but is "capillary," dispersed throughout the entire social body. Its characteristic agents are social scientists, expert witnesses, social workers, psychiatrists, teachers, progressive penologists, and the lay citizen who internalizes its categories and values. Above all, it is a power against which humanism is defenseless.

The reading of Foucault now under consideration takes him, then, to be rejecting humanism on strategic as well as on philosophical grounds. He is arguing, it is claimed, that the notions of subjectivity, autonomy, and selfhood to which the humanist appeals are in fact integral components of the disciplinary regime. Far from being genuinely critical, oppositional ideals with emancipatory force, they are actually the very norms and objects through which discipline operates. Selves and subjects in the proper sense came into existence only when the modern power/knowledge regime did. The humanist critic who appeals to them is thus not in a position to oppose that regime effectively. On the contrary, she or he is trapped in the doubling movement that defines the "age of Man."

Is this view defensible? The argument of *Discipline and Punish* consists in one extended historical example: the eighteenth-century European penal reform movement. This movement sought to end the *ancien régime*'s practice of torturing bodies and to replace it with a penal practice aimed at the criminal's mind. It would reorder the offender's mental representations in order to provoke self-reflection and enlightenment, thus rehabilitating the malefactor as an agent and subject. But, claims Foucault, humanist reform never materialized; it was immediately transformed into a normalizing, disciplinary mode of punishment in which the criminal was made the object of a technology of causal reconditioning.

There are obvious logical reasons to doubt that this argument establishes that humanism should be rejected on strategic grounds. It extrapolates from one case, over a hundred years old, to the general conclusion that the humanist conception of freedom as autonomy is today without critical force with respect to disciplinary institutions.

Moreover, a closer look at this case reveals an important new wrinkle. Foucault's account implies that the humanist penal reform movement contained a significant ambiguity. It was unclear whether the new object of punishment, the criminal's "mind" or "humanity," meant the capacity to choose rationally and freely (roughly, the capacities attributed by Kant to the noumenal self) or the causally conditioned seat or container of representations (roughly, the self posited by associationist psychology with the properties attributed by Kant to the empirical self). The result was that it was unclear whether the project of restoring the juridical subject meant provoking a process of *self*-reflection whereby the criminal would undergo *self*-change, a project that would require adopting vis-à-vis the criminal what Habermas calls "the stance of communicative interaction" (or dialogic persuasion), or whether it meant redoing the association of ideas via cognitive conditioning, a project that would mean adopting what Habermas calls "the stance of strategic action" (or technological control). Foucault's account suggests that the penal reform movement conflated these two objects and their corresponding projects and action orientations and so, in effect, contained within itself the seeds of discipline. It posited, at least in embryo, objectified, predictable, and manipulable Man, thus effectively opening the door to the behavioral engineers and welfare technologists.

But if this is so, then what the argument of *Discipline and Punish* discredits is not a proper humanism at all but, rather, some hybrid form resembling utilitarianism. (Nor should this surprise, given that the archvillain of the book is Jeremy Bentham, inventor of the Panopticon.) Thus, it does not follow that a nonutilitarian, Kantian, or quasi-Kantian humanism lacks critical force against the psychological conditioning and mind manipulation that are the real targets of Foucault's critique of disciplinary power. Recall that Habermas has devised a version of Kantian humanism that goes at least some of the way toward meeting the philosophical objections considered in the previous section of this essay.[18] He has elaborated a pragmatic reinterpretation of Kant's ethics, one that divorces the autonomy-heteronomy contrast from the vestiges of the foundational subject-object ontology it retained in Kant and that pegs it instead to the pragmatic distinction between communicative interaction and strategic action. This move strengthens the normative, critical force of the autonomy notion against discipline. It effectively condemns strategic action irrespective of whether the object of punishment be a body or a "soul" or a "self."

It seems plausible to me to follow this Habermassian line and still allow that Foucault is right to contend that in the context of punishment the outcome of Enlightenment penal reform was not merely contingent. It does indeed seem doubtful that the project of reaching agreement with a criminal, of positing her or him as an autonomous subject of conversation, could ever in fact be anything other than manipulation and control of linguistic behavior, given that *ex hypothesi* it is to be carried out in the quintessentially non-"ideal speech situation" of involuntary incarceration. The same may also hold for women in the bourgeois patriarchal family, students in institutions of compulsory education, patients in mental asylums, soldiers in the military — indeed, for all situations where the power that structures discourse is hierarchical and asymmetrical and where some persons are prevented from pressing their claims either by overt or covert force or by such structural features as the lack of an appropriate vocabulary for interpreting their needs.

But the fact that the humanist ideal of autonomous subjectivity is unrealizable, even co-optable, in such "disciplinary" contexts need not be seen as an argument against that ideal. It may be seen, rather, as an argument against hierarchical, asymmetrical power. One need not conclude, with Foucault, that humanist ideals must be rejected on strategic grounds. One may conclude instead, with Habermas, that it is a precondition for the realization of those ideals that the "power" that structures discourse be symmetrical, nonhierarchical, and hence reciprocal. Indeed, one may reinterpret the notion of autonomy so as to incorporate this insight, as Habermas has done. For him, autonomy ceases to refer to a "monologic" process of will formation wherein an isolated individual excludes all empirical needs, desires, and motives and considers only what is required by pure formal reason. Autonomy refers rather to an ideal "dialogic" process wherein individuals with equal right and power to question prevailing norms seek consensus through conversation about which of their apparently individual empirical needs and interests are in fact generalizable. In this interpretation, the cases of disciplinary domination described by Foucault in *Discipline and Punish* are instances not of autonomy but of heteronomy precisely because they involve modes of discourse production that do not meet the procedural requirements specified by the "ideal speech situation."

Furthermore, it is worth noting that any strategic argument against humanism depends on complex empirical considerations. The antihumanist must demonstrate that the actual character of the contemporary world really is such as to render humanism irrelevant and *dépassé*. She or he must show, for example, that it really is the modern bureaucratic welfare state and not other forms of repression or oppression that constitutes the chief threat to freedom in our era. For even a "utilitarian-humanist" can argue that, with all of its problems, the "carceral" society described in *Discipline and Punish* is better than the dictatorship of the party-state, junta, or Imam; that, *pace* Foucault, the reformed prison is preferable to the gulag, the South African or Salvadoran torture cell, and Islamic "justice"; and that in *this* world—which is the real world—humanism still wields its share of critical, emancipatory punch.

Moreover, for nonutilitarian humanists like Habermas, the continuing strategic relevance of humanism is broader still. It is not confined to the critique of premodern forms of domination but applies equally to more modern "disciplinary" forms of power.

3

There is yet another way of reading Foucault that remains to be considered. This way takes him to be rejecting humanism not simply on conceptual and/or strategic grounds but, rather, on substantive normative grounds. It holds that Foucault believes that humanism is intrinsically undesirable, that the conception of freedom as autonomy is a formula for domination *tout court*. Furthermore, some exponents of this line of interpretation, such as Hubert L. Dreyfus and Paul Rabinow, claim that Foucault is right to reject humanism on normative grounds.[19]

This reading is or ought to be the real target of Habermas's attack, for it denies that his pragmatic, dialogic reconceptualization of autonomy meets Foucault's objections. Habermas's point would have weight, it is claimed, if Foucault were merely arguing that discipline is the use of social science in utilitarian programs aimed at normalizing deviancy in contexts of asymmetrical or hierarchical power and that humanism is inefficacious against it. In fact, however, he is arguing a much stronger thesis. Foucault is claiming that even a perfectly realized autonomous subjectivity would be a form of normalizing, disciplinary domination.

This reading depends heavily on Foucault's more recent work: the first volume of his *History of Sexuality* and the lecture "Truth and Subjectivity", which previews the direction pursued in the subsequent volumes of the *History*.[20] These texts are seen as doing for the subject side of the Man doublet what *Discipline and Punish* did for the object side. They provide a genealogical account of the fabrication of the hermeneutical subject, a subject that is not the empirical, causally conditioned container of representations but, rather, the putatively free, quasi-noumenal subject of communicative interaction. Foucault demonstrates, it is claimed, that far from providing a standpoint for emancipation, the fabrication of this subject only seals Man's domination. The subjectification of Man is in reality his subjection.

This reading correctly notes that Foucault's later work focuses on a host of subjectifying practices. Central among these are those quintessentially humanist forms of discourse that aim at liberation and self-mastery via the thematization and critique of previously unthematized, uncriticized contents of the self: unarticulated desires, thoughts, wishes, and needs. Foucault seeks the origins of the notion that by hermeneutical decipherment of the deep, hidden meaning of such contents, one can achieve lucidity about the other in oneself and thus master it and become free. He traces the career of this notion from its beginnings in Stoic self-examination and early Christian penance to its modern variants in psychoanalysis and the allegedly pseudoradical politics of sexual liberation. Foucault aims to show that "truth is not naturally free," that it took centuries of coercion and intimidation to "breed a confessing animal."[21]

Certainly, early forms of hermeneutical subjectification involved the sort of asymmetrical, hierarchical distribution of power in which a silent authority commanded, judged, deciphered, and eventually absolved the confessional discourse and its author. But the reading now under consideration holds that Foucault does not assume that asymmetry and hierarchy are of the essence of disciplinary power. Nor does he believe, it is claimed, that they are what is most objectionable about it. On the contrary, one can imagine a perfected disciplinary society in which normalizing power has become so omnipresent, so finely attuned, so penetrating, interiorized, and subjectified, and therefore so invisible, that there is no longer any need for confessors, psychoanalysts, wardens, and the like. In this fully "panopticized" society, hierarchical, asymmetrical domination of some persons by others would have become superfluous; all would surveil and police themselves. The disciplinary norms would have become so thoroughly internalized that they would not be experienced as coming from without. The members of this society would, therefore, be autonomous. They would have appropriated the other as their own and made substance subject. Class domination would have given way to the kingdom of ends. The ideal speech situation would have been realized. But, it is claimed, this would not be freedom.

This picture of total, triumphant panopticism is held to be significant not empirically — as a prediction about the future course of historical development — but, rather, conceptually — for the new light it casts on the humanist ideals of autonomy and reciprocity. It suggests that these cannot, after all, be seen as genuinely oppositional ideals but are, rather, the very goals of disciplinary power. Conversely, it suggests that hierarchy and asymmetry are not, as humanists suppose, essential to that power but, rather, that they are only imperfections to be eliminated through further refinement. It suggests, therefore, that even Habermas's version of humanist ideals is internal to the disciplinary regime and devoid of critical, emancipatory force with respect to it. Thus, such ideals must be rejected on normative grounds.

Is this position defensible? Consider how a sophisticated Habermassian humanist might reply to the line of reasoning just sketched. Suppose she were to claim that what Foucault envisions as the realization of autonomous subjectivity is not that at all but only pseudoautonomy in conditions of pseudosymmetry; that despite appearances, the subject side and the object side do not really coincide yet; that the internalized other is still other; that self-surveillance is surveillance nonetheless and implies the hierarchical domination of one force by another; that the fact that everyone does it to herself or himself equally does not make it genuinely symmetrical self-rule of autonomous subjects.

I take it that a Habermassian humanist would be hard-pressed to make good such claims. By hypothesis, the members of the fully panopticized society are in an ideal speech situation, so that notion will have no critical force here. It will be necessary to invoke some other criterion to distinguish between "real" and "pseudo" autonomy, and it is not clear what such a criterion could possibly be.

Suppose, though, that the Habermassian humanist takes a different tack and grants Foucault his assumption of "real" autonomy and symmetry. Suppose that she simply digs in and says, "If that's discipline, I'm for it." This would be to concede that these humanist notions have no critical force with respect to the fully panopticized society. But it would also be to claim that this is no objection to them, since there is no good reason to oppose such a society. Such a society seems objectionable only because Foucault has described it in a way that invites the genetic fallacy, that is, because he has made it the outcome of a historical process of hierarchical, asymmetrical coercion wherein people have been, in Nietzschean parlance, "bred" to autonomy. But this is a highly tendentious description. Why not describe it instead as a form of life developed on the basis of new, emergent communicative competences, competences that, though perhaps not built into the very logic of evolution, nonetheless permit for the first time in history the socialization of individuals oriented to dialogic political practice? Why not describe it as a form of life that is desirable since it no longer takes human needs and desires as brute, given facts to be either satisfied or repressed but takes them, rather, as accessible to intersubjective linguistic reinterpretation and transformation? Such access, after all, would widen the sphere of practical-political deliberation and narrow that of instrumental-technical control and manipulation.

This response shifts the burden of argument back onto Foucault. By claiming that panoptical autonomy is not the horror show Foucault took it to be, the Habermassian humanist challenges him to state, in terms independent of the vocabulary of humanism, exactly what is wrong with this hypothetical society and why it ought to be resisted. Moreover, it would not suffice for this purpose for Foucault merely to invoke such terms as 'subjection' and 'normalization'. To say that such a society is objectionable because it is normalizing is to say that it is conformist or represents the rule of *das Man:* this, in effect, would be to appeal to something like authenticity, which (as Derrida and perhaps even the later Heidegger himself understood) is simply another version of autonomy, albeit a detranscendentalized one.

Ultimately, then, a normative rejection of humanism will require appeal to some alternative, posthumanist, ethical paradigm capable of identifying objectionable features of a fully realized autonomous society. It will require, in other words, nothing less than a new paradigm of human freedom. Only from the standpoint of such a paradigm can Foucault or his interpreters make the case for a normative rejection of humanism.

Foucault, however, does not offer an alternative, posthumanist ethical paradigm. He does occasionally suggest that protest urged in the name of the pleasures of our bodies may have greater emancipatory potential than that made in the name of the ideal of autonomy. But he neither justifies nor elaborates this suggestion. Nor does he give us convincing reasons to believe that claims couched in some new "body language" would be any less subject to mystification and abuse than humanist claims have been (see Chapter 3 of this volume).

It looks, therefore, as though the reading of Foucault as a normative rejectionist of humanism pushes us to choose between a known ethical paradigm and an unknown *x*. As long as we keep the discussion on this moral-philosophical plane, we are justified in siding with Habermas; we must balk at rejecting the idea of autonomy, at least until the Foucauldians fill in their x. But I suspect it will be more fruitful to hold off that conclusion for a while and to shift the debate onto a more hermeneutical and sociological plane. Let me rather recast the issue as a choice between two sets of fears or conceptions of danger.

Recall Foucault's nightmare of the fully panopticized society. Now consider that Habermas, too, describes a possible "brave new world" scenario for the future—but his version is the diametrical opposite of Foucault's. Habermas fears "the end of the individual," a form of life in which people are no longer socialized to demand rational, normative legitimations of social authority.[22] In this dystopian vision, they just cynically go along out of privatized strategic considerations, and the stance of communicative interaction in effect dies out.

Instead of asking which of these "brave new worlds" is the good one and which is the bad, we might ask which best captures our worst fears about contemporary social trends. But that question is too complex to be settled by exclusively moral-philosophical means. It is in part a question about empirical tendencies within contemporary Western societies and in part a question about the fears, and thus about the social identities and historical self-interpretations, of members of such societies. Hence, it is a question with an irreducible hermeneutical dimension: it demands that we weigh alternative ways of situating ourselves with respect to our past history and that we conceive ourselves in relation to possible futures, for example, as political agents and potential participants in oppositional social movements. To pose the issue in this way is to acknowledge the need for a *major* interdisciplinary, hermeneutical effort—an effort that brings to bear all the tools of historical, sociological, literary, philosophical, political, and moral deliberation in order to assess both the viability of our very strained and multivalent traditions and the possibilities of oppositional social movements. But once this is acknowledged, there is no assurance that such an effort can be contained within the terms of a choice between Habermas and Foucault.

This last point becomes especially salient when we consider that just such an interdisciplinary reassessment of humanism is now being undertaken by a social and intellectual movement without strong links to either Habermas or Foucault. I refer to the interdisciplinary community of feminist scholars and activists who are interrogating the concept of autonomy as a central value of male-dominated modern Western culture. Within this movement, a number of different perspectives on autonomy are being debated. At one end of the spectrum are those, like Simone de Beauvoir, who understand women's liberation precisely as securing our autonomy in the classical humanist sense.[23] At the other end are those, like Alison M. Jaggar, who reject autonomy on the grounds that it is an intrinsically masculinist value, premised on a mind-body, intellect-affect, will-nature dualism, linked to an invidious male-female dichotomy and positing woman (nature, affect, body) as the other to be mastered and suppressed.[24] In between are several mediating positions. There are those, like Carol Gould, who argue that autonomy is only one-half of a fully human conception of freedom and the good life and that it must be supplemented with the "feminine" values of care and relatedness that humanist ideology has denigrated and repressed.[25] There are those, influenced by Carol Gilligan, who claim that we need to acknowledge that there are now in operation two (currently gender-associated) moralities with two different concepts of autonomy correlated with public life and private life, respectively.[26] And there are those, like Iris Young, who insist that the task is, rather, to overcome the split between those moralities and to sublate the opposition between autonomy and "femininity" or humanism and antihumanism.[27]

We cannot at present anticipate the outcome of these debates, but we can recognize their capacity to resituate, if not altogether to displace, the normative dimension of the Habermas-Foucault dispute. For the feminist interrogation of autonomy is the theoretical edge of a movement that is literally remaking the social identities and historical self-interpretations of large numbers of women and of some men. Insofar as the normative dispute between Habermas and Foucault is ultimately a hermeneutical question about such identities and interpretations, it cannot but be affected, perhaps even transformed, by these developments.

Has Foucault, then, given us good reasons to reject humanism on normative grounds? Strictly speaking, no. But with respect to the larger question of the viability of humanism as a normative ideal, the results are not yet in; not all quarters have been heard from.

4

Is Michel Foucault a "Young Conservative"? Has he demonstrated the superiority of a rejectionist critique of modernity over a dialectical one? The scorecard, on balance, looks roughly like this.

First, when Foucault is read as rejecting humanism exclusively on conceptual and philosophical grounds, Habermas's charge misses the mark. Foucault is not necessarily aspiring to a total break with modern values and forms of life just because he rejects a foundationalistic metainterpretation of them. Indeed, the project of de-Cartesianizing humanism is in principle a laudable one. But, on the other hand, it is understandable that Habermas should take the line that he has, since Foucault has not done the conceptual work required to elaborate and complete a merely philosophical rejection of humanism.

Second, when Foucault is read as rejecting humanism on strategic grounds, Habermas's charge is on target. Foucault has failed to establish that a pragmatic, de-Cartesianized humanism lacks critical force in the contemporary world. On the contrary, there are grounds for believing that such humanism is still efficacious, indeed doubly so. On the one hand, it tells against still-extant forms of premodern domination; on the other hand, it tells against the forms of administratively rationalized domination described in *Discipline and Punish*. Foucault has not, then, made the case for strategic rejectionism.

Finally, when Foucault is read as rejecting humanism on normative grounds, moral-philosophical considerations support Habermas's position. Without a non-humanist ethical paradigm, Foucault cannot make good his normative case against humanism. He cannot answer the question, Why should we oppose a fully panopticized, autonomous society? And yet, it may turn out that there will be grounds for rejecting, or at least modifying and resituating, the ideal of autonomy. If feminists succeed in reinterpreting our history so as to link that ideal to the subordination of women, then Habermas's own normative paradigm will not survive unscathed. The broader question about the normative viability of humanism is still open.

All told, then, Michel Foucault is not a "Young Conservative." But neither has he succeeded in demonstrating the superiority of rejectionist over dialectical criticism of modern societies.

Notes

1. Jürgen Habermas, "Modernity versus Postmodernity," *New German Critique* 22 (Winter 1981): 3–14.

2. Habermas, "Modernity versus Postmodernity," and "The Entwinement of Myth and Enlightenment: Rereading *Dialectic of Enlightenment*," *New German Critique* 26 (Spring/Summer 1982): 13–30.

3. David C. Hoy, "Power, Repression, Progress: Foucault, Lukes, and the Frankfurt School," *Triquarterly* 52 (Fall 1981): 43–63, and "The Unthought and How to Think It" (American Philosophical Association, Western Division, 1982).

4. Hubert L. Dreyfus and Paul Rabinow, *Michel Foucault: Beyond Structuralism and Hermeneutics* (Chicago, 1982).

5. Hoy, "Power, Repression, Progress," and "The Unthought and How to Think It."

6. Dreyfus and Rabinow, *Michel Foucault*.

7. Martin Heidegger, "Overcoming Metaphysics," in *The End of Philosophy*, trans. Joan Stambaugh (New York, 1973), 84–110, and "The Age of the World Picture," in *"The Question concerning Technology" and Other Essays*, trans. William Lovitt (New York, 1977), 115–24.

8. Heidegger, "Overcoming Metaphysics"; "The Age of the World Picture"; "The Question concerning Technology," in *"The Question concerning Technology" and Other Essays*, 3–35; and "The Letter on Humanism," trans. Frank A. Capuzzi, in *Basic Writings*, ed. David Farrell Krell (New York, 1977), 189–242.

9. Heidegger, "The Letter on Humanism."

10. Michel Foucault, *The Order of Things: An Archaeology of the Human Sciences*, trans. pub. (New York, 1973), and *Discipline and Punish: The Birth of the Prison*, trans. Alan Sheridan (New York, 1979).

11. Foucault, *The History of Sexuality, Volume 1: An Introduction*, trans. Robert Hurley (New York, 1978), and "Truth and Subjectivity," Howison Lectures, University of California, Berkeley, 20–21 October 1980.

12. Foucault, *I, Pierre Riviére, Having Slaughtered My Mother, My Sister, and My Brother . . . : A Case of Parricide in the Nineteenth Century*, trans. Frank Jellinek (New York, 1975), and *Her-*

culine Barbin: Being the Recently Discovered Memoirs of a Nineteenth-Century French Hermaphrodite, trans. Richard McDougall (New York, 1980).

13. Hoy, "Power, Repression, Progress," and "The Unthought and How to Think It."

14. John Rawls, *A Theory of Justice* (Cambridge, Mass., 1971), and "Kantian Constructivism in Moral Theory," *Journal of Philosophy* 77, no. 9 (September 1980): 505–72; and Gerald Dworkin, "The Nature and Value of Autonomy" (1983).

15. Richard Rorty, "Postmodern Bourgeois Liberalism," *Journal of Philosophy* 80 (October 1983): 583–89, and "Solidarity or Objectivity?" in *Post-Analytic Philosophy,* ed. John Rajchman and Cornel West (New York, 1985), 3–19; and Michael Walzer, *Spheres of Justice: A Defense of Pluralism and Equality* (New York, 1983). For a discussion of Rorty, see my Chapter 5.

16. Louis Althusser, *For Marx,* trans. Ben Brewster (New York, 1970).

17. See, for example, essays by Philippe Lacoue-Labarthe and Jean-Luc Nancy in *Rejouer le politique* (Paris, 1982). For a discussion of this work, see my Chapter 4.

18. Habermas, *Legitimation Crisis,* trans. Thomas McCarthy (Boston, 1975).

19. Dreyfus and Rabinow, *Michel Foucault.*

20. Foucault, *The History of Sexuality,* vol. 1; "Truth and Subjectivity"; *The History of Sexuality,* vol. 2, *The Use of Pleasure,* trans. Robert Hurley (New York, 1983); and *The History of Sexuality,* vol. 3, *The Care of the Self,* trans. Robert Hurley (New York, 1986).

21. Foucault, "Nietzsche, Genealogy, History," in *Language, Counter-Memory, Practice: Selected Essays and Interviews,* ed. Donald F. Bouchard, trans. Bouchard and Sherry Simon (Ithaca, N.Y., 1977).

22. Habermas, *Legitimation Crisis.*

23. Simone de Beauvoir, *The Second Sex,* trans. H. M. Parshley (New York, 1961).

24. Alison M. Jaggar, *Feminist Politics and Human Nature* (Totowa, N.J., 1983).

25. Carol Gould, "Private Rights and Public Virtues: Women, the Family, and Democracy," in *Beyond Domination,* ed. Gould (Totowa, N.J., 1983).

26. Carol Gilligan, *In a Different Voice: Psychological Theory and Women's Development* (Cambridge, Mass., 1982).

27. Iris Young, "Humanism, Gynocentrism, and Feminist Politics," *Hypatia: A Journal of Feminist Philosophy* 3, special issue of *Women's Studies International Forum* 8, no. 3 (1985): 173–85.

Chapter 3
Foucault's Body Language:
A Posthumanist Political Rhetoric?

*You grab the girl by the wrist. "Enough of these disguises,
Lotaria! How long are you going to continue letting yourself be
exploited by a police regime?"*

*This time Sheila-Ingrid-Corinna cannot conceal a certain
uneasiness. She frees her wrist from your grasp. "I don't
understand who you're accusing, I don't know anything about
your stories. I follow a very clear strategy. The counterpower
must infiltrate the mechanisms of power in order to overthrow
it."*

*"And then reproduce it, identically! It's no use your
camouflaging yourself, Lotaria! If you unbutton one uniform,
there's always another uniform underneath!"*

Sheila looks at you with an air of challenge.

"Unbutton . . . ? Just you try . . . "

*Now that you have decided to fight, you can't draw back.
With a frantic hand you unbutton the white smock of Sheila the
programmer and you discover the police uniform of Alfonsina;
you rip Alfonsina's gold buttons away and you find Corinna's
anorak; you pull the zipper of Corinna and you see the
chevrons of Ingrid . . .*

*It is she herself who tears off the clothes that remain on her.
A pair of breasts appear, firm, melon-shaped, a slightly
concave stomach, the full hips of a fausse maigre, a proud
pubes, two long and solid thighs.*

"And this? Is this a uniform?" Sheila exclaims.

You have remained upset. "No, this, no . . . " you murmur.

*"Yes, it is!" Sheila cries. "The body is a uniform! The body
is armed militia! The body is violent action! The body claims
power! The body's at war! The body declares itself subject! The*

> *body is an end and not a means! The body signifies!*
> *Communicates! Shouts! Protests! Subverts!"*
> —Italo Calvino, *If on a Winter's Night a Traveler*

A long and distinguished tradition of modern, normative social criticism and historical interpretation has developed around the humanist notions of autonomy, reciprocity, mutual recognition, dignity and human rights. These in turn depend, usually, upon a metaphysics of subjectivity. Clearly, the social thought of Kant, Hegel, Marx, Husserl, Sartre, and Habermas derives its normative force from such notions and (with the possible exceptions of Marx and Habermas) from such a metaphysics. Recently, however, Michel Foucault has offered a different sort of social criticism and historical interpretation, a "posthumanist" one, which explicitly rejects the metaphysics of subjectivity. For Foucault, the subject is merely a derivative product of a certain contingent, historically specific set of linguistically infused social practices that inscribe power relations upon bodies. Thus, there is no foundation, in Foucault's view, for critique oriented around the notions of autonomy, reciprocity, mutual recognition, dignity, and human rights. Indeed, Foucault rejects these humanist ideals as instruments of domination deployed within the current "disciplinary power/knowledge regime."

Whence, then, does Foucault's work, his description of "the carceral society," for example, derive *its* critical force? How does Foucault make it look so ugly and menacing without appealing to the humanist ideals associated with the concept of the subject? Does he presuppose some alternative, posthumanist normative standpoint, and if so, what justifies *it?* Does he presuppose some alternative metaphysic, say, one of bodies? Or is his critique radically antifoundationalist, and if so, to what sort of justification can it lay claim?

Foucault himself is far from having a single, consistent position on these issues. But a number of things are nonetheless clear. He has not, in fact, elaborated any substantive, normative alternatives to humanism. Indeed, like some members of the Frankfurt school, he is openly suspicious of attempts to formulate a positive, theoretical basis for critique. He assumes that such efforts are implicitly totalitarian because totalizing, that they must be normalizing because normative.[1] But even as he rejects the project of a new, posthumanist *moral theory,* Foucault in effect proclaims the need for a new *vocabulary* or *rhetoric* of social criticism.[2] To continue to use the modern humanist vocabulary and rhetoric is, he claims, to enhance and perpetuate the very form of life he wishes to oppose. Hence, the need for a new *critical paradigm.*

It is the project of a critique without traditional normative foundations, a critique rooted in a postmodern *rhetoric* rather than in a postmodern *theory,* that I wish to explore here. I shall do so by means of an examination of some rather unsystematic remarks of Foucault's, remarks that in effect sketch some requirements for a new critical paradigm and suggest, albeit in a very tentative and abstract fashion, what such a paradigm might look like. I shall focus, in other words, on that strand of his thought that is not content simply to be humanism's own immanent counterdiscourse — its critical, self-reflective conscience, as it were — but that aspires rather to "transgress" or transcend humanism and to replace it with something new.[3] The interesting result of these considerations, to give away the ending, is that in the light of all the difficulties exposed, good old-fashioned modern humanism, or some properly detranscendentalized version thereof, comes to appear increasingly attractive.

Let me begin by noting that it is one thing to criticize an entrenched political vocabulary and another to stop using it. Not only does Foucault not elaborate a substantive postmodern alternative to humanism, he continues to make tacit use of the same humanist rhetoric he claims to be rejecting and delegitimating. *Discipline and Punish,* for example, even as it indicts humanist reform for complicity in disciplinary power, depends for its *own* critical force on the reader's familiarity with and commitment to the modern ideals of autonomy, reciprocity, dignity, and human rights.[4] What else but one's attachment to such notions — at least as the ideals of one's culture, if not as the unavoidable foundational categories of moral reflection per se — explains the revulsion generated by Foucault's graphic depiction of processes for the production of "docile-useful bodies"?

Now, the fact that Foucault continues to speak (or at least to murmur) the language of humanism need not be held against him. Every good Derridean will allow that there is not, at least for the time being, any other language he could speak. Wary, perhaps, of the dangers of the "false sortie,"[5] Foucault himself acknowledges that he cannot simply and straightaway discard at will the normative notions associated with the metaphysics of subjectivity. He admits that

> When today one wants to object in some way to the disciplines and all
> the effects of power and knowledge that are linked to them, what is it
> that one does, concretely, in real life . . . if not precisely appeal to this
> canon of right, this famous, formal right, that is said to be bourgeois,
> and which in reality is the right of sovereignty?[6]

But even as he cannot help but have recourse to the rhetoric of "right" against discipline, Foucault is not content with it. He claims that it is inadequate for several reasons. First, the rights vocabulary is foundationalistic; it purports to be "Morality's Own Language," to paraphrase Richard Rorty, to be grounded, that is, in "the nature of persons as they really are in themselves" apart from their participation in contingent, historically specific regimes of social practices. This inadequacy might be corrigible were it not also the case, according to Foucault, that rights talk functions in contemporary society as a language of mystification, obscuring the actual processes of social domination and helping to produce the subjects of those processes.

Foucault's account of the mystificatory functioning of humanist rhetoric depends upon some assumptions about historical temporality that help define his *own* project of a posthumanist political rhetoric. These assumptions come to light in the curious fact that he charges rights rhetoric with two seemingly mutually contradictory offenses.

On the one hand, right is not the proper normative standard for the critical thematization of discipline because it is *anachronistic*. It harks back to an earlier period in which power had not yet become thoroughly diffused throughout the entire social body via everyday, disciplinary micropractices. Thus, Foucault holds that the psychoanalytic critique of fascism, however admirable, was "in the last analysis a historical 'retrovision'," because it was couched in the categories of law, right, and sovereignty.[7]

But on the other hand, Foucault *also* rejects the standard of right (or "sovereignty," as he sometimes calls it) on the grounds that it is precisely *contemporary* with the disciplinary regime and, thus, is internal to and complicit with it. He says,

It is not through recourse to sovereignty against discipline that the effects of disciplinary power can be limited, because sovereignty and disciplinary mechanisms are two absolutely integral constituents of the general mechanism of power in our society.[8]

It is no doubt this rejection of contemporaneous critique that is in play when Foucault intimates that Marxism may be inadequate because it opposes the regime of "bio-power" in the latter's own terms, to wit, in the name of "life."[9]

Of course, Foucault cannot, strictly speaking, have it both ways and hold that right is simultaneously anachronistic to and contemporary with discipline. In fact, he reconciles the apparent contradiction by claiming that modern power operates through precisely this heterogeneity between the disciplinary practices and the atavistic ideological and juridical organization of right. Right, in other words, exactly because it is *anachronistic,* has the *contemporary* ideological function of masking disciplinary domination and thus contributes to it.

But be that as it may, what is important here is that Foucault wants to rule out in principle any critical paradigm that is either anachronistic to or contemporary with the regime it is to critique. Neither the vocabulary of the past nor that of the present is adequate. Clearly, this leaves only the vocabulary of the future. Foucault seems to assume that an adequate critique of discipline must await the appearance of an entirely new political rhetoric, which in his scheme of things is tantamount to a new moral vision.

If one wants to look for a non-disciplinary form of power, or rather, to a struggle against disciplines and disciplinary power, . . . one should turn . . . towards the possibility of a new form of right, one which must indeed be anti-disciplinarian, but at the same time liberated from the principle of sovereignty.[10]

This puts Foucault in a position similar to that of the later Heidegger, the position of awaiting an *Ereignis* revealing a new direction of cultural development utterly discontinuous with the dying one of modern humanism. But since Foucault does not share Heidegger's critique of the will, his brand of "waiting" is not one of essentially passive receptivity ("Only a God can save us now") but, rather, one of multiple local resistances carried out in the name of no articulable positive ideals. It seems, then, that Foucault's assumptions about historical temporality and critique condemn him to a politics of negation.

But Foucault does make one rather tentative move to go beyond this stance of place-holding resistance while waiting for the dawning of a new postdisciplinary, posthumanist standard of right. He drops an occasional hint as to what such a standard might look like or at least as to where one might appropriately be sought. These hints are puzzling, however, because the alternative they suggest seems vulnerable to precisely the sorts of objections that in Foucault's eyes vitiated humanism: it seems to involve a retreat from antifoundationalism and a turn toward a new metaphysics—one of bodies—and it may be no less subject to co-optation and mystification than Foucault claims humanist critique has been.

Foucault concludes the first volume of his *History of Sexuality* with the suggestion that "the rallying point for the counterattack against the deployment of sexuality ought not to be sex-desire, but bodies and pleasures."[11] The reasons for the rejection of "sex-desire" are the characteristic deconstructive and demystifying ones. "Sex," according to Foucault, is a fictitious object invented in the late eighteenth century that functions as an instrument of domination in the regime of bio-power. It did not exist until the modern power/knowledge regime

> group[ed] together, in an artificial unity, anatomical elements, biological functions, conducts, sensations and pleasures, and . . . [made] use of this fictitious unity as a causal principle, an omnipresent meaning, a secret to be discovered everywhere.[12]

Sex has a role in the modern regime as an epistemic object and a target of power; it justifies asymmetrical procedures of coercion and intimidation and induces the formation of habits of *self*-surveillance and *self*-policing. But sex corresponds to nothing apart from this role. It simply *is* this role, an object-within-a-set-of-practices.

Of course, in this respect sex is no different from anything else in Foucault's scheme of things. Absolutely everything is socially constructed in his view. But not everything is "fictitious" in the way that sex is. What is different about sex is that, unlike many other objects-within-practices, it purports to refer to a transcendent entity existing apart from, and identifiable independently of, any social practices whatsoever. 'Sex,' then, is the name a particular historical power regime gives to an illusory object that it posits as existing outside all power regimes and as subject to repression and distortion by them. Sex, therefore, is an illusory object through which the current regime channels protest so as to integrate and feed that protest into the mechanisms of its own functioning. Protests in the name of sex merely continue to articulate the organization of sexuality proper to the regime. "We must not think that by saying yes to sex, one says no to power; on the contrary, one tracks along the course laid out by the general deployment of sexuality."[13]

In a fashion that parallels his treatment of "Man" and the subject, then, Foucault rejects "sex-desire" as a normative category on two analytically distinct but functionally interrelated counts: (1) it is foundationalistic, and (2) it is an instrument of domination. As he did in the case of "Man" and the subject, Foucault assumes that this means that sex is an instrument of domination *tout court,* that it has no critical, emancipatory force vis-à-vis the current regime.

Instead, Foucault suggests resistance in the name of "bodies and pleasures." But how does this standard escape the difficulties that plagued sex-desire? It must be that either the body-pleasure notion is not fictitious in the way that sex is or that it does not function as an instrument of domination within the current deployment of sexuality.

What could it mean to say that bodies are not fictitious in the way that sex is? Could it be that Foucault exempts bodies from his general thesis that everything is interpretation all the way down? Could it be, in other words, that he holds that the body is not simply an object-within-a-regime-of-practices but is, rather, a transcendental signified?

There is some evidence for this reading in *Discipline and Punish* in Foucault's claim that however various penal practices constitute or institute their respective objects, it is always really the body that is being punished. When the sovereign tortures malefactors' bodies, when the reformers rehabilitate juridical subjects, when the disciplinarians normalize deviants, all are in fact applying force to bodies. It is always the body that is contested.

But if indeed Foucault does hold the view that the body is a transcendental signified and if it is for *this* reason that he claims that bodies are the appropriate basis for postmodern political critique, how does he himself avoid the sort of foundationalism for which he attacks humanism?

In fact, Foucault does not identify any positive characteristics of bodies "as they really are in themselves" apart from the ways in which they are historically "invested." Nor does he derive any universal normative political ideals from this putative suprahistorical corporeality. On the contrary, he calls his project the study of the history of the political technology of the body. He insists that this is neither the history of what people have said and thought about the body nor that of some identical, selfsame referent prior to history. Rather, it is a history of the politically and historically invested body, of the distinctive ways in which various successive power/knowledge regimes institute the body as an object within their respective techniques and practices. For example, there is the tortured body of the *ancien régime,* the object of the "art of unbearable sensations"; then there is the mechanical, analyzable body of Galilean science, the object of calculable spatiotemporal forces and motions; and there is also the natural, organic body of discipline, the trainable, manipulable object of *dressage* and eventually the "docile-useful body."

Clearly, none of these is the body *simpliciter.* Rather, each is the body already invested with some historically specific form of power. Indeed, the notion of the body *simpliciter,* as a substratum prior to power, upon which power inscribes its figures, drops out of the picture altogether. That sort of body would be merely another version of the *Ding-an-sich,* since it can never be encountered and has no identifiable properties whatsoever. Foucault's antifoundationalism requires him to reject such a notion. He cannot consistently appeal to it either to ground a post-humanist political vision or to justify his historical interpretations.

If this is so, one may ask, With what right does Foucault continue to speak of the body *simpliciter* at all? What justifies him in calling his work a history of the political technology of "*the* body"? What justifies his assumption that the various invested bodies just mentioned are all species of the same genus? If there is no identifiable common referent underlying them all, why organize the material in this way, and why give the body any special role in political critique?

In order to avoid an ill-advised retreat from his antifoundationalist position to a metaphysical one, Foucault should probably answer these questions as a pragmatist would. He should say that although there is no *ontological* basis for organizing his discourse about the succession of power/knowledge regimes in terms of how they institute bodies as opposed to in some other terms, there *is* a *pragmatic* basis, in that such discourse provides critical insights that help us cope. It is, in that sense, the most efficacious discourse for thematizing the problematic of emancipation in modern societies.

But if the claim in *Discipline and Punish* that it is really always a question of bodies boils down, in effect, to the claim that "body language" has greater emancipatory potential than the alternatives, then we need to ask whether this latter claim is really so. Is "body language" really more efficacious than "rights language" or "desires language" or "needs-and-interests language"?

Foucault's reply will no doubt be that rights language and the others function as instruments of domination within the disciplinary power regime, whereas body language does not. But addressing the first half of this reply, one can say that even if rights talk does so function, it does not follow that it is wholly inefficacious or devoid of critical force. Foucault himself has cited cases in which opposition groups have appropriated entrenched vocabularies for their own purposes and turned them against those who had used them to exclude and oppress.

He notes, for example, that those disqualified as ''perverts'' in the vocabulary of the new nineteenth-century *scientia sexualis* defended their legitimacy in a counterdiscourse employing some of that vocabulary's own terms.[14] Now, if a ''strategic reversal'' was possible in that case, why might not something similar occur in the case of rights talk? Why does Foucault dismiss such a possibility out of hand? Why does he assume that rights talk has no emancipatory potential whatsoever, that it is reducible without remainder to its putative current mystificatory function?

Perhaps Foucault believes that the track record of humanist rhetoric is so miserable as to be compromised beyond all possibility of redemption. But if so, might not one dispute his historiography? Surely, one need be neither a Whiggish proponent of the ideology of progress nor a foundationalistic positivist in matters of epistemology in order to doubt that he has done justice to the ''emancipatory moment'' in the history of humanism. In any event, the decision on whether to reject rights rhetoric surely demands both a more judicious weighing of such considerations than Foucault gives us and an examination of the available alternatives.

This brings me to the second half of the claim that I have just attributed to Foucault, namely, that body language does not currently function as an instrument of disciplinary domination. This is no doubt true, but only trivially so: since no one now speaks this body language, it has *no* function, domination-engendering or otherwise, in the current regime. It therefore satisfies Foucault's requirement that an adequate critical rhetoric or paradigm be radically external or future-situated. But this only shows, in my view, how insufficient—indeed, how bizarre—Foucault's criterion is, for the same thing could be said of any of an indefinitely large number of other currently unspoken, unborn languages. What justifies the suggestion that the one having to do with bodies and their pleasures is the one we now need? Why does *it* in particular seem promising as an antidisciplinary strategem?

One way to answer this question is to appeal to the tactical value of body language as a counter to the ''ideophilia'' of humanist culture.[15] The rhetoric of bodies and pleasures, in other words, can be said to be useful for exposing and opposing, in highly dramatic fashion, the undue privilege modern western culture has accorded subjectivity, sublimation, ideality, and the like. But this is to treat Foucault's suggestion as a flashy strategic ploy aiming to *épater les bourgeois*. Unless more can be said about the uses of body talk for thematizing at least some of the major social and political issues of the day—issues such as the prospects for democratic, nonbureaucratic, nonauthoritarian socialism; the ecological crisis; scientism, technologism, and the deformation of public life; sexism, racism, homophobia, national and religious chauvinisms; the relations between modern and traditional cultures; disarmament; mass culture; the family; poverty—unless body talk can speak in some way to these, Foucault's proposal might understandably be thought jejune.

What, then, might body language better permit us to say and do about such things than the vocabulary of humanism can? Here is where my capacity to imagine a plausible Foucauldian response runs out. I can form no concrete picture of what resistance to the deployment of sexuality in the regime of bio-power in the name of bodies and their pleasures would be like. Or, to the extent that I can, it is one that, by the most ironic of coincidences, resembles the hedonistic utilitarianism of the very architect of panopticism himself, Jeremy Bentham. Still more troubling, though, is the thought that since the disciplinary deployment of sexuality has, according to Foucault, produced its own panoply of bodily pleasures (including those associated with the sadomasochistic, hunter-prey, cat-and-mouse scenarios described in the first volume of *The History of Sexuality*)— since, in other words, disciplinary power has thoroughly marked the only bodies that we potential protesters have—it is not clear how claims in the name of the pleasures of our bodies would have any greater critical leverage on the regime than, say, claims in the name of the rights traditionally recognized but *not generally realized* in modern Western culture.

Indeed, it probably follows from Foucault's own antifoundationalistic assumptions that there is no normative archimedean point for political critique. No vocabulary whatsoever is intrinsically immune from all possibility of co-optation and misuse. To abandon as illusory the philosophical quest for Morality's Own Language is to admit that, given the right circumstances, any normative concept, emancipatory ideal, or political rhetoric can, might, and likely will be used as an instrument of domination.[16] And by the same token, it is to recognize that no critical paradigm need be reduced without remainder to that status, since "strategic reversals" are sometimes possible. The moral here is that claims couched in the language of the pleasures of our bodies are no more intrinsically immune from co-optation and abuse than are claims made in any other vocabulary. Their capacity to generate critical leverage and escape co-optation is entirely relative to their situation.

It seems, then, that the best one can do now is to take a hard look at Foucault's social critique and ask straightforwardly, What is it, after all, that strikes us as objectionable about the regime of discipline and bio-power so graphically depicted there? Can we sum up our objections more efficaciously by saying that panoptical practices and the like produce an offensive economy of bodies and pleasures or by saying that they fail to respect the rights that express our sense of how persons ought to be treated?

I suspect that the second formulation will strike most people as more trenchant. Most people will object to the modern power regime on the grounds that (1) it objectifies people and negates the autonomy one usually prefers to accord them, and that (2) it is premised upon hierarchical and asymmetrical relations and negates the reciprocity and mutuality usually valued in human relations. But to put matters thus is to suggest that there may after all be some emancipatory potential surviving in humanism. It is to suggest the possibility of the sort of immanent critique that consists in condemning the institutions of a culture for their failure to realize its own widely accepted ideals.

Yet it may be argued that what strikes most people as more trenchant is not the last word. I concede that there is something disturbingly conservative in this approach. The objections just formulated are couched in the vocabulary of modern Western normative theory, and the intuitions that support them are not innocent of that theory and that tradition. On the contrary, these intuitions are themselves saturated with the presuppositions of the last several centuries of our culture. It seems question-begging, therefore, to take them as the standard when what is to be decided is the desirability of a revolution in political culture that would result in some major restructuring of our intuitions, presuppositions, and vocabulary. It seems, in other words, overly tendentious to assume that we will or should retain our current standards.

But once we have recognized this problem, there is no getting around the fact that our current standards are the only ones we currently have. It is true that we may not be stuck with them forever, that a revolution in political culture may occur (although, of course, there is no guarantee that that would be an improvement—by *whomever's* standards). But in the absence of such a revolution—which is to say in the absence of some positive, concrete, palpable alternative social vision or exemplar capable of winning our loyalty and restructuring our way of seeing—the standards we have are the standards we have. This is so however reflexively self-conscious we are about the fact that it is *we* who have them. So when someone who offers no convincingly articulated alternative comes along and tells us that our attempts to critique discipline in terms of humanism testify only to our immersion in the disciplinary matrix and in fact are moves deployed to articulate and strengthen that matrix, a healthy dose of skepticism is in order—provided, of course, that such skepticism does not degenerate into the sort of blind adherence to tradition that rules out receptivity to new critical paradigms, if and when these emerge.

If this conclusion seems unduly hard on Foucault, it might be well to recall that it follows from an analysis of one strand of his thought only—the strand that aspires to "transgress" or transcend humanism and replace it with something new. It is this "transgressive" Foucault who appears to lack genuine political seriousness, to be wanting in the theoretical, lexical, and critical resources necessary to sustain a viable political vision.

But to leave matters thus would be to ignore the *other* strand of Foucault's thought—the strand that in effect constitutes humanism's own immanent counterdiscourse or critical conscience. This is the strand that aspires less to overthrow humanism than to keep it honest. It offers no solutions of its own but only an extremely keen nose for sniffing out hypocrisy, cant, and self-deception, on the one hand, and the historical logic whereby "modes of humanistic knowledge and practice escape the good intentions of their formulators and supporters, on the other."[17] This is the muckraking, Socratic Foucault, the Foucault who has done more, perhaps, than anyone since Marx to expose and warn against the enormous variety of ways in which humanist rhetoric has been and is liable to misuse and co-optation. To *this* Foucault we owe a profound debt of gratitude.

But even this more evenhanded conclusion may not seem entirely satisfactory. Despite (or perhaps because of) its eminent reasonableness, one might feel uneasy with an interpretation that subdivides Foucault in this way and selects out for approval only that portion of his thought that is, to put a Derridean gloss on it, recuperable within the humanist closure. One might, in other words, wish to find some way of better appreciating the *un*recuperable Foucault.

Two possibilities suggest themselves. First, one could follow Derrida further and see the immanentist Foucault and the transgressive Foucault as two phases of a deconstructive "double gesture." The nonidentity of these phases would then be the "interval" marking the text as the sort of "bifurcated writing" necessary to "*dis*place" (rather than *re*place) humanism.[18] Intriguing as this is, it is unclear what the political implications of such a reading would be. Is displacement reform? Revolution? Or some third, new, possibility? Does it mean that the immanentist Foucault is simply a tactic deployed in the service, ultimately, of the transgressive Foucault? And if so, do not all of the foregoing objections to the latter reassert themselves?

There is perhaps another, simpler way in which one might appreciate the unrecuperable Foucault. One might take a hint from Susan Sontag, who writes:

> Great writers are either husbands or lovers. Some writers supply the solid virtues of a husband: reliability, intelligibility, generosity, decency. There are other writers in whom one prizes the gifts of a lover, gifts of temperament rather than of moral goodness. Notoriously, women tolerate qualities in a lover—moodiness, selfishness, unreliability, brutality—that they would never countenance in a husband, in return for excitement, an infusion of intense feeling. In the same way, readers put up with unintelligibility, obsessiveness, painful truths, lies, bad grammar—if, in compensation, the writer allows them to savor rare emotions and dangerous sensations. And, as in life, so in art both are necessary, husbands and lovers. It's a great pity when one is forced to choose between them.[19]

Foucault, one might conclude, isn't much good as a husband; one wouldn't want, politically speaking, to cohabit with him indefinitely. But he makes a very interesting lover indeed. His very outrageousness in refusing standard humanist virtues, narrative conventions, and political categories provides just the jolt we occasionally need to dereify our usual patterns of self-interpretation and renew our sense that, just possibly, they may not tell the whole story.

Notes

1. Foucault himself does not explicitly argue these assumptions. However, his teacher, Georges Canguilhem, attempted to demonstrate an internal relation between the normative and the normalizing in medicine; see *Le normal et le pathologique* (Paris, 1966). Why such a relation should be thought to hold more generally has not, to my knowledge, been plausibly articulated.

2. The centrality of rhetoric, as opposed to epistemology and ethics, in Foucault's project has been noted by Hayden White; see his "Michel Foucault," in *Structuralism and Since: From Lévi-Strauss to Derrida,* ed. John Sturrock (Oxford, 1979). The contrast between a moral *vocabulary* and a moral *theory* is developed by Richard Rorty in "Method, Social Science, and Social Hope," in *Consequences of Pragmatism: Essays, 1972–1980* (Minneapolis, 1982).

3. The distinction between these two strands in Foucault's thought was impressed upon me as a result of James Bernauer's comments on an earlier draft of this paper read at a meeting of the Society for Phenomenology and Existential Philosophy on 29 October 1981 in Evanston, Illinois. Professor Bernauer's comments emphasized what I call the strand of "immanentism" in Foucault, whereas my paper emphasizes what I call the "transgressive" strand. Clearly, both are present in Foucault. I shall return to the contrast between them at the end of the paper.

4. I argue this thesis in "Foucault on Modern Power: Empirical Insights and Normative Confusions"; see Chapter 1 of this volume.

5. The "false sortie" is Jacques Derrida's expression for the abstract and premature effort whereby one catapults oneself outside the metaphysical closure only to end up reproducing it; see "The Ends of Man," *Philosophy and Phenomenological Research* 30, no. 1 (September 1969): 56.

6. Foucault, "Two Lectures," in *Power/Knowledge,* ed. Colin Gordon trans. Gordon et al. (New York, 1980), 108.

7. Foucault, *The History of Sexuality, Volume I: An Introduction,* trans. Robert Hurley (New York, 1978), 150.

8. Foucault, "Two Lectures," 108.

9. Foucault, *The History of Sexuality,* 144–45.

10. Foucault, "Two Lectures," 108.

11. Foucault, *The History of Sexuality,* 157.

12. Ibid. 154.

13. Ibid. 156.

14. Ibid. 134. The example and the general point are found in Jonathan Arac, "The Function of Foucault at the Present Time," *Humanities in Society,* 3, no. 1 (Winter 1980): 73–86.

15. I owe this term to James Bernauer (see n. 3 above). The point was also suggested to me by Hayden White.

16. See Richard Rorty, "Method, Social Science, and Social Hope."

17. Bernauer; see n. 3 above.

18. See Derrida, "Positions: Interview with Jean-Louis Houdebine and Guy Scarpetta," in *Positions,* trans. Alan Bass (Chicago, 1981), 41–42.

19. Susan Sontag, "Camus' *Notebooks,*" in *"Against Interpretation" and Other Essays* (New York, 1966), 52. I am grateful to Martin Jay for calling this passage to my attention.

Part 2

On the Political and the Symbolic

Chapter 4
The French Derrideans:
Politicizing Deconstruction or
Deconstructing the Political?

In the summer of 1980 a conference entitled "The Ends of Man: Spin-offs of the Work of Jacques Derrida" ("Les fins de l'homme: A partir du travail de Jacques Derrida") was held at Cérisy, France. Participants included many French philosophers in and around the Derridean circle as well as a number of American literary critics. Readers of the proceedings of this event are likely to find that the most interesting—and, as it subsequently turned out, the most fruitful—portion of the meeting was the "Political Seminar."[1] Here, at last, were raised explicitly all the questions that have long been bugging those who have followed the career of Derrida's writings and their peculiar reception in the United States: Does deconstruction have any political implications? Does it have any political significance beyond the byzantine and incestuous struggles it has provoked in American academic lit crit departments? Is it possible—and desirable—to articulate a deconstructive politics? Why, despite the revolutionary rhetoric of his writings circa 1968[2] and despite the widespread assumption that he is "of the Left," has Derrida so consistently, deliberately and dexterously avoided the topic of politics? Why, for example, has he danced so nimbly around the tenacious efforts of interviewers to establish where he stands vis-à-vis Marxism?[3] Why has he continued "to defer indefinitely" the encounter of deconstruction with "the text of Marx" that he has on occasion promised? Or is there *already* a politics implicit

Research for this article was supported by a much appreciated grant from The University of Georgia Research Foundation.

in his work? If so, what is it, and is it a tenable one? What problems does Derrida's very complex relationship with Heidegger pose for those wishing to politicize deconstruction? What sort of politics is possible at "the end of metaphysics" or "in the wake of deconstruction"? What sort of political thought remains possible once one has deconstructed all the traditional bases of political reflection? Is it possible to rethink the political from a Derridean standpoint? What might such an effort look like?

Participants in the "Political Seminar" at Cérisy proposed a number of mutually incompatible answers to these questions. Not surprisingly, the chief upshot of the sessions was the proliferation of further questions and a recognition that an ongoing, systematic inquiry was needed if these were ever to be satisfactorily resolved. A few months later the Center for Philosophical Research on the Political was launched at the Ecole Normale Supérieure in Paris. Under its auspices, as organized by Strasbourg philosophers Jean-Luc Nancy and Philippe Lacoue-Labarthe, a group composed mainly of philosophers, including but not limited to many of the Cérisy participants, has since been pursuing the inquiry.[4] The center holds about six meetings a year to hear and discuss papers both by people whom I shall call "members" (people who attend regularly, have been associated with or influenced by Derrida, and have not necessarily done previous work directly oriented to specifically political questions) and by people whom I shall call "nonmembers" (people who do not attend regularly, have not been especially identified with deconstruction, and whose work has long been explicitly concerned with politics—for example, Claude Lefort, former Althusserians Etienne Balibar and Jacques Rancière, and *Esprit* editor Paul Thibaud). Papers presented during the first year of the center's existence, along with the text of its inaugural, founding statement, have been collected and published under the title *Rejouer le politique*.[5] The second year's papers have appeared in another volume, *Le retrait du politique*.[6]

The central trajectory of the center's work, especially as defined by the members' papers that appear in these volumes, is an interesting and original one. It is a trajectory that will probably surprise many American readers both pro-and anti-deconstruction, for it is deeply marked with Heideggerian and Arendtian motifs and is profoundly suspicious of the sorts of projects for politicizing deconstruction or articulating a deconstructive politics that have appeared in the United States.[7] In order to understand this unexpected line of thought, to see why and how it has taken the form it has, and eventually to assess its merits, it is necessary to look first at the discussions of the Cérisy "Political Seminar."

Two of the Cérisy presentations, though extremely well-conceived and well-written and though marked by a number of original and provocative themes, could be said to have been predictable. Each of these sought to isolate what its author considered the most fundamental "gesture" of Derridean deconstruction and to determine its political significance. Each treated that gesture as the basis for a politics of deconstruction and tried to elaborate it into a substantive, pro-grammatic political orientation. It will come as no surprise to readers of Derrida that the two papers in question fastened upon different gestures and thus pre-sented different—indeed, opposing—deconstructive politics.

What we might call the "left gesture" and hence the left version of decon-structive politics was presented by literary critic Gayatri Chakravorty Spivak.[8] Although she conceded that "Derrida no longer invokes this project" (511), Spi-vak nevertheless oriented her paper to the apocalyptic closing of his 1968 essay "The Ends of Man." The project of deconstruction, she quoted approvingly, is that of "a radical shake-up [ébranlement], [which] can come only from the out-side [and which] takes place [se joue] in the violent relationship—be it 'linguis-tic' . . . or ethnological, economic, political, or military—between *all* of the West and its other."[9] The aim, in other words, is to pave the way for revolution, to destabilize the West by forcing it to confront the other, which it excludes. For Spivak, this other is "women, . . . the non-Western world, . . . the victims of capitalism" (513). But, she argued, "*all* the relations between East and West are today written in terms of the possibility of the production, maximally, of absolute surplus value and, minimally, of relative surplus value; and this is not only in the 'pure' sense of an effect in excess of a text" (511). In her view, it was Derrida himself who showed that "the working body, although it be a text, is certainly not one text among others" and that "the economy is not one domain among others" (511). Thus, concluded Spivak, the discourse of deconstruction cannot continue to exclude that of political economy. To persist in reducing the latter to "the status of [a] precritical method duped by its own axiomatic" is to be duped oneself in turn (507). It is to fall back "into a precritical, ideological space" (513), to reproduce the very gesture of marginalization-exclusion that Derrida himself has repeatedly condemned ever since his 1967 *Speech and Phenomena* (508). It is to establish a "binary opposition" by means of "a certain ethico-political decision" establishing "centralized norms by means of strategic exclu-sions" (506). This ignores the "most important 'political' lesson" to be learned from Derrida: theory is a practice; one must be careful "not to exclude the other term of a polarity or the margins of a center"; one must "put in question the normative character of the institutions and disciplines in and by which we live" (506).

Thus for the sake of the project of a "radical shake-up of the West from the outside," Spivak urged deconstruction to deconstruct its own exclusion of polit-ical economy. She claimed that a subtle reading of Marx would reveal a decon-structor *avant la lettre*. Contemporary Derrideans should follow Marx's example and "confront the false other of philosophy, make a performative or revolution-ary contingency erupt into [it, make] felt the heterogeneity of being and knowl-edge and of being and doing." They should decenter their own discourse, "open it onto an 'outside' constituted by ethical-political contingencies" (514).

The discussion that followed Spivak's Cérisy presentation did not directly confront or challenge the political orientation she proposed. Instead, participants noted that there were metaphysical elements in Marxism themselves in need of deconstruction: the presupposition of a "quasi-divine" labor power producing more than it consumes; the elaboration of that labor power as the "source or origin of surplus value for the sake of assigning a proper terminus (a *propre*) to the movement, really produced by nothing, of production of surplus value"; the concepts of disappropriation, mediation, and appropriation.[10] But subsequent developments in the "Political Seminar" soon revealed that many of the participants did not share Spivak's commitment to a politicized deconstruction in the service of Marxism, however nonclassical.

If Spivak's version of deconstructive politics was anchored in the apocalyptic closing gesture of "The Ends of Man," the next presentation proposed an alternative politics based on the explicit rejection of that gesture. French philosopher Jacob Rogozinski titled his paper "Deconstruct the Revolution."[11] He argued that, *pace* Spivak, the "inaugural gesture" of deconstruction, the one that opens its field of operation, is the *rejection* of the radical cut or break (*coupure*). To her citation from "The Ends of Man," Rogozinski counterposed the following passage from *Positions:* "I do not believe in decisive ruptures, in an unequivocal 'epistemological break,' as it is called today. Breaks are always, and fatally, reinscribed in an old cloth that must continually, interminably be undone."[12] There is, then, no transgression that is unrecuperable, that cannot be reinstalled within the closure it tries to exceed. Indeed, it is the impossibility of a break that makes deconstruction necessary. For Derrida, claimed Rogozinski, the idea of such a break is a mere ruse of the system, a wily strategy by means of which it recuperates protest. Hence, an even wilier counterstrategy is called for. Deconstruction can only be a "double game, a double writing." It must substitute for the violent, eruptive temporality of the break (and of Spivak's Marxism) a temporality of its own: one of patient, enduring, interminable work, Penelopean or Sisyphean labor, "an acute vigilance and perhaps a silent distress" (518).

Hence, argued Rogozinski, a politics of deconstruction can be inaugurated only by a rejection of revolution. It must deconstruct revolution as the metaphysical project of an impossible radical break. It must expose the latter's "archeteleological structure," which projects an origin and an end, promising an "end of man" (communism, the proletariat) as the total reappropriation of his *propre* and as the return to the *parousia* of his presence. It must show that Marxism, qua project of revolution, is "the last avatar of political metaphysics" (520).

But, continued Rogozinski, a deconstructive politics that was content simply to deconstruct the metaphysics of the *propre* in political philosophy would not be adequate. It would fail to see that in political philosophy *before* Marx this metaphysics functioned as a guard against the tyranny and Terror that was its "inadmissable other.'' For in order to define the conditions of legitimate authority, the tradition always conjured up the figure of the gravest danger, the most extreme decay of *Mitsein*. And it elected to link the latter in every case to a disturbance of the *propre*. The demand for the *propre,* then, was always the antistrophe in a chorus bewailing the menace of tyranny. This tradition reached its apogee in Hegel, where the gesture of *Aufhebung*–qua absolute reappropriation of absolute loss — became the guard protecting against Terror. In the sections of the *Phenomenology* that treat the French Revolution, the *Aufhebung* was the mechanism for overcoming the unthinkable horror of a death *sans phrase;* it overcame the meaningless, uncompensated death that issued from the revolutionary assertion of the absolute, abstract freedom of unmediated self-consciousness. In place of this ''death worse than death,'' the *Aufhebung,* qua recovery of the *propre,* substituted a ''beautiful death under the yoke of the Law'' (521–22).

It follows, *pace* Spivak, that it is Hegel, not Marx, who is the deconstructor *avant la lettre.* For Hegel, claimed Rogozinski, conceives Terror as the foreclosure of *différance,* as the actualized presence of the absolute. In opposition to Terror, Hegelian political philosophy is established ''in the shelter of *différance.*'' It exiles the absolute to another world outside history and time, refrains from attempting to realize it here and now, defers it to eternity. It maintains differentiations within civil society as well as the differentiation between civil society and the state. Thus it takes account of *différance.* by accepting and reinscribing differences at the heart of social space. Hegelian politics, then, preserves a nondialectical, un*aufheb*able cleavage (522–23).

But this puts it in diametric opposition to Marxism, which seeks dialectically to overcome or abrogate *différance* in its ''utopia of the totally transparent, self-reconciled '*une-société*''' (523). Marxian politics thus attacks ''the stronghold of discretion protecting the reserve of the absolute'' and unleashes revolutionary Terror. If the *propre* is metaphysics's guard against Terror, its ''inadmissable other,'' then Marxism is ''the lowering of that guard [and] hence (unhappily) the least metaphysical of projects'' (523). Quoting Adorno, Rogozinski concluded that deconstruction must side with Hegel against Marx; it ought not simply deconstruct metaphysics but should be ''in solidarity with metaphysics in the moment of its fall'' (523).

Rogozinski ended his paper by formulating what he saw as deconstruction's present dilemma: on the one hand, it inaugurates itself by rejecting the radical break and contents itself with the sort of patient, faithful, disinterested endurance that corresponds to a politics of resistance. But, on the other hand, it does so in the name of another, more radical rupture; invoking the apocalyptic tone par excellence, ''it sets its sights on the '*outre-clôture*' [and] surrenders to the fascination of the beyond, seek[ing] the 'Orient of its text,' the other space beyond the frontiers delimiting Western metaphysics'' (523). Deconstruction contains, thus, two different calls to *différance,* two different intonations and intensities. One calls us to a politics of resistance that preserves *différance* as a guard against Terror. The other calls us to a "wholly other politics," one of revolution more radical than has ever been conceived, one that celebrates *différance* as "absolute danger" and "the monstrosity of the future" (524). Deconstruction slides incessantly—strategically, it would claim—between a politics of revolution and a politics of resistance. It says that the alternatives are undecidable and lingers on the threshold, refusing to choose. But, concluded Rogozinski, "Now you have no choice: you must choose. The impossible choice of your death presses you more and more. You are required to choose, and quickly, between a 'beautiful death' under the yoke of the Law, and that other monstrous death that is worse than death" (525).

The discussion following this remarkable tour de force was lively and contentious.[13] If the seminar participants were unwilling to accept Spivak's reading of Marx, they did not like Rogozinski's any better. Many speakers objected to his hypostatization of *the one* Marxism and *the one* project of revolution; they appealed to the variety of Marxian and revolutionary theories, parties, and political tendencies. But the most interesting response was that of Derrida himself, who delivered some of his most straightforward and revealing remarks to date on the topic of politics. Derrida claimed to agree with the broad lines of the argument but to disagree with Rogozinski's conclusions. He said that he had deliberately not produced a discourse against revolution or Marxism, in order to avoid contributing to the "anti-Marxist concert" of the 1968 period. He did not, and *does* not, want to weaken "what Marxism and the proletariat can constitute as a force in France" (527). Despite his distrust of the idea of revolution qua *metaphysical* concept, he does not "devalue what [this idea] could contribute . . . as a force of 'regroupment' [*rassemblement*]" (527).

So, for the sake of the traditional leftist aim of not splitting the Left, Derrida claimed to have adopted a "complex," "encumbered" strategy. He had refrained from a frontal attack while marking a series of "virtual differences or divergences" from the revolutionary project. This strategy was marked in his writings, he said, by "a sort of withdrawal or retreat [*retrait*], a silence on Marxism—a blank signifying . . . that Marxism was not attacked like such and such other theoretical comfort . . . This blank was not neutral . . . It was a perceptible political gesture" (527). But having defended this strategy as appropriate to the political context in 1968, Derrida did not protest when Jean-Luc Nancy replied that it had now become necessary to substitute a reading of Marx for this "blank" (528).

Whether such a reading is actually produced—and if it is, what it looks like—remains to be seen. But what is evident even now is Derrida's determination to avoid or reject the Spivak-Rogozinski alternative. His own Cérisy paper was a refusal of the alternative between an apocalyptic and an antiapocalyptic discourse.[14] And this refusal seemed in tune with the general sentiment in the

"Political Seminar." Indeed, the refusal to choose between the two political orientations proposed there was later to become in effect the "inaugurating gesture" of the Center for Philosophical Research on the Political. For in an implicit repetition of a philosophical move at least as old as Kant, the members of the center have refused to defend one side of the antinomy against the other and have instead retreated to a deeper level of analysis which interrogates the conditions of possibility shared by both.

This move was already foreshadowed at Cérisy in a presentation by Jean-Luc Nancy, made outside the framework of the "Political Seminar." In "The Free Voice of Man," Nancy explored the important and difficult problem of the status of the various quasi-ethical imperatives or obligations—the *il faut*'s—in Derrida's writings: *il faut déconstruire la philosophie; il faut penser l'écriture; il faut entendre doublement;* and so on.[15] More important than his solution, it seems to me, was Nancy's way of posing the issue. He began by invoking Heidegger's response in "The Letter on Humanism" to the question, When are you going to produce an ethics? Nancy noted that Heidegger rebuffed the suggestion, arguing that an ethics, like a logic or a physics, made sense only within the confines of the metaphysical tradition and that the task of thought at the end of metaphysics was to think the "unthought" of that tradition—to think, in this case, the prior, enabling background, itself nonethical, upon which the domain of the ethical is instituted. Nancy argued that Derrida would have to make a similar response to the demand to produce an ethics, especially, he claimed, were such a demand to understand ethics as the translation into practice of a philosophical theory. For Nancy endorsed what he took to be Heidegger's view of the matter: namely, that ethics is metaphysical insofar as it has been conceived in the Western tradition as *the practical effectuation of the philosophical,* that is, as the effectuation in practice of theoretical knowledge and thus as presupposing the prior establishment of the domain of the philosophical. Nancy inferred that deconstruction "does its duty" (*fait son devoir*) when it rebuffs the demand for an ethics and instead deconstructs that demand, showing where it comes from and interrogating the "essence" (in Heidegger's sense of the "transcendentale") of the ethical.

Although the Center for Philosophical Research on the Political has never explicitly addressed the question of the relation between ethics and politics, it has in fact proceeded as if the two were analogous. It has subjected the political to a line of interrogation paralleling that which Nancy proposed for the ethical. This has been tantamount to refusing Spivak's and Rogozinski's demands that it produce a politics of deconstruction—the practice of the theory—while offering instead to deconstruct the political.

The outlines of this program were already visible in two other presentations at the Cérisy "Political Seminar." Christopher Fynsk broached the problem of the political by noting a certain doubleness in Derrida's work.[16] On the one hand, there is the *retrait* of or from politics in his writings; Derrida avoids any direct

engagement with political questions and resists demands for an explicit, immediate politicization of his work. But, on the other hand, and at the same time, he
claims that his practice *is* political and that philosophical activity in general is a
political practice. Fynsk sought to explain this apparent contradiction by noting
that it has become a truism of the modern age that politics is the horizon of every
practice, that every act is necessarily inscribed within the domain of the political,
presupposing political institutions and producing political effects. But, he argued, this "self-evident" omnipresence of the political makes it difficult to as-
sign any determinate meaning to the term 'politics.' When everything is political, the sense and specificity of the political recedes, giving rise to still another
inflection of the expression *le retrait du politique*: the retreat or withdrawal of the
political. Henceforth, this expression will evoke Hannah Arendt's diagnosis of
modernity as the age in which the sphere of the political is engulfed by the socioeconomic, in which the public space for normative deliberation about common ends is overrun by administrative decisionmaking, interestbrokering, and
obsession with the (putatively prepolitical) problems of "national housekeep-
ing"— a diagnosis, incidentally, in which Marxism appears as the culmination
of the sad trend.[17]

The theme of the *retrait du politique* was later to become a leitmotiv of the
center's work. It was further elaborated at Cérisy by Philippe Lacoue-Labarthe.[18]
He cited Derrida's remark in "The Ends of Man" that there is an "essential belonging-to-one-another [*co-appartenance*] of the political and the philosophical." This remark, claimed Lacoue-Labarthe, posed the question of "the bond
indissociably uniting the philosophical and the political" (494). Paraphrasing
Heidegger's claims about technology,[19] he argued that "the unconditional [or to-
tal] domination of the political in the modern age represents the completion of a
philosophical program. In the [self-evident omnipresence of the] political today,
the philosophical reigns" (494). This was to echo Nancy's view, itself inspired by
Heidegger, that the tendency in contemporary culture to see everything as political presupposes a prior determination of the political as the practical effectuation
of the philosophical. Given this analysis, Lacoue-Labarthe defended Derrida's
retreat (*retrait*) from politics as the necessary response to the withdrawal (*retrait*)
of the political. Those who would oppose the reign of the philosophical, he
claimed, cannot avoid such a retreat (494).

But, Lacoue-Labarthe went on to argue, this retreat from the political cannot
be a simple gesture. It is not as if one can turn away from the political and move
on to something else. On the contrary, today there is not and cannot be something
other than the political. To retreat from the political, then, is not to move into a
retraite (a nonpolitical refuge or haven) (495); it is rather to step back from "our
passionate obsession with the political" in order to interrogate it. It is to refuse
the "intimidation" of the political, especially as exercised by Marxism (495).
One resists the pressure to produce a deconstructive politics and instead ques-

tions the *obviousness* of the political. One interrogates the "essence of the political" (497).

The discussion following Fynsk's and Lacoue-Labarthe's Cérisy presentations
turned on a number of issues that have continued to be subjects of controversy
among the center's members.[20] One of these was the question of the adequacy of
the Heideggerian assumption of a basic unity or homogeneity of Western metaphysics that permits one to speak of "*the philosophical*" in the singular. Another
was the question, raised by American literary critic David Carroll, of the applicability of the notion of "the total domination of the political" outside France —
in the United States, for example. More generally, French philosopher Sarah Kof-
man questioned the appropriateness of supposing a quasi-Heideggerian
framework. Why appeal to Heidegger, she asked, in order to think the political
implications of deconstruction, given the enormous differences separating the respective political practices of Heidegger and Derrida? Lacoue-Labarthe's response underlined a distinction that was to become canonical for the center: one
can recognize, he claimed, that there may be a stratum of thought common to
Heidegger and Derrida vis-à-vis *the political (le politique)* without ignoring the
differences between them at the level of *politics (la politique)*. On the other hand,
distinguishing between *le politique* and *la politique* in this way does not obviate
the necessity of asking if and how the two are related. There must come a point,
claimed Lacoue-Labarthe — as there surely did, alas, for Heidegger — at which
one's *politics* encroaches upon one's conception of *the political*.

Nearly all the major themes of the center's work were already broached in the
Cérisy presentations of Nancy, Fynsk, and Lacoue-Labarthe: the theme of the *retrait du politique* (with its double signification of, first, the disengagement from
and resistance to the insistent demands of, for instance, Spivak and Rogozinski
for a politics of deconstruction, and, second, the receding of the specificity of the
political in the contemporary truism that "everything is political"); the theme of
the *essence of the political* (the program of interrogating the constitution and institution of the political in Western culture); the theme of the *essential belonging-
to-one-another of the political and the philosophical* (the way in which the constitution and institution of the political is related to that of the philosophical); and
the theme of the distinction between *le politique* and *la politique*. Together, these
themes comprise a decision to replace the project of politicizing deconstruction
with the project of deconstructing the political.

That project and its salient themes were elaborated more systematically in the
"Ouverture," or inaugural lecture, delivered by Nancy and Lacoue-Labarthe at
the first meeting of the Center for Philosophical Research on the Political on 8
December 1980.[21] This remarkable document is worth explicating at some
length. The authors begin by explaining their choice of a name for the center.
They claim that in calling the workspace they wish to create the "Center for
Philosophical Research on the Political," they intend to suggest a double aim:

first, they envision a *philosophical* interrogation of the political, one that excludes other possible approaches; but, second, this philosophical interrogation is not one that supposes that philosophy is itself privileged or unproblematic—on the contrary, it also problematizes philosophy, by interrogating the latter's relation to the political (12–13).

The justification for the first of these aims runs as follows: empirical investigation of the political—investigation aimed at establishing a political science or a political theory or at discovering or inventing a new concept of the political—is excluded because it can no longer be "decisive." Such investigation itself issues from and is determined by a preestablished philosophical field—one that is old, past, closed. Discourses claiming to be independent of the philosophical, whether by treating the political itself as an autonomous positive domain or by subordinating it to some other autonomous positive domain (for instance, the economic or the psychoanalytic), are not in fact independent. Rather, they have philosophical presuppositions—and not for reasons that are merely accidental. These discourses *necessarily* bear the marks of the "essential belonging-to-one-another" of the philosophical and the political in the Western tradition (13–14).

It is this "essential belonging-to-one-another" that justifies as well the second prong of the center's double aim. In Western culture ever since the contemporaneous institution of philosophy and the Greek polis, there has always been a reciprocal implication of the political and the philosophical such that neither is anterior or exterior to the other. Indeed, this reciprocal implication is part and parcel of what Nancy and Lacoue-Labarthe take to be our current predicament (14–15). We live, say the authors of the "Ouverture," in the age of the "total domination of the political." It is the age of the completion, or fulfillment (*l'accomplissement*), of the philosophical *in* the political, in a sense precisely analogous to that in which Heidegger claimed that metaphysics was completed, or fulfilled, *in* modern technology.[22] We necessarily act within the "closure of the political" (15). Sartre was right, though not in the way he thought, when he claimed that Marxism was the unsurpassable horizon of our time. This is true when it is construed as meaning that socialism ("really existing socialism") is the most complete realization of the drive to impose philosophy on existence. *Philosophy* is what is being completed and effectuated in the discourse analyzed by Rogozinski: the great "enlightening," progressive, secular-eschatological discourse of revolution as humanity's self-reappropriation and self-actualization (though it does *not* follow that one should therefore endorse the counterdiscourse of the *nouveaux philosophes* [16]).

In Nancy and Lacoue-Labarthe's view, to recognize our confinement in the closure of the political is to realize that despite real possibilities of revolt here and there (in truth, less here than there), History-with-a-capital-*H* is finished. We can no longer accept theories offering global political solutions to inhumanity, for we have seen, Nancy and Lacoue-Labarthe claim, that the project of social transparence, of the utopian homogenization of the "social bond," leads to totalitarianism. Indeed, if the definition of totalitarianism is the universalization of one domain of reference to the point where it usurps and excludes all others, then the epoch of the completion of the philosophical in the political is the totalitarian age par excellence (16–17).

But, say the authors, the project of interrogating the philosophical essence of the political is not equivalent to simply denouncing, from the outside, as it were, by means of a simple *political* critique, the various metaphysical programs for founding the political or for programming existence philosophically. Rather, the work of the center must take into account the fact that such denunciations — which are now commonplace — are themselves internal to and determined by the development of philosophy. They are part of an epochal process akin to what Nietzsche called "European nihilism" and to what Heidegger called "the overcoming of metaphysics": a process wherein philosophy is undermining its own foundations, delegitimating its own authority, *de*instituting itself.[23] Deconstruction is itself an immanent component of this process (17–18).

Nancy and Lacoue-Labarthe infer that recognition of the closure of the political and of the self-deinstitution of philosophy requires us to think the *re-trait du politique* in two senses: first, as a *withdrawal* on our part from the blinding self-evidence of the political, which marks our confinement in its closure; and, second, as a *retracing* of the political from the standpoint of its essence. Moreover, we are required to distinguish rigorously between the political (*le politique*) and politics (*la politique*) (18).

That last distinction complicates the character of the center's work. On the one hand, say the authors, to deconstruct the political and the essential belonging-to-one-another of the political and the philosophical is *not* to take a *political position;* it is rather to question the very *position* of *the political*. The task, in other words, is not *to institute a new politics* but, rather, to *think the institution of the political* in Western thought (15). But, on the other hand, they claim that the work of the center is not and cannot be a retreat to apoliticism (18). There is and can be no nonpolitical *outre-clôture* to which one could safely emigrate; besides, it is unavoidable that the center's work will produce political effects (20). So to interrogate the essence of the political cannot be to discard or sublimate political or class struggles. Such struggles are the givens of the age and there is no way around them (24). It follows, for Lacoue-Labarthe and Nancy, that the *retrait du politique* must itself be a political gesture, albeit a somewhat unusual one. It permits one to "exceed something of the political" — but not by a *sortie* outside the political (18–19). It is a kind of *engagement* — but one that does not consist in pledging oneself to one or another politics (19).

The authors of the "Ouverture" go on to argue that the "engaged" character of the center's work requires it to reexamine a variety of received political notions. For example, it can no longer accept the traditional left maxim, invoked by

Derrida at Cérisy, that enjoins silence on certain matters in order to avoid harming the Left. To keep such silence today, they claim, is to court a far greater risk, namely, the very extinction of every Left (20). Thus, the center must address itself to Marxism. In doing this, it need not start from scratch but may critically appropriate some important recent work by nondeconstructionist thinkers, for example, Claude Lefort's work on the "lacuna of the political" in Marx. Marx's neglect of the political, along with his early project of negating the state as a separate instance in society, which in the East has meant the incursion of the state into all social instances, should be rethought from the standpoint of the center's problematic. It should be related to the way in which the question of the specificity of the political has repeatedly surfaced in such diverse Marxian currents as Council Communism, Gramscism, Althusserianism, and Maoism. The center should also address the question of the temporary form of the political that becomes necessary in the revolutionary transition to communism (the dictatorship of the proletariat—a form that is encrusted in the socialist countries). Nor should the center ignore the question of the ultimate form of the political, given the project of overcoming the split between civil society and the state, that is, the complete engulfment of the political by the social (20–21).[24]

In addition to work on Marx and Marxism, Nancy and Lacoue-Labarthe propose a line of inquiry oriented to thinkers like Heidegger and Bataille, who have produced discourses "at the extreme limit or border of the political." These discourses sought, unsuccessfully, to exceed the political by avoiding the presupposition of the *subject,* a presupposition that has always marked more properly metaphysical political discourses, paradigmatically those of Hegel. Heidegger and Bataille attempted to locate an *outre-sujet* of the political (22–23); they failed, however, and ended up inadvertently reintroducing quasi-subjectivities, thereby confirming that "behind the self-evidence of the political is dissimulated the self-evidence of the subject" (23). From this, the authors of the "Ouverture" infer that the center must rethink the state, power, and political struggles without assuming the "arche-teleological domination of the subject" (24).

In order not to presuppose the subject, it will be necessary, they claim, to problematize the very notion of the "social bond," for that notion has always been thought as a relationship among previously constituted subjects. Consequently, it too can be seen as a "limit question" of the political, one that must repeatedly surface as such in the tradition. Thus, argue Lacoue-Labarthe and Nancy, the center should interrogate the diverse forms in which the problematic of "the other" repeatedly arises in political philosophy: the questions of "forms of sympathy," conflict, and *Mitsein* (24–25). A reading of Freud, for example, may demonstrate how the motifs of sociality and alterity make the question of the "social bond" a limit question for psychoanalysis, one that it can neither avoid nor resolve. On their reading of Freud, the birth or fabrication of the subject arises from its bond to the paradigm of subjectivity represented "in the form of the Father'' (25–26). But, they suggest, this bond is achieved only with the concomitant withdrawal of what is neither subject nor object, "the mother." Despite the danger that such a formula may give rise to a host of *Schwärmerei,* one could say, claim the authors of the "Ouverture," that "behind the political (if it must be identified with the Father), [lies] 'the mother'" (26).

It is here, say Lacoue-Labarthe and Nancy, that the work of the center rejoins the Derridean source of its inspiration. In trying to think a process in which something recedes as the political is installed, they ask, What nondialectical negativity, what nonunity and nontotality withdraws or recedes or is divided or subtracted in the fabrication of the "social bond" (26)? For the essence of the political cannot be an originary social organism or harmony or communion, any more than it can be a partition of functions and differences. Nor can it be anarchy. It must, rather, be "the an-archy of the archē itself" (27). In other words, the question of the *retrait du politique* rejoins the general problematic of the opening of the *trace* as elaborated by Derrida (27).

Thus, in their "Ouverture," Nancy and Lacoue-Labarthe sketch a program for rethinking the political from the standpoint of deconstruction. It is a program that, in its purity and rigor, is far more faithful to the spirit of Derrida's work than the latter's own comparatively simplistic leftist remarks at Cérisy. But it also— indeed, *therefore*–reveals all the more starkly the limitations of deconstruction as an outlook seeking to confront the political.

Consider again the way in which the center's project emerged: In the rhetoric and politics of Gayatri Spivak, the Derrideans found themselves face-to-face with the authentic political expression of Derridean *apocalypticism:* revolution as a celebration of the "monstrousness" of the "wholly other." But this in the end is only a pose, one that does not do justice to the depths of the historical experience from which deconstruction emerged. Rogozinski was right to detect a "silent distress" beneath Derridean bravado. It is the existential distress of a specific cultural experience: the experience of nihilism in the immediate wake of the historical *dépassement* of Marxism. Rogozinski's own politics of resistance, however inadequate to the complexities of contemporary social reality, remains the authentic expression of the deep, *tragic* current underlying deconstruction's compulsive playfulness. When sounded against that tragic strain, Derrida's political line about not splitting the Left rings false. Hence, Nancy and Lacoue-Labarthe have little difficulty in showing that it travesties the rigorous ethos of deconstruction—an ethos that they seek to maintain, even as Derrida threatens to abandon it.

The standpoint of Nancy and Lacoue-Labarthe, then, is founded on the collapse of three political orientations, three versions of *la politique:* Spivak's, Rogozinski's, and Derrida's. The authors of the "Ouverture" reject each of the three—and rightly, in my view—as inadequate. But it is telling that, in doing so, they do not debate their opponents on the latter's own—*political*—terms. Rather, they refuse the very genre of political debate and in this way, too, maintain the ethos of deconstruction. For there is one sort of difference that deconstruction cannot tolerate: namely, difference as dispute, as good old-fashioned political fight. And so, Nancy and Lacoue-Labarthe are utterly — one might say, terribly — faithful to deconstruction in refusing to engage in political debate.[25]

But this leaves them poised between the horns of a dilemma. On the one hand, they long, with all the poignancy evoked by Rogozinski, for a post-Marxian politics, a genuine "engagement." But, on the other hand, the supposed historical unavailability at present of a viable political stance, of *une politique,* aborts that longing and drives them back to *le politique,* to the philosophical interrogation of the political.

It seems, then, that the "Ouverture" of Lacoue-Labarthe and Nancy is the scene of a dialectic of aborted desire, a scene replete with tensions that threaten to shatter it. But if this is so, then it is likely that their project, like deconstruction itself, is only a temporary way station on the exodus from Marxism now being traveled by the French intelligentsia. It is not and cannot be a permanent resting place. Indeed, the subsequent career of the Center for Philosophical Research on the Political tends to bear this out.

The fragility of the center's project could be surmised from the fact that during the first year of its existence, only two of the papers presented directly pursued the program laid out in the "Ouverture." Not surprisingly, these were written by Nancy and Lacoue-Labarthe, respectively. In "The Juri-Diction of the Hegelian Monarch," Nancy provided a deconstructive reading of *The Philosophy of Right* that showed how the problem of the social bond was a limit question for a thought about the political that presupposed the self-evidence of the subject.[26] In "Transcendence Ends in Politics," Lacoue-Labarthe investigated both the "essential belonging-to-one-another" of the political and the philosophical and also the relation between *le politique* and *la politique* in Heidegger's Nazi-era writings.[27]

The second year of the center's existence brought some attempts on the part of members at criticism of the "Ouverture" program. Denis Kambouchner questioned the exclusion of empirical work and argued that Nancy and Lacoue-Labarthe were in danger of succumbing to idealism.[28] Philippe Soulez adduced some Lacanian considerations against the formula: "Behind the political [qua Father, lies] 'the mother.'"[29] But it was the intervention of nonmember Claude Lefort that provoked the most unambiguous expression of the fragility of the program of sublimating the desire for *la politique* in an interrogation of *le politique.*

The subject of Lefort's paper was the differences between democracy and totalitarianism.[30] It elicited, in response, the most interesting section of yet another text by Lacoue-Labarthe and Nancy.[31] At the closing session of the center's second year, the principal organizers sought to take stock of the previous two years' work and to see how things stood in relation to the questions posed in the

"Ouverture." After reprising a number of that document's salient themes and replying to the charge of idealism, they try to locate their own conception of totalitarianism in relation to Lefort's. Nancy and Lacoue-Labarthe distinguish two senses of 'totalitarianism'. First, there is their own very general sense suggested in the notion of "the total domination of the political." This sense concerns the universalization of the political to the point of usurping and excluding every other domain of reference. It finds symptomatic expression in the contemporary truism that "everything is political." This generalized sense of 'totalitarianism' is not empirical, they claim, although it does permit the thematization of certain salient "facts" of the age: the Arendtian paradox of the disappearance of the specificity of the political in its very domination; the confounding of the political with other instances, such as the socioeconomic, the technological, the cultural, and the psychological; and the consequent banalization of the political. The result of the rise of totalitarianism in this sense, they say, is that nowhere can even the slightest specifically political question be posed; nowhere can the question of a new politics have the slightest chance of emerging—none of which, however, prevents "politics as usual" from being carried on (188–89).

Nancy and Lacoue-Labarthe distinguish this first sense of totalitarianism from a second, narrower one. The latter emerges from political-scientific analyses—by, for example, Arendt and Lefort—of notable cases like nazism, fascism, Stalinism, and Soviet-type societies. Here, totalitarianism is a response to the "crisis of democracy." Following the erosion of authority, traditions, and religion, modern democracy rests on a desubstantialized and disincarnated form of power. Thus, it institutes a version of the political that is bereft of metaphysical foundations, devoid of transcendence. The result is a "delocalization" of the political: the dismemberment of the political body "which is no longer one except in the pure dispersion of suffrage," and the consequent surrender of political affairs to the play of interests. Responding, then, to this democratic "impasse," totalitarianism in the narrow sense is the attempt at a mad, frenzied resubstantialization and reincarnation of the political body. It remolds the political by force so as willfully to impose transcendence and unity (189–90).

Nancy and Lacoue-Labarthe claim that their adherence to the first, generalized sense of totalitarianism does not lead them to reject this second, more specific sense. The latter, too, must continue to be investigated "in all its (apparent) heterogeneity" with the former (190). But, they go on to argue, such investigation should be informed by certain questions suggested by the generalized sense of totalitarianism: Isn't the "reincarnation" notion applicable, above all, to a first (albeit still-extant), pure, radically brutal historical face of totalitarianism? And hasn't there since been installed, in the "democratic" societies, under the general domination of systems governed by technical and performative criteria, a second, inconspicuous, insidious, "soft" form of totalitarianism?[32] Isn't this "soft totalitarianism" a response, *internal to democracy,* to the "democratic crisis"—

one that, unlike "hard totalitarianism," does not assume the guise of a rebuke (*redressement*)? Isn't it the case, then, that despite the crying differences, a certain ready-made and widely circulating opposition between totalitarianism and democracy is rather too simple? Granted, "we don't have camps, and our police, whatever their 'technological advancedness,' are not omnipresent political police. But this doesn't mean, however, that the democracy we have is that described by Tocqueville. And if the democracy of Tocqueville contained the germ of classical totalitarianism, there is no guarantee that ours is not in the process of secreting something else, a brand new form [*une forme inédite*] of totalitarianism" (191).

With explicit reference to the work of Hannah Arendt, Nancy and Lacoue-Labarthe link the withdrawal of the political in "soft totalitarianism" to the rise of the "economic-socio-techno-cultural complex," a complex that is no longer simply the state. They claim that this complex is characterized by (1) the triumph of the *animal laborans,* (2) the colonization of the public space by a *gesellschaftlich* sociality, such that common life is governed by considerations pertaining to subsistence and not by genuinely public or political ends, and (3) the loss of authority as a distinct element of power, a loss concomitant with the loss of liberty. They argue that these characteristics of soft totalitarianism demonstrate the insufficiency of simple critiques of classical totalitarianism. If classical totalitarianism proceeds from the "incorporation and presentation of transcendence," then soft totalitarianism proceeds from the *dissolution* of transcendence, a dissolution that pervades and thus homogenizes every sphere of life, eliminating alterity (191–92).

The *retrait du politique,* therefore, is the withdrawal of the transcendence or alterity of the political vis-à-vis other social instances. But, say Lacoue-Labarthe and Nancy, it does not follow that the task is to achieve a new political transcendence. That, indeed, is the program of classical totalitarianism. The task is rather to interrogate the way in which the *retrait* requires us to displace and reelaborate the concept of political transcendence, to think a "wholly transformed" transcendence or alterity of the political (192–93).

Reinstalling a (nontotalitarian) alterity of the political today, they claim, would require the following: (1) the overcoming of the present dissociation of *power* (material constraint) from *authority* (transcendence), (2) the repair of the presently disrupted relation of the community to what Arendt called "immortality" (a this-worldly immortality in which the community preserves the words and deeds of mortals through remembrance), and (3) the restoration of the community's capacity to represent its communality to itself in the political sphere (193–94).

Nancy and Lacoue-Labarthe go on to interweave these quasi-Arendtian observations with more properly Heideggerian motifs. The *retrait du politique,* they claim, is not a wholly privative phenomenon. Rather, it is a withdrawal that releases or delivers something else: it makes something appear—namely, the possibility, indeed the necessity, of retracing the political anew. Furthermore, it is probably the case that what receded or withdrew is something that had never occurred in the first place; it is doubtful that the polis described by Arendt ever existed. But Nancy and Lacoue-Labarthe deny that the task is to make it occur now, or to pull the political out of its withdrawal, or even to achieve a new founding of the political. They want, instead, to pose what they take to be a more fundamental question: To what is the *retrait du politique* linked? Is it linked to the withdrawal of the unity, totality, and effective manifestation of the community (194–95)?

Thus, Nancy and Lacoue-Labarthe paraphrase Heidegger in claiming that from or in the withdrawal of the political, the political "itself" arises as a question and as an exigency. What is released is the opening of a question: On the basis of what, against what, is the closure of the political traced? The answer is not simply: on the basis of, or against, the nonpolitical (an answer popularized by Pierre Clastres's defense of anarchism, *Society against the State*).[33] It is, rather: on the basis of, or against, the "essence of the political," the essence that is withdrawn in the total completion of the political in the "techno-social" (195–96).

Provisionally, several things may be said, claim Nancy and Lacoue-Labarthe, about the "essence of the political." This essence is masked by various metaphysical programs that purport to ground the political domain on a transcendent foundation. Chief among these in the modern period is the attempt to found the political on a preconstituted, preindividuated autonomous subjectivity. It is no wonder, then, that those seeking to avoid foundationalism often substitute the notion of human finitude for that of autonomous subjectivity. But that substitution is by itself insufficient for the center's purposes: it is not guaranteed to lead beyond the politics of liberal democracy. Moreover, since finitude devolves upon immersion in an always already given, contingent sociohistorical matrix, it fails to problematize, but rather takes for granted, the existence of the social bond. In other words, it forecloses those questions that Nancy and Lacoue-Labarthe earlier took as crucial to their project: the questions circulating around the shadowy, enigmatic figure of "the mother," namely, the questions of the social constitution of identity, of the constitution of social identity, and of a prepolitical, "originary" sociality (196–97).

Nancy and Lacoue-Labarthe claim that these themes lead back to the problem of the specificity of the political—to the "philosophical fact" that at least since Aristotle, the being together of human beings, of the *zoon politikon,* is not based on the factual given of needs and the vital necessities of life. It is based rather on that other given: the sharing in ethical or evaluative speech. It is the excess of this second given over the first, of "living well" over mere "life" or social "living together," that defines the *zoon politikon.*[34] And it is the question of a "good" over and above every organization of needs and regulation of forces that remains in *retrait* today and thereby opens the question of the political (13).

This most recent statement of Nancy and Lacoue-Labarthe's program is notable for the sharp relief into which it throws the dilemma I noted earlier. On the one hand, the authors seek to resist the pressure to produce a politics, and they strive instead to maintain a pure, rigorous, deconstructive, quasi-transcendental interrogation of the political. But, on the other hand, they entertain the not-so-secret hope that the thought engendered by means of this approach will yield insights that will be relevant to *la politique*. Hence, there is an incessant sliding back and forth between two heterogeneous levels of analysis, a constant venturing toward the taking of a political position and a drawing back to metapolitical philosophical reflection.

This oscillation is clearly visible in the treatment of totalitarianism. The thesis about "hard" and "soft" totalitarianism is patently a *political position*, a venture into *la politique*. For totalitarianism is without doubt a *politically contested notion*. Nancy and Lacoue-Labarthe concede as much when they counterpose their conception to that of Lefort, arguing that the latter is not adequate to think the character of contemporary Western societies. Here, they are supposing a *specific interpretation of social reality*, a view that is not merely deconstructive and philosophical but *empirical, normative*, and *critical*. They are confronting the *political* problem of the character and meaning of contemporary scientific-technological culture. And this necessarily brings them into dialogue—indeed, into conflict—with competing *political* positions and interpretations. On the one hand, they must contest Lefort and other theorists of Soviet-type societies. But also, and on the other hand, whether they admit it or not, they must contest competing theories of Western political culture—most prominently, perhaps, those of Habermas and Foucault, not to mention Marx and Weber. Only if they are willing to enter the fray against such alternatives can they possibly make good their claims about "the total domination of the political" and "soft totalitarianism."

But just when such straightforwardly empirical and political argumentation is called for, just when *la politique* is about to be broached in earnest, Nancy and Lacoue-Labarthe remove themselves from the scene of conflict and draw back into quasi-Heideggerian speculation. They reflect on the "essence of the political," the "delivery of the question of the political," "finitude," the "social bond," an "originary sociality," "the mother," and a "wholly transformed alterity." The problem is not that such speculation is in itself useless or irrelevant. It is rather that it functions for Nancy and Lacoue-Labarthe as a means of avoiding the step into politics to which the logic of their own hopes and thought would otherwise drive them.

This is evident in a somewhat different way in their treatment of the Arendtian themes of the receding of the specificity of the political in the rise of the "economic-socio-techno-cultural complex"; the triumph of the *animal laborans;* the

colonization of the public space by *gesellschaftlich* sociality; the loss of authority, of this-worldly immortality, of the transcendence or alterity of the political
vis-à-vis "life," needs, and the prepolitical in general. With the introduction of
such themes, Nancy and Lacoue-Labarthe verge once again upon politics proper.
Indeed, they urge these themes against the politics of Lefort, whom they take to
be insufficiently critical of contemporary "democratic" societies. But just when
one would expect them to continue in this Arendtian vein, to call for a new or
renewed transcendence or alterity of the political, to bring into being now the
"politicity" of a polis that may never have existed—just at this point they draw
back once again and explicitly deny that any such *normative political* tasks and
conclusions follow. Instead, they conclude that one must think the *retrait*, the
essence, the tracing of the closure, and the rest.

Similarly, when Nancy and Lacoue-Labarthe invoke Aristotle at the close of
their text, they stop just short of embracing any normative political conclusions.
They appeal to the excess of "living well" over mere life, of the sharing in ethical or evaluative speech over mere need and necessity. They claim that it is the
question of a "good" over and above every organization of needs and regulation
of forces that opens the question of the *retrait* of the political today. But it is
significant that they do not proceed from these remarks to call for an institution or
restitution of noninstrumental, normative, political deliberation about "the good
life." It is significant that, instead, they note parenthetically that this "good"
beyond every organization of needs and regulation of forces is one that they
"charge with no moral weight" (198).

What these discussions of totalitarianism, Arendt, and Aristotle show, in my
view, is the fragile, slippery character of the tightrope on which Nancy and Lacoue-Labarthe are walking. They are engaged in a sort of balancing act, one that
probably cannot be maintained with much fruitfulness for very long. It is likely
that either one of two things will happen. Either they will try to maintain the
rigorous exclusion of politics, and especially of empirical and normative
considerations—in which case the political import of their philosophical work
will diminish. Or they will cross the line and enter upon concrete political
reflection—in which case their work will become increasingly empirical and normative and therefore increasingly *contested*. In either case, one avenue appears
to be excluded, the one to which Nancy and Lacoue-Labarthe apparently hope to
keep—namely, the middle way of a philosophical interrogation of the political
that somehow ends up producing profound, new, politically relevant insights
without dirtying any hands in political struggle.

This impasse is quite intractable. But one ought not, on that account, underestimate the importance of the questions Nancy and Lacoue-Labarthe are asking.
When they probe the meaning, character, and boundaries of the domain of the
political as instituted in Western civilization, the historical transformations that
domain has undergone since its Greek beginnings, and its specifically modern

(and, we might add, postmodern) features, they broach issues that are central to contemporary political reflection. This is evident in the way their project links up with two more specific sets of empirically and normatively anchored questions.

First, and most explicitly, Nancy and Lacoue-Labarthe broach a series of issues concerning the relation between the political and economic dimensions of contemporary societies. These issues have arisen as a result of the concurrent development of welfare state capitalism in the West and authoritarian state socialism in the East (where they reached a new pitch of articulateness and insistence in Poland, in Solidarity's struggle for an "autonomous civil society"). From the Western perspective, these issues can be decisively formulated: When, in the late modern period, even capitalist economic production is socialized to the point of defying the label "private enterprise"; when, therefore, justice requires that the domain of the political be *quantitatively* enlarged so as to include the previously excluded "social question," and when, *pace* Arendt, politics must, as a result, become political economy, what *qualitative* transformations of the political are needed to prevent its being overrun by instrumental reason and reduced to administration? What transformations can stem the homogenizing and antidemocratic tendencies that accompany the blurring of the division between civil society and the state (both in its communist form of rule by a centralized state planning apparatus and in its capitalist form of rule by a combined corporate and state-bureaucratic managerial elite)? How can both participatory democracy and the qualitative diversity of human experience be fostered in the face of these developments? What new, still uninvented postliberal and post-Marxian models of democratic, decentralized, socialist, or mixed political economies can do justice both to the specificity of the political and to its connectedness with the socioeconomic?[35]

Second, but far more obliquely, the center's problematic links up with a range of issues concerning the relationship between the political and the familial or domestic dimensions of contemporary societies. When they problematize the contemporary truism that "everything is political" and suggest instead that "behind the political (if it must be identified with the Father), lies the 'mother,'" Nancy and Lacoue-Labarthe at once gesture at and recoil from questions now being posed by Western feminists. Indeed, the contrast between their silence here and their volubility concerning Marxism has the significance of a symptom, since the current wave of feminist scholarship is without doubt the most advanced post-Marxian interrogation of the political now in progress[36] — an interrogation, one should note, that remains engaged while problematizing extant concepts and institutions of the political and that avoids the snares of transcendentalism by incorporating empirical and normative elements into its philosophical critique.

Like it or not, then, Nancy and Lacoue-Labarthe are de facto engaged in a covert dialogue with a movement that is questioning the relationship between the political and the familial. When this is acknowledged, a number of issues cry out for explicit consideration: If, as Arendt contended, the institution of the political in the West depended upon, indeed was the flip side of, the institution of the familial; and if the familial, as a sphere of inequality and exploitation, can no longer be immune from critique and transformation, then how must and ought the political sphere change as well? For example, if, as Arendt argued, modern political culture, including Marxism, has been deformed by its obsession with the production of food and objects to the neglect of symbolic action; and if, *pace* Arendt, this is nowhere more evident than in the undervaluation and privatization of women's childrearing work (which—as the cultivation of persons—is symbolic action par excellence, then how might an equitable reorganization of childrearing, one that put it at the center of public concern, help to revitalize and transform the political? Finally, if women's traditional domestic activities, including the emotional servicing of men and children, have contributed to the development of enclaves (at least) of distinctive women's cultures with distinctive women's values, and if these values, which include nurturance, caring, affectivity, and nonviolence, have been denigrated and occluded in a sexist and androcentric political culture that privileges autonomy, sovereignty and instrumental reason, then how might the political be transformed if women's cultures were liberated from domesticity and permitted to infuse public life?

Together, these two sets of questions form the outer horizon of Nancy and Lacoue-Labarthe's work. That this is so is, for me, a large part of the interest and importance of that work. But it is also an indication of its limitations. For to begin to answer these questions in earnest is of necessity to abandon transcendental and deconstructive discourse for inquiry of a different sort. It remains for the Center for Philosophical Research on the Political to join the ranks of those seeking to rise to this challenge.

Postscript:

The preceding account was written in the fall of 1982.

On 16 November 1984, Philippe Lacoue-Labarthe and Jean-Luc Nancy announced that they were indefinitely suspending the activities of the Center for Philosophical Research on the Political. In a memorandum sent to members, they claimed that the center had ceased to be a place where one could advance the project of interrogating "the essence of the political." That project required that all questions concerning the political be kept open and that all certitudes be bracketed, but this was no longer the case at the center. On the contrary, during the previous two years, a certain facile, taken-for-granted consensus had settled in and closed off the opening in which radical questioning had, for a time, been possible. This consensus bore on three principal concerns. First, "totalitarianism," originally the sign of a series of questions about the similarities and differences among a variety of historical and contemporary societies, had congealed into a "simple and vehement designation of *the sole* political danger . . . henceforth incarnated by regimes of Marxist provenance." Second, Marxism, too, had ceased to be a question and had become—simply—past, outmoded, obsolete, an unfortunate nineteenth-century ideology to which one now opposed conceptions of a somehow still relevant eighteenth century—conceptions of liberty (as opposed to equality) and of right (as opposed to politics). Finally, the political itself had acquired the one-dimensional signification of a danger and an impasse, so that it was no longer possible to consider the character and organization of collective identity and sovereignty—which meant that "the ethical or the aesthetic, even the religious" had come to be privileged over the political. The result was the surrender of the very object of the center's interrogation and, simultaneously, the triumph of apoliticism. But this was, in reality, capitulation to a determinate political position, namely, the "economic neoliberalism" and "political neoconformism" now sweeping France, a born-again liberalism arising from what it proclaims to be the ashes of Marxism.

This, of course, is only one side of the story. Lacking the other side(s), one might well hesitate to offer an analysis. Nonetheless, I cannot resist pointing out that the demise of the center recapitulates its constitutive dilemma.

In their memorandum, Nancy and Lacoue-Labarthe note that in dissolving the center they are responding to a political exigency. Indeed, they have taken what, from one point of view, appears to be a straightforwardly political stand: they are opposing anti-Marxist neoliberalism. But from another point of view, the situation is more complicated. The dominant thrust of their dissolution memorandum is not to marshal *political* arguments against the neoliberals; it is, rather, to accuse them of violating the transcendental pact, of breaking faith with the interrogation of the essence of the political. The problem, in other words, is less that their opponents have bad politics than that they have politics—which is a fair guess as to how the neoliberal tendency won hegemony in the center in the first place.

Moreover, there is a sense in which the neoliberal position represents one—if not *the*—legitimate working out of at least some of Nancy and Lacoue-Labarthe's own views. What they now excoriate as "apoliticism," for example, is a not wholly unfaithful elaboration of their own theme of "the total domination of the political." After all, that theme was always inherently ambiguous. It compounded Heidegger's already overblown suspicion of technology and Arendt's already too categorical suspicion of "the social" into an even more global and undifferentiated suspicion of the political, thereby seeming to surrender the possibility of *political* opposition to administration and instrumental reason. No wonder, then, that some members concluded that henceforth such opposition must be waged under the banner of "the ethical or the aesthetic, even the religious."

A similar argument could doubtless be made with respect to anti-Marxism. In fact, of the three issues discussed in the dissolution memorandum, only one—namely, totalitarianism—is altogether unambiguous. For only with respect to that issue do Nancy and Lacoue-Labarthe assert themselves unequivocally. First, they reject a use of the term 'totalitarianism' that would put them in lockstep with NATO, and *that* is a political stand. Second, they insist on conceptual distinctions adequate to the empirical complexity of contemporary social reality, East *and* West, and *that* is a posttranscendental methodological stand. "Totalitarianism," then, remains the site of the most advanced strand of their thought, the strand that could, in principle, lead beyond the current impasse and transform their problematic.

Two years ago I argued that the Center for Philosophical Research on the Political would be but "a temporary way station on the exodus from Marxism now being traveled by the French intelligentsia [and not] a permanent resting place." Now the precise character of the journey—its possible and actual destinations—is more evident. One route runs through the Center for Philosophical Research on the Political to "apolitical neoliberalism." Another, barely visible, would require French post-Marxists to develop links with German Critical Theory and Anglo-American socialist feminism. Given the larger currents of contemporary French culture, including widespread disillusionment with the Mittérrand government, the pressures to take the first route are enormous. That Nancy and Lacoue-Labarthe nonetheless refuse it is certainly to their credit. Still, one hopes they will soon venture forth from their transcendental safe house.

Notes

1. See *Les fins de l'homme: A partir du travail de Jacques Derrida* (Paris, 1981); hereafter cited as *Fins*.

2. See, especially, the essay whose title provided that of the conference: Derrida, *"The Ends of Man,"* trans. Edouard Morot-Sir, Wesley C. Piersol, Hubert L. Dreyfus, and Barbara Reid, *Philosophy and Phenomenological Research* 30, no. 1 (September 1969): 31–57.

3. See Derrida, "Positions: Interview with Jean-Louis Houdebine and Guy Scarpetta," in *Positions,* trans. Alan Bass (Chicago, 1981), 37–96.

4. The present account covers only the first two years of the center's existence.

5. *Rejouer le politique* (Paris, 1982); hereafter cited as *Rejouer*.

6. *Le retrait du politique* (Paris, 1983); hereafter cited as *Retrait*.

7. See for example, Michael Ryan, *Marxism and Deconstruction: A Critical Articulation* (Baltimore, 1982). Related work by Gayatri Chakravorty Spivak will be discussed below.

8. Spivak, "Il faut s'y prendre en s'en prenant à elles," in *Fins,* 505–15; hereafter cited parenthetically, by page numbers, in my text. The translations are my own.

9. Derrida, "The Ends of Man," 56. I have altered the translation slightly.

10. Discussion transcribed in *Fins,* 515–16.

11. Jacob Rogozinski, "Déconstruire la revolution," in *Fins,* 516–26; hereafter cited parenthetically, by page numbers, in my text. The translations are my own.

12. Derrida, "Semiology and Grammatology: Interview with Julia Kristeva," in *Positions,* 24.

13. Discussion transcribed in *Fins*, 526–29; hereafter cited parenthetically, by page numbers, in my text. The translations are my own.

14. Derrida, "D'un ton apocalyptique adopté naguère en philosophie," in *Fins*, 445–79.

15. Nancy, "La voix libre de l'homme," in *Fins*, 163–82.

16. Christopher Fynsk, "Intervention," in *Fins*, 487–93.

17. See Hannah Arendt, *The Human Condition* (Chicago, 1958).

18. Lacoue-Labarthe, "Intervention," in *Fins*, 493–97; hereafter cited parenthetically, by page numbers, in my text. The translations are my own.

19. Martin Heidegger, "The Question concerning Technology," in *"The Question concerning Technology" and Other Essays*, trans. William Lovitt (New York, 1977), and "Overcoming Metaphysics," in *The End of Philosophy*, trans. Joan Stambaugh (New York, 1973).

20. Discussion transcribed in *Fins*, 497–500.

21. Nancy and Lacoue-Labarthe, "Ouverture," in *Rejouer*, 11–28; hereafter cited parenthetically, by page numbers, in my text. The translations are my own.

22. See n. 19 above.

23. See Friedrich Nietzsche, "European Nihilism," in *The Will to Power*, ed. Walter Kaufmann, trans. Walter Kaufmann and R. J. Hollingdale (New York, 1968); and Heidegger, "Overcoming Metaphysics." See also Heidegger, *Nihilism*, trans. Frank A. Capuzzi, vol. 4 of *Nietzsche* (New York, 1982).

24. Cf. Karl Marx, "On the Jewish Question, Part I," and "Contribution to the Critique of Hegel's *Philosophy of Right*," both in *The Marx-Engels Reader*, ed. Robert C. Tucker, 2d ed. (New York, 1978).

25. Several of the formulations in this paragraph and in the preceding one were suggested to me by John Brenkman.

26. Nancy, "La jurisdiction du monarch hegelien," in *Rejouer*, 51–90; an English translation by Mary Ann Caws and Peter Caws appears in *Social Research* 49, no. 2 (Summer 1982): 481–516.

27. Lacoue-Labarthe, "La transcendence finit dans la politique," in *Rejouer*, 171–214; an English translation by Peter Caws appears in *Social Research* 49, no. 2 (Summer 1982): 405–40.

28. Denis Kambouchner, "De la condition la plus générale de la politique," in *Retrait*, 113–58.

29. Philippe Soulez, "La mère est-elle hors-jeu de l'essence du politique?" in *Retrait*, 159–82.

30. Claude Lefort, "La question de la democratie," in *Retrait*, 71–88.

31. Lacoue-Labarthe and Nancy, "Le retrait du politique," in *Retrait*, 183–200; hereafter cited parenthetically, by page numbers, in my text. The translations are my own.

32. Nancy and Lacoue-Labarthe credit group member Jean-François Lyotard with this notion; they cite his book *La condition postmoderne: Rapport sur le savior* (Paris, 1979).

33. Pierre Clastres, *La société contre l'état* (Paris, 1974).

34. See Aristotle, *Politics*, bk. 1.

35. Recent (but not wholly successful) attempts to address such questions include André Gorz, *Farewell to the Working Class*, trans. Michael Sonenscher (London, 1982); and Michael Walzer, *Spheres of Justice* (New York, 1983).

36. Among the many works one could cite here, see Alison M. Jaggar, *Feminist Politics and Human Nature* (Totowa, N.J., 1983); Susan Moller Okin, *Women in Western Political Thought* (Princeton, 1979); Linda Nicholson, *Gender and History: The Failure of Social Theory in the Age of the Family* (New York, 1986); Lorenne M. G. Clark and Lynda Lange, eds., *The Sexism of Social and Political Theory: Women and Reproduction from Plato to Nietzsche* (Toronto, 1979); Carol Gilligan, *In a Different Voice: Psychological Theory and Women's Development* (Cambridge, Mass., 1982); Nancy Hartsock, *Money, Sex, and Power* (New York, 1983); and Iris Young, "Impartiality and the Civic Public," Seyla Benhabib, "The Generalized and the Concrete Other," and Maria Markus, "Women, Success, and Civil Society," all in *Feminism as Critique*, ed. Seyla Benhabib and Drucilla Cornell (Minneapolis, 1987). For my own take on these issues, see my Chapter 8.

Chapter 5
Solidarity or Singularity?
Richard Rorty between Romanticism and Technocracy

*Nothing can serve as a criticism of a final vocabulary save
another such vocabulary; there is no answer to a redescription
save a re-re-redescription.*
—Richard Rorty, *Contingency, Irony, and Solidarity* [1]

Consider a somewhat cartoonish characterization of the Romantic impulse.
Think of this impulse as the valorization of individual invention understood as
self-fashioning. A Romantic impulse of this sort would lionize the figure of the
extraordinary individual who does not simply play out but, rather, rewrites the
cultural script his sociohistorical milieu has prepared for him. It would represent
this individual as a "genius" or "strong poet," irrespective of the field of his
inventiveness. Science, politics, whatever—from the standpoint of the Romantic
impulse, every arena of invention would be a branch of literature in an extended
sense, just as every significant act would be an aesthetic act and every making a
self-making. Here, novelty would be valued for its own sake; it would be the
sheer difference between what is merely found or inherited, on the one hand, and
what is made or dreamed up ex nihilo, on the other, that would confer value and
importance. Insofar as the Romantic impulse figures such difference making as
the work of extraordinary individuals, insofar as it treats them and their work as
the source of all significant historical change, insofar as it views history largely
as the succession of such geniuses, it becomes aestheticizing, individualist, and

I am grateful to Jonathan Arac for suggesting this title as well as for extending the invitation that
provided the occasion for writing this essay. I benefited from helpful discussions with Jonathan Arac,
Sandra Bartky, Jerry Graff, Carol Kay, Tom McCarthy, Linda Nicholson, Joe Rouse, Michael
Williams, and Judy Wittner and from stimulating questions from members of the audience at The
English Institute, Harvard University, August 1987. Richard Rorty generously provided copies of un-
published drafts of several essays cited here.

elitist. It is, in short, the impulse to father oneself, to be *causa sui,* to separate from one's community. Thus, the masculine pronoun is appropriate.[2]

Now contrast this cartoon version of the Romantic impulse with an equally cartoonish characterization of the pragmatic impulse. Take the latter to consist in an impatience with differences that do not make a difference. Take it as a distaste for baroque invention and for useless epicycles, for whatever does not get to the point. Thus, the pragmatic impulse would be goal-directed and purposive; it would care less for originality than for results. Problems solved, needs satisfied, well-being assured, these would be its emblems of value. For the Romantic's metaphorics of poetry and play, it would substitute a metaphorics of production and work. It would scorn gears that engage no mechanism, tools that serve no useful purpose, Rube Goldberg contraptions that do no real work. Indeed, from the standpoint of this impulse, words would be tools and culture an outsize tool kit, to be unceremoniously cast off in the event of obsolescence or rust. The pragmatic impulse, then, would be bright and busy. It would prefer the civic-mindedness of the problem-solving reformer to the narcissism of the self-fashioning poet. Its hero would be the fellow who gets the job done and makes himself useful to his society, not the one who's always preening and strutting his stuff. Moreover, the pragmatic impulse would see history as a succession of social problems posed and social problems solved, a succession that is in fact a progression. Crediting progress to the account of common sense, technical competence and public-spiritedness, its ethos would be reformist and optimistic, its politics liberal and technocratic.

If these cartoonlike characterizations do not do justice to the complexities of the Romantic and pragmatic traditions, I trust that they nonetheless mark out two recognizable strands in the recent writings of Richard Rorty. These writings, in my view, are the site of a struggle between just such a Romantic impulse and a pragmatic impulse. Moreover, it is a struggle that neither impulse seems able decisively to win. Sometimes one, sometimes the other gains a temporary advantage here or there. But the overall outcome is stalemate.

It is symptomatic of Rorty's inability to resolve this contest that he oscillates among three different views of the relationship between Romanticism and pragmatism, poetry and politics. These, in turn, carry three different conceptions of the social role and political function of intellectuals.

The first position I call the "invisible hand" conception. It is the view that Romanticism and pragmatism are "natural partners." Here, the "strong poet" and the "utopian reform politician" are simply two slightly different variants of the same species. Their respective activities are complementary if not strictly identical, providing grist for the same liberal democratic mill.

The second position I call the "sublimity or decency?" conception. It is the view that Romanticism and pragmatism are antithetical to each other, that one has to choose between the sublime "cruelty" of the strong poet and the beautiful "kindness" of the political reformer. This view emphasizes the "dark side" of Romanticism, its tendency to aestheticize politics and, so, to turn antidemocratic.

Evidently, the "invisible hand" conception and the "sublimity or decency?" conception are converses of one another. Thus, each can be read as a critique of the other. Rorty's third position, which I call the "partition" position, represents a compromise. If Romanticism and pragmatism are not exactly "natural partners" but if, at the same time, one is not willing to abandon either of them, then perhaps they can learn how to live with each other. Thus, Rorty has recently outlined the terms of a truce between them, a truce that allots each its own separate sphere of influence. The Romantic impulse will have free rein in what will henceforth be "the private sector." But it will not be permitted any political pretensions. Pragmatism, on the other hand, will have exclusive rights to "the public sector." But it will be barred from entertaining any notions of radical change that could challenge the "private" cultural hegemony of Romanticism.

An ingenious compromise, to be sure. Yet compromises based on partition are notoriously unstable. They tend not truly to resolve but only temporarily to palliate the basic source of conflict. Sooner or later, in one form or another, that conflict will out.

1. The Sorelian Temptation

Consider the role the Romantic impulse plays in Rorty's thought. Recall his insistence on the difference between vocabularies and propositions. It is precisely the tendency to confound them, to treat vocabularies as if they could be warranted like propositions, that is for him the cardinal sin of traditional philosophy. In Rorty's view, vocabulary choice is always underdetermined. There are no non-question-begging arguments, no reasons not already couched in some vocabulary, that could establish once and for all that one had the *right* vocabulary. To pretend otherwise is to seek the metaphysical comfort of a God's-eye view.

Now consider, too, how much hinges on vocabulary shifts, in Rorty's view. The mere redistribution of truth-values across a set of propositions formulated in some taken-for-granted vocabulary is a paltry thing compared to a change of vocabulary. With vocabulary shifts, urgent questions suddenly lose their point, established practices are drastically modified, entire constellations of culture dissolve to make room for new, heretofore unimaginable ones. Thus, vocabulary shifts are for Rorty the motor of history, the chief vehicles of intellectual and moral progress.

Consider, finally, exactly how it is, according to Rorty, that vocabulary shifts occur. A vocabulary shift is the literalization of a new metaphor, the application across-the-board of somebody's new way of speaking, the adoption by an entire community of some poet's idiosyncrasy. It follows that poets, in the extended sense, are "the unacknowledged legislators of the social world."[3] It is their chance words, coming like bolts from "outside logical space," that determine the shape of subsequent culture and society.

The Romantic impulse in Rorty is the impulse that thrills to the sublimity of metaphor, the headiness of "abnormal discourse." When he is under its sway, Rorty figures the culture hero as the poet, allowing the latter to outrank not only the priest and the philosopher but even the pragmatist's traditional heroes, the scientist and the reform politician. In general, then, it is Rorty's Romantic impulse that dictates his "utopian ideal" of "an aestheticized culture," a culture with no other goal than to create "ever more various, multi-colored artifacts," no other purpose than "to make life easier for poets and revolutionaries."[4]

The Romantic impulse is fairly strong in Rorty. But it is not an impulse with which he's entirely comfortable. And for good reason. Consider what a politics that gave free rein to the Romantic impulse would look like. Recall the individualist, elitist, and aestheticist character of that impulse, its deification of the strong poet, its fetishization of creation ex nihilo. It takes only the squint of an eye to see here the vision of a Georges Sorel: a "sociology" that classifies humanity into "leaders" and "masses," a "theory of action" whereby the former mold the latter by means of a sheer "triumph of the will," a "philosophy of history" as an empty canvas awaiting the unfettered designs of the poet-leader.[5]

I take it that something like this Sorelian nightmare is what disturbs the sleep of Richard Rorty. For a long time now he has been at pains to show that his own Romantic streak does not lead down this road, that his own "utopian vision" of an "aestheticized culture" is liberal and democratic rather than Sorelian and potentially fascistic.

2. The Invisible Hand; or, Better Living through Chemistry and Poetry

One way in which Rorty has sought to exorcize the Sorelian demon is by providing a positive political defense of his own version of Romanticism. Thus, he has tried to portray the Romantic dimension of his thought as compatible with—indeed, even as fostering—the apparently opposing pragmatic dimension. More strongly, he has tried to show that the two dimensions are "natural partners," that the fit between them is extremely tight and that the strong poet is the democrat personified.

The chief strategy here is to link poetizing with community-mindedness, Romantic making with social identification. Thus, Rorty argues that in giving up Kantian buttresses for liberal views, one goes from "objectivity" to "solidarity." For to cease pinning our hopes on such God substitutes as Reason, Human Nature, and the Moral Law is to start pinning them on one another.[6]

Likewise, Rorty claims that the aesthetic stance and the moral stance are not antithetical. On the contrary, they are not even distinct—for in adopting the aes-

thetic attitude, we "dedeify" or disenchant the world, thereby promoting toler-
ance, liberalism, and instrumental reason.[7] The refusal to mortgage culture making to ahistorical authorities liberates us for "experimentalism" in politics, for
that simultaneously utopian and down-to-earth sort of "social engineering" that
is the very soul of moral progress.

Moreover, claims Rorty, to treat the strong poet as one's hero and role model is
"to adopt an identity which suits one for citizenship in an ideally liberal state,"
since there is a "fairly tight" fit, supposedly, between the freedom of intellectuals and "the diminution of cruelty."[8] We see practices of earlier ages as cruel and
unjust only because we have learned how to redescribe them. And we have done
that only by virtue of vocabulary shifts owing to the metaphors of poets. Thus,
contrary to initial appearances, it is not really elitist to "treat democratic societies as existing for the sake of intellectuals."[9] In fact, only by making society safe
for poets can we insure that language keeps changing—and only by ensuring that
language keeps changing can we prevent the normalization of current practices
that might later look cruel and unjust. Thus, to make society safe for poets is to
help make it safe for everyone.

Finally, claims Rorty, a culture organized for the sake of poetry and play
would foster "decency" and "kindness." It would diminish or equalize the lia-
bility to a specifically human form of suffering, namely, the humiliation that
comes from being redescribed in someone else's terms while one's own vocabulary is peremptorily dismissed. The best safeguard against this sort of cruelty is
an awareness of other people's vocabularies. Such an awareness in turn is best
acquired by reading lots of books. Thus, a culture that fostered a cosmopolitan
literary intelligentsia would promote the greatest happiness of the greatest
number.[10]

In short, Rorty claims that cultural innovation and social justice go together.
They are united in the liberationist metaphorics of liberal societies, where history
is figured as a succession of emancipations: serfs from lords, slaves from plan-
tation owners, colonies from empires, labor from the unlimited power of capital.
Since both are dominated by these images of liberation, Romanticism in the arts
goes with democracy in politics.[11]

In all these arguments what is really at stake is the accusation of elitism. Rorty
seeks to rebut the charge that a Romantic politics must elevate liberty over equality, sacrificing the greatest happiness of the greatest number on the altar of the
strong poet. His general approach is to invoke a version of the old trickle-down
argument: liberty in the arts fosters equality in society; what's good for poets is
good for workers, peasants, and the hard-core unemployed.

Here, then, is the Rorty who has sought a seamless joining of Romanticism
and pragmatism. Adopting an "invisible hand" strategy, he has tried to show that
aesthetic play and liberal reformist politics are but two sides of the same coin,

that what promotes one will also promote the other, that we can have Better Living through the Marriage of Chemistry and Poetry.

These arguments do not represent Rorty at his most persuasive. On the contrary, they tend to raise far more questions than they answer. For example, is to say goodbye to objectivity really to say hello to solidarity? Surely, there is no relation of logical entailment between antiessentialism and loyalty to one's society. Nor is there even any contingent psychological or historical connection if modern Western societies are considered any measure. Moreover, why assume a quasi-Durkheimian view according to which society is integrated by way of a single monolithic and all-encompassing solidarity? Why not rather assume a quasi-Marxian view according to which modern capitalist societies contain a plurality of overlapping and competing solidarities?

Furthermore, is it really the case that societies that produce the best literature are also the most egalitarian? Do poets' interests and workers' interests really coincide so perfectly? And what about women's interests, given that, Rorty's use of the feminine pronoun notwithstanding, his poets are always figured as sons seeking to displace their cultural fathers? Moreover, does poetizing really dovetail so neatly with social engineering? How does the down-to-earth, results-oriented character of the latter square with the extravagant playfulness of the former? For that matter, why is "social engineering" the preferred conception of political practice? And why is equality cast in terms of "kindness" and "decency"? Why is it made to hinge on a virtue of the literary intelligentsia, on the latter's supposed inclination to forebear humiliating others? Why is equality not instead considered in terms of equal participation in poetizing, culture making, and politics?

3. Sublimity or Decency? Or, The Dark Side of Romanticism

As usual, no one states the case against the invisible hand "solution" better than Rorty himself. Recently, he has acknowledged that there is a "dark side" of Romanticism, a side he now designates as "ironism." By ironism, Rorty means the modernist literary intellectual's project of fashioning the best possible self by continual redescription. Identifying himself as such an ironist, Rorty wonders whether it really is possible to combine "the pleasures of redescription" with sensitivity to "the sufferings of those being redescribed." He fears that the ironist demand for maximum cultural freedom may indeed be elitist, compatible with indifference to the sufferings of nonpoets. Ironism, he concedes, is by definition reactive, requiring a nonironist public culture from which to be alienated. Thus, even in a postmetaphysical culture, ironism cannot be the generalized attitude of the entire social collectivity; it can be the attitude of only one stratum of society, a literary intelligentsia or cultural elite. Moreover, there is no denying that ironism can be cruel. It delights in redescribing others instead of taking them in their own terms. There is no question but that this is often humiliating, as when a child's favorite possessions are set next to those of a richer child and thereby made to seem tacky. To make matters worse, the ironist cannot claim that in redescribing others he is uncovering their true selves and interests, thereby empowering them and setting them free. Only the metaphysically minded politician can promise that. It follows that even were the ironist to profess support for liberal politics, he could not be very "dynamic" or "progressive."[12]

Considerations like these lead Rorty to a dramatic reversal of his earlier view. Now he no longer assumes that to substitute making for finding is to serve one's community, that to say goodbye to objectivity is to say hello to solidarity. On the contrary, Rorty now discerns a "selfish," antisocial motive in Romanticism, one that represents the very antithesis of communal identification. He finds that the Romantic's search for the sublime is fueled by a desire for disaffiliation, a need to "cut loose from the tribe." Thus, behind the strong poet's love for what is original and wholly new lurks a secret contempt for what is familiar and widely shared. This is especially disturbing when what is familiar and shared is a commitment to democracy. In a culture supposedly already organized around a metaphorics of liberation and social reform, to seek new, more vivid, less hackneyed metaphors is to court political disaster.

Thus, Rorty voices a new worry that Romanticism and pragmatism do not mix. Whereas pragmatism is community-minded, democratic, and kind, Romanticism now seems selfish, elitist, and cruel. Whereas the pragmatist aims to solve the problems and meet the needs of his ordinary fellow citizens, the Romantic ironist is more likely to dismiss these as trite, uninteresting, and insufficiently radical.

Accordingly, soi-disant left-wing poststructuralists are deluded in thinking they "serve the wretched of the earth" by rejecting the currently disseminated liberal political vocabulary. On the contrary, what they really do is express the traditional vanguardist contempt for their fellow human beings. Heideggerians, deconstructionists, neo-Marxists, Foucauldians, and assorted New Leftists— these are not differences that make a difference. All are potential Sorelians who confuse the ironist-intellectual's special yen for the sublime with society's general need for the merely beautiful.[13]

It is in this vein that Rorty has recently taken care explicitly to distinguish the pragmatic from the Romantic conception of philosophy. He argues that Romanticism and pragmatism represent two distinct reactions against metaphysics and that they ought not to be conflated with each other. Granted, both reject the traditional view of "philosophy as science"—as the search, that is, for a permanent neutral matrix for inquiry. But whereas Romanticism wants to replace this with a view of "philosophy as metaphor," pragmatism prefers to substitute the view of "philosophy as politics." It follows that the two approaches differ sharply in their images of the ideal person: in the metaphor view this must be the poet, whereas in the political view it is the social worker and the engineer. Granted, both perspectives are holistic; both distinguish abnormal discourse from normal discourse, the invention of a new metaphor from its literalization or social application. But they part ways over the value of turning live metaphors into dead metaphors by disseminating them in the service of society. For the Romantic, this sort of applied poetry is the vilest hackwork, whereas for the pragmatist it is exactly what the best metaphors are made for. It follows that the two views entail very different social attitudes. In the Romantic view, the social world exists for the sake of the poet. In the pragmatic view, on the other hand, the poet exists for the sake of the social world.[14]

In this rather more complicated scenario, then, there are not one but two alternatives to objectivity. Only one of these leads to solidarity and democracy; the other leads to vanguardism if not to fascism. Here, Rorty frames the issue as Romanticism versus pragmatism. He treats the two impulses as antithetical to one another, and he forces a choice. Romanticism or pragmatism? Sublimity or decency? Strong poetry or dead metaphors? Self-fashioning or social responsibility? One cannot have it both ways.

Or can one?

4. The Partition Position

In his most recent essays, Rorty refuses to choose between sublimity and decency, Romanticism and pragmatism. He has instead contrived a new formulation aimed at letting him have it both ways: he will split the difference between Romanticism and pragmatism along a divide between private and public life.

The idea is that two things that cannot be fused into one may nonetheless coexist side by side if clear and sharp boundaries are drawn between them. Now, sublimity cannot be fused with decency, nor strong poetry with social responsibility. But if each were allotted its own separate sphere and barred from interfering with the other, then they might just make passably good neighbors.

This, then, is the strategy of Rorty's "partition" position: to bifurcate the map of culture down the middle. On one side will be public life, the preserve of pragmatism, the sphere where utility and solidarity predominate. On the other side will be private life, the preserve of Romanticism, the sphere of self-discovery, sublimity, and irony. In the public sphere, one's duty to one's community takes precedence; social hope, decency, and the greatest happiness of the greatest number are the order of the day. In the private sphere, by contrast, the reigning cause is one's duty to oneself; here, one may disaffiliate from the community, attend to the fashioning of one's self and, so, deal with one's "aloneness."[15]

Thus, Rorty wishes to preserve both ecstasy and utility, "the urge to think the Unthinkable" and "enthusiasm for the French Revolution."[16] But only by strictly isolating them from one another. Indeed, he now claims that it is the desire to overcome the implacable split between public and private life that is at the root of many theoretical and political difficulties. This desire, it turns out, is common to metaphysics and its ironist critique, to Marxism and to various non-Marxist forms of radical politics. It is what led even the later Heidegger astray, causing him to confound what was actually his private need to get free of some local, personal authority figures named Plato, Aristotle, and Kant with the destiny of the West.[17]

Rorty claims that there is a lesson to be learned from the difficulties of all these opponents of liberalism: When irony goes public, it gets into trouble. Thus, ironist theory has to stay private if it is to stay sane.[18]

It turns out, happily, that there is a way to neutralize the nonliberal political implications of radical thought—it is to deny that radical thought has any political implications. So, Heidegger was simply mistaken in imagining his work had any public relevance. Ditto for all those would-be leftists who aim to make political hay of deconstruction, postmodernism, Foucauldianism, and neo-Marxism. In fact, the sole use of ironist theory is a private one: to bolster the self-image and aid the self-fashioning of the literary intelligentsia.

Clearly, the partition position entails a revised view of the social role and political function of intellectuals. The strong poet as heretofore conceived must be domesticated, cut down to size and made fit for private life. He must become the aesthete, a figure denuded of public ambition and turned inward.[19] Thus, the intellectual will be king in the castle of his own self-fashioning, but he will no longer legislate for the social world. Indeed, the intellectual will have no social role or political function.

It is a measure of the domesticated status of Rorty's aesthete that he may pursue sublimity only on his "own time, and within the limits set by *On Liberty*."[20] He may think ironic thoughts involving cruel redescriptions within the privacy of his own narcissistic sphere, but he must not act on them in any way that might cause pain or humiliation to others. This means that the aesthete must have a bifurcated final vocabulary, a vocabulary split into a public sector and a private sector. The private sector of the aesthete's final vocabulary will be large and luxuriant, containing all manner of colorful and potentially cruel terms for redescribing others. The public sector of his vocabulary, on the other hand, will be smaller, consisting of a few flexible terms, like 'kindness' and 'decency', that express his commitment to the politics of liberalism.[21]

The partition position represents a new and extremely interesting development in Rorty's thinking. It is his most sophisticated effort to date to take seriously the problem of reconciling Romanticism and pragmatism. And yet this position is seriously flawed. It stands or falls with the possibility of drawing a sharp boundary between public life and private life. But is this really possible? Is it really possible to distinguish redescriptions that affect actions with consequences for others from those that either do not affect actions at all or that affect only actions

with no consequences for others?[22] Surely, many cultural developments that occur at some remove from processes officially designated as political are nonetheless public. And official political public spheres are by no means impermeable to
developments in cultural public spheres,[23] since cultural processes help shape social identities, which in turn affect political affiliations. Moreover, the social
movements of the last hundred or so years have taught us to see the power-laden,
and therefore political, character of interactions that classical liberalism considered private. Workers' movements, for example, especially as clarified by Marxist theory, have taught us that the economic is political. Likewise, women's
movements, as illuminated by feminist theory, have taught us that the domestic
and the personal are political. Finally, a whole range of New Left social movements, as illuminated by Gramscian, Foucauldian, and, yes, even by Althusser-
ian theory, have taught us that the cultural, the medical, the educational—
everything that Hannah Arendt called "the social," as distinct from the private
and the public—that all this, too, is political.[24] Yet Rorty's partition position requires us to bury these insights, to turn our backs on the last hundred years of
social history. It requires us, in addition, to privatize theory. Feminists, especially, will want to resist this last requirement, lest we see our theory go the way
of our housework.

5. Abnormal Discourse Reconsidered

None of Rorty's three positions represents a satisfactory resolution of the tension
between pragmatism and Romanticism. The invisible hand position fails because
to say goodbye to objectivity is not necessarily to say hello to a single, unitary
solidarity and because what's good for poets is not necessarily good for workers,
peasants, and the hard-core unemployed. The sublimity-or-decency position fails
because not all radical theorizing is elitist, antidemocratic, and opposed to collective concerns and political life. Finally, the partition position fails because final vocabularies do not neatly divide into public and private sectors, nor do actions neatly divide into public and private.

   If none of the three proffered solutions is adequate, then it may be worthwhile
to reconsider the terms of the original dilemma. We might take a closer look at
the categories and assumptions that inform Rorty's thinking about culture and
politics.

   Begin with the key distinction in Rorty's framework, the contrast between normal discourse and abnormal discourse. In fact, Rorty oscillates between two
views of abnormal discourse. The first view is the one developed in *Philosophy
and the Mirror of Nature,* and it is derived from the work of Thomas Kuhn. It is
the simple negation of the discourse of normal science, that is, of discourse in
which interlocutors share a sense of what counts as a problem or question, as a
well-formed or serious hypothesis, and as a good reason or argument. Abnormal

discourse, then, is discourse in which such matters are up for grabs. It involves a plurality of differentiable if not incommensurable voices, and it consists in an exchange among them that is lively if somewhat disorderly. Call this "the poly-logic conception" of abnormal discourse.

Now, contrast the polylogic conception with another conception of abnormal discourse that is also found in Rorty, a monologic conception. The monologic view is the Romantic-individualist view in which abnormal discourse is the pre-rogative of the strong poet and the ironist theorist. It is a discourse that consists in a solitary voice crying out into the night against an utterly undifferentiated back-ground. The only conceivable response to this voice is uncomprehending rejec-tion or identificatory imitation. There is no room for a reply that could qualify as a different voice. There is no room for interaction.

Clearly, these two different conceptions of abnormal discourse correspond to the two different impulses I identified earlier. The monologic view develops un-der the spur of Rorty's Romantic impulse, whereas the polylogic view is fed by his pragmatic impulse. In addition, the monologic view maps onto Rorty's no-tions of radical-theory-cum-strong-poetry and privacy, whereas the polylogic view maps onto his notions of practice, politics, and publicity.

At one level this mapping makes good sense. It seems that Rorty is perfectly right to want a polylogic politics instead of a monologic politics — indeed, per-fectly right to reject a monologic politics as an oxymoron. However, at another level, there is something profoundly disturbing here. It is the sharply dichoto-mous character of the resulting map of culture, the abstract and unmediated op-position between poetry and politics, theory and practice, individual and com-munity.

Consider the impact of the monologic conception of abnormal discourse on the various regions of Rorty's map of social space. The monologic conception, we have seen, is individualistic, elitist, and antisocial. Moreover, it is associated by Rorty with radical theorizing, which is itself treated as a species of poetizing. As a result, radical theorizing assumes individualistic connotations, becoming the very antithesis of collective action and political practice. Radical theory, in other words, gets inflected as a sphere apart from collective life, a sphere of pri-vacy and of individual self-fashioning. It becomes aestheticized, narcissized, and bourgeoisified, a preserve where strivings for transcendence are quarantined, rendered safe because rendered sterile.

Now, this privatized, narcissistic conception of radical theory has two impor-tant social consequences. First, there can be no legitimate cultural politics, no genuinely political struggle for cultural hegemony; there can only be Oedipal re-volts of genius sons against genius fathers. Second, there can be no politically relevant radical theory, no link between theory and political practice; there can only be apolitical ironist theory and atheoretical reformist practice. Thus, both culture and theory get depoliticized.

The privatization of radical theory takes its toll, too, on the shape of the political. In Rorty's hands, politics assumes an overly communitarian and solidary character, as if in reaction against the extreme egotism and individualism of his conception of theory. Thus, we can supposedly go straight from objectivity to solidarity, from the metaphysical comfort of traditional philosophy to the communitarian comfort of a single "we." Here, Rorty homogenizes social space, assuming tendentiously that there are no deep social cleavages capable of generating conflicting solidarities and opposing "we's." It follows from this assumed absence of fundamental social antagonisms that politics is a matter of everyone pulling together to solve a common set of problems. Thus, social engineering can replace political struggle. Disconnected tinkerings with a succession of allegedly discrete social problems can replace transformation of the basic institutional structure. And the expert social problem solver and top-down reformer can replace organized social movements of people collectively articulating their own interests and aspirations; thus the political agent comes to be typified as the social worker or the engineer instead of as, say, the membership of the National Welfare Rights Organization or of the Clamshell Alliance. Moreover, with no deep rifts or pervasive axes of domination, practice can float entirely free of theory. If there are no mechanisms of subordination inscribed in the basic institutional framework of society, then a fortiori there can be no need to theorize them. Thus, politics can be detheoreticized.

Clearly, this cultural map presupposes a substantive political diagnosis, one with which I shall later take issue. But it also possesses a noteworthy formal feature: Rorty's conceptions of politics and of theory are obverses of one another. If theory is hyperindividualized and depoliticized, then politics is hypercommunalized and detheoreticized. As theory becomes pure *poiēsis,* politics approaches pure *technē.* Moreover, as theory is made the preserve of pure transcendence, politics is banalized, emptied of radicalism and of desire. Finally, as theory becomes the production ex nihilo of new metaphors, politics must be merely their literalization; politics must be application only, never invention.

It is paradoxical that such a dichotomous picture should be the upshot of a body of thought that aimed to soften such received dichotomies as theory versus practice, aesthetics versus morality, science versus literature. It is also paradoxical that what was supposed to be a political "polylogue" comes increasingly to resemble a monologue.

Consider that Rorty makes nonliberal, oppositional discourses nonpolitical by definition. He associates such discourses with Romanticism, the quest for the uncharted. They are made the prerogative of free-floating intellectuals who are "bored" with widely disseminated vocabularies and who crave "the new" and "the interesting." Radical discourses, then, are inflected as a turning away from the concerns of collective life. Rorty thus casts the motive for oppositional discourse as aesthetic and apolitical. He casts the subject of such discourses as the lone, alienated, heroic individual. And he casts the object or topic of radical discourses as something—anything—other than the needs and problems of the social collectivity.

With radical discourses thus aestheticized and individualized—indeed, oedipalized and masculinized—political discourse, in turn, is implicitly deradicalized. Political discourse in fact is restricted by Rorty to those who speak the language of bourgeois liberalism. Whoever departs from that vocabulary simply lacks any sense of solidarity. Likewise, it turns out that the adherents of bourgeois liberalism have a monopoly on talk about community needs and social problems. Whoever eschews the liberal idiom must be talking about something else—about, say, individual salvation.

Thus, in Rorty's recent essays social solidarity and nonliberal discourses are seen as antithetical to one another. Discourse rooted in solidarity and oriented to collective concerns is restricted to liberal problem solving. Nonliberal discourse, on the other hand, is reduced to aestheticism, apoliticism, and Romantic individualism.

Clearly, this way of mapping the discursive terrain effects some significant exclusions. There is no place in Rorty's framework for *political* motivations for the invention of new idioms, no place for idioms invented to overcome the enforced silencing or muting of disadvantaged social groups. Similarly, there is no place for *collective* subjects of nonliberal discourses, hence, no place for radical discourse communities that contest dominant discourses. Finally, there is no place for *nonliberal* interpretations of social needs and collective concerns, hence, no place for, say, socialist-feminist politics. In sum, there is no place in Rorty's framework for genuinely radical political discourses rooted in *oppositional* solidarities.

Consequently, Rorty ends up supposing there is only one legitimate political vocabulary, thereby betraying his own professed commitment to a polylogic politics. This, too, is a paradoxical result for a thought that seemed always to insist on the decisive importance of vocabulary choice for the framing of issues. In any case, and whatever his intentions, by dichotomizing private and public, singular individual and homogeneous community, Rorty cuts out the ground for the possibility of democratic radical politics.

How can we build this possibility back into the picture? How can we retrieve a version of pragmatism that is compatible with radical democracy, polylogic abnormal political discourse, and socialist-feminist politics?

6. Recipe for a Democratic-Socialist-Feminist Pragmatism

Rorty has recently summarized the aim of his latest round of essays: "to separate . . . 'postmodernism' from political radicalism[,] polemics against 'the metaphysics of presence' from polemics against 'bourgeois ideology', criticisms of

Enlightenment rationalism and universalism from criticisms of liberal, reformist, political thought.''[25]

In contrast, I would like to summarize *my* aim in the present paper: to separate pragmatism from cold war liberalism, polemics against traditional foundationalist philosophy from polemics against social theory, criticisms of Romantic Sorelian politics from criticisms of radical democratic-socialist-feminist politics.

Let me conclude by sketching very roughly how such a separation can be effected. Since the point is to show that one can indeed put asunder what Rorty hath joined together, my sketch will be a recipe for an alternative combination, a democratic-socialist-feminist pragmatism.[26]

Begin with the sort of zero-degree pragmatism that is compatible with a wide variety of substantive political views, with socialist feminism as well as bourgeois liberalism. This pragmatism is simply antiessentialism with respect to traditional philosophical concepts like truth and reason, human nature and morality.[27] It implies an appreciation of the historical and socially constructed character of such categories and of the practices from which they get their sense, thereby suggesting at least the abstract possibility of social change. This sort of zero-degree pragmatism is a useful, though hardly all-sufficing, ingredient of socialist feminism.

Then, add the kind of zero-degree holism that combines easily with radical democratic politics. This holism is simply the sense of the difference between the frame of a social practice and a move within it. It implies an appreciation of the way background institutions and habits prestructure the foreground possibilities available to individuals in social life. This zero-degree holism does not necessarily lead to conservative politics. On the contrary, it is a necessary ingredient for any politics that aspires to radical social transformation as opposed to simple amelioration.

Next, add a keen sense of the decisive importance of language in political life. Mix with the pragmatism and the holism until you get a distinction between making a political claim in a taken-for-granted vocabulary and switching to a different vocabulary. This distinction clears a space for those far-reaching redescriptions of social life at the heart of every new political vision, from bourgeois liberalism to Marxism to contemporary feminism. This distinction also allows for contestatory interactions among competing political vocabularies. It thus makes conceivable the sort of robust, polylogic, abnormal discourse that is essential to radical democratic politics in a multicultural society.

Now, add a view of contemporary societies as neither hyperindividualized nor hypercommunalized. This view should allow for social divisions capable of generating multiple, competing solidarities and multiple, competing political vocabularies. It should allow also for inequality and for power. Thus, it should distinguish dominant from subordinated solidarities, hegemonic from counterhegemonic vocabularies. This view of society should be mixed with the preceding ingredients to get a keen sense of social contestation.

Contestation, in turn, should be broadly conceived to include struggle over cultural meanings and social identities, as well as over more narrowly traditional political stakes like electoral office and legislation. It should encompass struggles for cultural hegemony, the power to construct authoritative definitions of social situations and legitimate interpretations of social needs. This broad sense of contestation allows for a politics of culture that cuts across traditional divisions between public and private life. It allows also for the possibility of radical democratic social movements: broad, informally organized, collective formations wherein politics and poetry form an unbroken continuum as struggles for social justice shade into the unleashing of creativity.

Next, add a view of social change as neither determined by an autonomous logic of history nor as simply contingent and utterly inexplicable. Consider the agents of historical change to be social movements rather than extraordinary individuals. Avoid a rigid, dichotomous opposition between playing the game in the same old way and starting completely from scratch, between boring, stable, frozen normality and the sudden, novel bolt from the blue. Avoid also a dichotomy between sheer invention and mere application, between the heretofore undreamt of and its routinization. Instead, see these extremes as mediated in the social practice of social movements. See such practice as spanning the gulf between the old and the new, as application that is always at the same time invention. This allows for the possibility of a radical politics that is not Sorelian, not the expression of the elitist and masculinist will to the Wholly Other. It allows for the possibility of a radical democratic politics in which immanent critique and transfigurative desire mingle with one another.

Next, add the view that (multiplicity and contestation notwithstanding) contemporary societies are organized around a basic institutional framework. Of course, any precise characterization of the structure of this framework will suppose contestable political commitments and a contestable political vocabulary. Nonetheless, suppose that among the candidates for core elements of this framework are ingredients like the following: an organization of social production for private profit rather than for human need; a gender-based division of social labor that separates privatized childrearing from recognized and remunerated work; gender- and race-segmented paid labor markets that generate a marginalized underclass; a system of nation-states that engage in crisis management in the form of segmented social welfare concessions and subsidized war production.

Now, add to this the possibility that the basic institutional framework of society could be unjust, that it could work to the systematic detriment of some social groups and to the systematic profit of others. Stir with the preceding ingredients to get a sense of the possible political uses of a critical social theory. Consider, for example, the utility of a theory that could specify links among apparently discrete social problems via the basic institutional structure, thereby showing "how things, in the broadest sense, hang together, in the broadest sense."[28] Or consider the utility of a social theory able to distinguish system-conforming reforms that perpetuate injustices, on the one hand, from radical and empowering social changes, on the other hand.

Next, add some distinctions among different kinds of theories. Distinguish, for example, traditional, ahistorical foundationalist theories, as in Epistemology or Moral Philosophy, from the ironist pragmatic metatheories that provide their critique. Then, distinguish both of these from a third kind of theory, to wit, first-order, substantive social theory that is nonfoundational, fallibilistic, and historically specific. Now, use these distinctions to avoid throwing out the baby of critical social theory with the bathwater of traditional philosophy. Use them, also, to avoid conflating social theory with Heideggerian bathos, private irony or oedipal high jinks. Instead, use these distinctions to make room for politically relevant radical social theory and thus for theoretically informed radical democratic politics.

Then, add a non-Leninist, nonvanguardist conception of the role of intellectuals in radical left-wing democratic politics. Think of such intellectuals first and foremost as members of social groups and as participants in social movements. Think of them, in other words, as occupying specifiable locations in social space rather than as free-floating individuals who are beyond ideology. Think of them, in addition, as having acquired as a result of the social division of labor some politically useful occupational skills: for example, the ability to show how the welfare system institutionalizes the feminization of poverty or how a poem orientalizes its subject. Think of them as potentially capable of utilizing these skills both in specialized institutions like universities and in the various larger cultural and political public spheres. Think of them, thus, as participants on several fronts in struggles for cultural hegemony. Think of them, also, alas, as mightily subject to delusions of grandeur and as needing to remain in close contact with their political comrades who are not intellectuals by profession in order to remain sane, level-headed, and honest.

Combine all these ingredients with a nonindividualist, nonelitist, nonmasculinist utopian vision. Articulate this utopian vision in terms of relations among human beings instead of in terms of individuals considered as separate monads. Imagine new relations of work and play, citizenship and parenthood, friendship and love. Then, consider what sort of institutional framework would be needed to foster such relations. Situate these relations in the institutional framework of a classless, multicultural society without racism, sexism or heterosexism—an international society of decentralized, democratic, self-managing collectivities.

Combine all the above ingredients and season to taste with social hope. Garnish with just the right mix of pessimism of the intellect and optimism of the will.

Notes

1. Richard Rorty, "Private Irony and Liberal Hope," in *Contingency, Irony, and Solidarity* (Cambridge), 1989/, 80.

2. It is worth recalling that one of Rorty's heroes is Harold Bloom, especially the Bloom of *The Anxiety of Influence* (New York, 1973). My own view of the masculinist character of Rorty's Romantic impulse has been influenced by the feminist critique of Bloom by Sandra M. Gilbert and Susan Gubar in *The Madwoman in the Attic: The Woman Writer and the Nineteenth-Century Literary Imagination* (New Haven, Conn., 1979).

3. This is Rorty, echoing Shelly, in "Philosophy as Science, as Metaphor, and as Politics," in *The Institution of Philosophy: A Discipline in Crisis?*, ed. Avner Cohen and Marcelo Descal (Peru, Illinois, forthcoming).

4. Rorty, "The Contingency of Community," *London Review of Books,* 24 July 1986, 11,13. A revised version of this essay appears under the title "The Contingency of a Liberal Community" in *Contingency, Irony, and Solidarity.*

5. The choice of Sorel as the personification of this possibility is mine, not Rorty's. He tends rather to represent it with Lenin. In my view, Lenin is far less appropriate here than Sorel. The "sociology," "theory of action," and "philosophy of history" I have sketched bear little resemblance to Lenin's and much to Sorel's. Moreover, Sorel's much greater ambiguity in terms of standard notions of "Right" and "Left" better captures the flavor of the sort of political Romanticism I am trying to characterize here. Finally, Rorty's choice of Lenin as the personification of Romanticism run amok is an anti-Marxist political gesture that I do not wish to repeat. In general, Rorty shows no awareness of the tradition of Western Marxism nor of attempts within Marxism to find alternatives to vanguardist conceptions of the relation between theory and practice.

6. Rorty, "Solidarity or Objectivity?" in *Post-Analytic Philosophy,* ed. John Rajchman and Cornel West (New York, 1985), 3–19.

7. Rorty, "The Priority of Democracy to Philosophy," in *The Virginia Statute of Religious Freedom,* ed. Merrill Peterson and Robert Vaughan (Cambridge, 1988), 39–40. See also his "From Logic to Language to Play," *Proceedings and Addresses of the American Philosophical Association* 59, no. 5 (June 1986): 747–53.

8. Rorty, "The Contingency of Community," 14.

9. Ibid.

10. Rorty, "Private Irony and Liberal Hope," 89, 94–95.

11. Rorty, "Liberal Hope and Private Irony." (unpublished manuscript).

12. Rorty, "Private Irony and Liberal Hope," 87–91.

13. Rorty, "Habermas and Lyotard on Postmodernity," in *Habermas and Modernity,* ed. Richard J. Bernstein (Cambridge, Mass. 1985); "Method, Social Science, and Social Hope," in *Consequences of Pragmatism: Essays, 1972–1980* (Minneapolis, 1982); and "Thugs and Theorists: A Reply to Bernstein," *Political Theory* 15, no. 4 (November 1987): 564–80.

14. Rorty, "Philosophy as Science, as Metaphor, and as Politics."

15. Rorty, "The Priority of Democracy to Philosophy," 37.

16. Rorty, "Habermas and Lyotard on Postmodernity," 175.

17. Rorty, "Self–creation and Affiliation: Proust, Nietzche, and Heidegger," in *Contingency, Irony, and Solidarity*, 100, 110, 114, 118–21.

18. Ibid., 120.

19. I am grateful to Michael Williams for the suggestion that Rorty's view of the intellectual here is that of the aesthete.

20. Rorty, "Posties," *London Review of Books,* 3 September 1987, 11.

21. Rorty, "Private Irony and Liberal Hope," 92–93.

22. This problem is posed but by no means resolved in Mill's *On Liberty.*

23. I use the expression 'official political' here to signal the existence of social arenas not officially recognized as political that should nonetheless be understood as political. For a discussion of this issue, see Chapter 8 of this volume.

24. To insist on the power-laden, and therefore political, character of these matters is not necessarily to authorize unlimited state intervention. One can favor, instead, the use of nongovernmental counterpowers like social movements and democratic political associations. This is the view of many feminists, myself included, on pornography: pornography that is harmful to women in a diffuse rather than a direct way is better opposed via boycotts, pickets, counterpropaganda, and consciousness-raising than by state censorship.

25. Rorty, "Thugs and Theorists," 564.

26. The recipe form has a number of advantages, not least of which is a certain gender resonance. In choosing this genre, I am taking seriously Rorty's implicit assimilation of theorizing to housework. For me, however, this means deprivatizing housework rather than privatizing theory. It also suggests a nontechnocratic and more genuinely pragmatic view of the relation between theory and practice, since cooks are expected to vary recipes in accordance with trial and error, inspiration, and the conjunctural state of the larder. Finally, the recipe form has the advantage of positing the outcome as a concoction rather than as a system or synthesis. It thus avoids those hyperbolic forms of theoretical totalization of which the democratic Left has rightly grown suspicious.

27. Rorty, "Pragmatism, Relativism, and Irrationalism," in *Consequences of Pragmatism,* 162.

28. This is one of Rorty's favorite positive characterizations of philosophy. He attributes the characterization to Wilfred Sellars.

Part 3

Gender and the Politics of Need Interpretation

Chapter 6
What's Critical about Critical Theory?
The Case of Habermas and Gender

To my mind, no one has yet improved on Marx's 1843 definition of critical theory as "the self-clarification of the struggles and wishes of the age."[1] What is so appealing about this definition is its straightforwardly political character. It makes no claim to any special epistemological status but, rather, supposes that with respect to justification there is no philosophically interesting difference between a critical theory of society and an uncritical one. However, there is, according to this definition, an important political difference. A critical social theory frames its research program and its conceptual framework with an eye to the aims and activities of those oppositional social movements with which it has a partisan, though not uncritical, identification. The questions it asks and the models it designs are informed by that identification and interest. Thus, for example, if struggles contesting the subordination of women figured among the most significant of a given age, then a critical social theory for that time would aim, among other things, to shed light on the character and bases of such subordination. It would employ categories and explanatory models that revealed rather than occluded relations of male dominance and female subordination. And it would demystify as ideological any rival approaches that obfuscated or rationalized those relations. In this situation, then, one of the standards for assessing a

I am grateful to John Brenkman, Thomas McCarthy, Carole Pateman, and Martin Schwab for helpful comments and criticism; to Dee Marquez and Marina Rosiene for crackerjack word processing; and to The Stanford Humanities Center for financial support.

113

critical theory, once it had been subjected to all the usual tests of empirical adequacy, would be: How well does it theorize the situation and prospects of the feminist movement? To what extent does it serve the self-clarification of the struggles and wishes of contemporary women?

In what follows, I am going to presuppose the conception of critical theory that I have just outlined. In addition, I am going to take as the actual situation of our age the scenario I just sketched as hypothetical. On the basis of these presuppositions, I want to examine the critical social theory of Jürgen Habermas as elaborated in *The Theory of Communicative Action* and related recent writings.[2] I intend to read this work from the standpoint of several specific questions: In what proportions and in what respects does Habermas's critical theory clarify and/or mystify the bases of male dominance and female subordination in modern societies? In what proportions and in what respects does it challenge and/or replicate prevalent ideological rationalizations of such dominance and subordination? To what extent does it, or can it be made to, serve the self-clarification of the struggles and wishes of the contemporary women's movement? In short, with respect to gender, what is critical and what is not in Habermas's social theory?

This would be a fairly straightforward enterprise were it not for one thing: apart from a brief discussion of feminism as a ''new social movement'' (a discussion I shall consider anon), Habermas says virtually nothing about gender in *The Theory of Communicative Action*. Now, according to my view of critical theory, this is a serious deficiency, but it need not stand in the way of the sort of inquiry I am proposing. It simply necessitates that one read the work in question from the standpoint of an absence, that one extrapolate from things Habermas does say to things he does not, that one reconstruct how various matters of concern to feminists would appear from his perspective had those matters been thematized.

Thus, in section 1 of this essay, I examine some elements of Habermas's social-theoretical framework in order to see how it tends to cast childrearing and the male-headed modern restricted nuclear family. In section 2, I look at his account of the relations between the public and private spheres of life in classical capitalist societies and try to reconstruct the unthematized gender subtext. And finally, in section 3, I consider Habermas's account of the dynamics, crisis tendencies, and conflict potentials specific to contemporary Western welfare state capitalism, so as to see in what light it casts contemporary feminist struggles.[3]

1. The Social-Theoretical Framework: A Feminist Interrogation

Let me begin by considering two distinctions central to Habermas's social-theoretical categorial framework. The first of these is the distinction between the symbolic reproduction and the material reproduction of societies. On the one hand, claims Habermas, societies must reproduce themselves materially; they must successfully regulate the metabolic exchange of groups of biological individuals with a nonhuman, physical environment and with other social systems. On the other hand, societies must reproduce themselves symbolically; they must maintain and transmit to new members the linguistically elaborated norms and patterns of interpretation that are constitutive of social identities. Habermas claims that material reproduction comprises what he calls "social labor." Symbolic reproduction, on the other hand, comprises the socialization of the young, the cementing of group solidarity, and the transmission and extension of cultural traditions.[4]

This distinction between symbolic and material reproduction is in the first instance a functional one: it distinguishes two different functions that must be fulfilled more or less successfully if a society is to survive. At the same time, however, the distinction is used by Habermas to classify actual social practices and activities. These are distinguished according to which one of the two functions they are held to serve exclusively or primarily. Thus, according to Habermas, in capitalist societies, the activities and practices that make up the sphere of paid work count as material reproduction activities since, in his view, they are "social labor" and serve the function of material reproduction. On the other hand, the childrearing activities and practices that in our society are performed without pay by women in the domestic sphere—let us call them "women's unpaid childrearing work"—count as symbolic reproduction activities since, in Habermas's view, they serve socialization and the function of symbolic reproduction.[5]

It is worth noting, I think, that Habermas's distinction between symbolic and material reproduction is susceptible to two different interpretations. The first of these takes the two functions as two objectively distinct "natural kinds" to which both the actual social practices and the actual organization of activities in any given society may correspond more or less faithfully. Thus, childrearing practices would in themselves be symbolic reproduction practices, whereas the practices that produce food and objects would in themselves be material reproduction practices. And modern capitalist social organization—unlike, say, that of archaic societies—would be a faithful mirror of the distinction between the two natural kinds, since it separates these practices institutionally. This "natural kinds" interpretation is at odds with another possible interpretation, which I shall call the "pragmatic-contextual" interpretation. It would not take childrearing practices to be in themselves symbolic reproduction practices but would allow for the possibility that, under certain circumstances and given certain purposes, it could be useful to consider them from the standpoint of symbolic reproduction—for example, if one wished to contest the view, dominant in a sexist political culture, according to which this traditionally female occupation is merely instinctual, natural, and ahistorical.

Now I want to argue that the natural kinds interpretation is conceptually inadequate and potentially ideological. I claim that it is not the case that childrearing practices serve symbolic as opposed to material reproduction. Granted, they comprise language teaching and initiation into social mores — but also feeding, bathing, and protection from physical harm. Granted, they regulate children's interactions with other people — but also their interactions with physical nature (in the form, for example, of milk, germs, dirt, excrement, weather, and animals). In short, not just the construction of children's social identities but also their biological survival is at stake — and, therefore, so is the biological survival of the societies they belong to. Thus, childrearing is not per se symbolic reproduction activity; it is equally and at the same time material reproduction activity. It is what we might call a "dual aspect" activity.[6]

However, the same is true of the activities institutionalized in modern capitalist paid work. Granted, the production of food and objects contributes to the biological survival of members of society. But it also, and at the same time, reproduces social identities. Not just nourishment and shelter *simpliciter* are produced but culturally elaborated forms of nourishment and shelter that have symbolically mediated social meanings. Moreover, such production occurs via culturally elaborated social relations and symbolically mediated, norm-governed social practices. The contents of these practices as well as the results serve to form, maintain, and modify the social identities of persons directly involved and indirectly affected. One need only think of an activity like computer programming for a wage in the U.S. pharmaceutical industry to appreciate the thoroughly symbolic character of "social labor." Thus, such labor, like unpaid childrearing work, is a "dual aspect" activity.[7]

Thus, any distinction between women's unpaid childrearing work and other forms of work that is drawn in terms of reproduction functions cannot be a distinction of natural kinds. If any distinction is to be drawn at all, it must rather be a pragmatic-contextual distinction for the sake of focalizing what is in each case actually only one aspect of a dual aspect phenomenon. And this, in turn, must find its warrant in relation to specific purposes of analysis and description, purposes that are themselves susceptible to analysis and evaluation and that need, therefore, to be justified through argument.

But if this is so, then the natural kinds classification of childrearing as symbolic reproduction and of other work as material reproduction is potentially ideological. It could be used, for example, to legitimize the institutional separation of childrearing from paid work, a separation that many feminists, myself included, consider a linchpin of modern forms of women's subordination. It could be used, in combination with other assumptions, to legitimate the confinement of women to a "separate sphere." Whether Habermas himself uses it to those ends will be considered shortly.

The second component of Habermas's categorial framework that I want to examine is his distinction between "socially integrated action contexts" and "system integrated action contexts." Socially integrated action contexts are those in which different agents coordinate their actions with one another by reference to some form of explicit or implicit intersubjective consensus about norms, values, and ends, consensus predicated on linguistic speech and interpretation. System-integrated action contexts, on the other hand, are those in which the actions of different agents are coordinated with one another by the functional interlacing of unintended consequences, while each individual action is determined by self-interested, utility-maximizing calculations typically entertained in the idioms—or, as Habermas says, in the "media"—of money and power.[8] Habermas considers the capitalist economic system to be the paradigm case of a system-integrated action context. By contrast, he takes the modern restricted nuclear family to be a case of a socially integrated action context.[9]

Now this distinction is a rather complex one. As I understand it, it contains six analytically distinct conceptual elements: functionality, intentionality, linguisticality, consensuality, normativity, and strategicality. However, I am going to set aside the elements of functionality, intentionality, and linguisticality. Following some arguments developed by Thomas McCarthy in another context, I assume that in both the capitalist workplace and the modern restricted nuclear family the consequences of actions may be functionally interlaced in ways unintended by agents; that, at the same time, in both contexts agents coordinate their actions with one another consciously and intentionally; and that in both contexts agents coordinate their actions with one another in and through language.[10] I assume, therefore, that Habermas's distinction effectively turns on the elements of consensuality, normativity, and strategicality.

Once again, I think it useful to distinguish two possible interpretations of Habermas's position. The first takes the contrast between the two kinds of action contexts as registering an absolute difference. Thus, system-integrated contexts would involve absolutely no consensuality or reference to moral norms and values, whereas socially integrated contexts would involve absolutely no strategic calculations in the media of money and power. This "absolute differences" interpretation is at odds with a second possibility, which takes the contrast rather as registering a difference in degree. According to this second interpretation, system-integrated contexts would involve some consensuality and reference to moral norms and values but less than do socially integrated contexts. In the same way, socially integrated contexts would involve some strategic calculations in the media of money and power but less than do system-integrated contexts.

Now I contend that the absolute differences interpretation is too extreme to be useful for social theory and that, in addition, it is potentially ideological. In few if any human action contexts are actions coordinated absolutely nonconsensually and absolutely nonnormatively. However morally dubious the consensus and however problematic the content and status of the norms, virtually every human action context involves some form of both of them. In the capitalist marketplace, for example, strategic, utility-maximizing exchanges occur against a horizon of intersubjectively shared meanings and norms; agents normally subscribe at least tacitly to some commonly held notions of reciprocity and to some shared conceptions about the social meanings of objects, including what sorts of things are considered exchangeable. Similarly, in the capitalist workplace, managers and subordinates, as well as co-workers, normally coordinate their actions to some extent consensually and with some explicit or implicit reference to normative assumptions, though the consensus be arrived at unfairly and the norms be incapable of withstanding critical scrutiny.[11] Thus, the capitalist economic system has a moral-cultural dimension.

Likewise, few if any human action contexts are wholly devoid of strategic calculation. Gift rituals in noncapitalist societies, for example, previously taken as veritable crucibles of solidarity, are now widely understood to have a significant strategic, calculative dimension, one enacted in the medium of power if not in that of money.[12] And, as I shall argue in more detail later, the modern restricted nuclear family is not devoid of individual, self-interested, strategic calculations in either medium. These action contexts, then, though not officially counted as economic, have a strategic, economic dimension.

Thus, the absolute differences interpretation is not of much use in social theory. It fails to distinguish, for example, the capitalist economy—let us call it "the official economy"[13]—from the modern restricted nuclear family, for both of these institutions are mélanges of consensuality, normativity, and strategicality. If they are to be distinguished with respect to mode of action-integration, the distinction must be drawn as a difference of degree. It must turn on the place, proportions, and interactions of the three elements within each.

But if this is so, then the absolute differences classification of the official economy as a system-integrated action context and of the modern family as a socially integrated action context is potentially ideological. It could be used, for example, to exaggerate the differences and occlude the similarities between the two institutions. It could be used to construct an ideological opposition that posits the family as the "negative," the complementary other, of the (official) economic sphere, a "haven in a heartless world."

Now which of these possible interpretations of the two distinctions are the operative ones in Habermas's social theory? He asserts that he understands the reproduction distinction according to the pragmatic-contextual interpretation and not the natural kinds one.[14] Likewise, he asserts that he takes the action-context distinction to mark a difference in degree, not an absolute difference.[15] However, I propose to bracket these assertions and to examine what Habermas actually does with these distinctions.

Habermas maps the distinction between action contexts onto the distinction between reproduction functions in order to arrive at a definition of societal modernization and at a picture of the institutional structure of modern societies. He holds that modern societies, unlike premodern societies, split off some material reproduction functions from symbolic ones and hand over the former to two specialized institutions — the (official) economy and the state — which are system-integrated. At the same time, modern societies situate these institutions in the larger social environment by developing two other institutions, which specialize in symbolic reproduction and are socially integrated. These are the modern restricted nuclear family, or "private sphere," and the space of political participation, debate, and opinion formation, or "public sphere"; together they constitute what Habermas calls the two "institutional orders of the modern lifeworld." Thus, modern societies "uncouple," or separate, what Habermas takes to be two distinct but previously undifferentiated aspects of society: "system" and "lifeworld." Hence, in his view, the institutional structure of modern societies is dualistic. On the one side stand the institutional orders of the modern lifeworld, the socially integrated domains specializing in symbolic reproduction, that is, in socialization, solidarity formation, and cultural transmission. On the other side stand the systems, the system-integrated domains specializing in material reproduction. On the one side stand the nuclear family and the public sphere; on the other side stand the (official) capitalist economy and the modern administrative state.[16]

What are the critical insights and blind spots of this model? Let us attend first to the question of its empirical adequacy. And let us focus, for the time being, on the contrast between "the private sphere of the lifeworld" and the (official) economic system. Consider that this aspect of Habermas's categorial divide between system and lifeworld institutions faithfully mirrors the institutional separation in male-dominated, capitalist societies of family and official economy, household and paid workplace. It thus has some prima facie purchase on empirical social reality. But consider, too, that the characterization of the family as a socially integrated, symbolic reproduction domain and the characterization of the paid workplace, on the other hand, as a system-integrated material reproduction domain tends to exaggerate the differences and occlude the similarities between them. For example, it directs attention away from the fact that the household, like the paid workplace, is a site of labor, albeit of unremunerated and often unrecognized labor. Likewise, it does not make visible the fact that in the paid workplace, as in the household, women are assigned to, indeed ghettoized in, distinctively feminine, service-oriented, and often sexualized occupations. Finally, it fails to focalize the fact that in both spheres women are subordinated to men.

Moreover, this characterization presents the male-headed nuclear family, qua socially integrated institutional order of the modern lifeworld, as having only an extrinsic and incidental relation to money and power. These "media" are taken as definitive of interactions in the official economy and the state administration but as only incidental to intrafamilial ones. But this assumption is counterfactual. Feminists have shown through empirical analyses of contemporary familial decision making, handling of finances, and wife battering that families are thoroughly permeated with, in Habermas's terms, the media of money and power. They are sites of egocentric, strategic, and instrumental calculation as well as sites of usually exploitative exchanges of services, labor, cash, and sex — and, frequently, sites of coercion and violence.[17] But Habermas's way of contrasting the modern family with the official capitalist economy tends to occlude all this. It overstates the differences between these institutions and blocks the possibility of analyzing families as economic systems, that is, as sites of labor, exchange, calculation, distribution, and exploitation. Or, to the degree that Habermas would acknowledge that they can be seen in that way too, his framework would suggest that this is due to the intrusion or invasion of alien forces, to the "colonization" of the family by the (official) economy and the state. This, too, however, is a dubious proposition (I shall discuss it in detail in section 3 below).

Thus, Habermas's model has some empirical deficiencies: it is not easily able to focalize some dimensions of male dominance in modern societies. Yet it does offer a conceptual resource suitable for understanding *other* aspects of modern male dominance. Consider that Habermas subdivides the category of socially integrated action contexts into two subcategories. On the one hand, there are "normatively secured" forms of socially integrated action. These are actions coordinated on the basis of a conventional, prereflective, taken-for-granted consensus about values and ends, consensus rooted in the precritical internalization of socialization and cultural tradition. On the other hand, there are "communicatively achieved" forms of socially integrated action. These involve actions coordinated on the basis of explicit, reflectively achieved consensus, consensus reached by unconstrained discussion under conditions of freedom, equality, and fairness.[18] This distinction, which is a subdistinction within the category of socially integrated action, provides Habermas with some critical resources for analyzing the modern restricted male-headed nuclear family. Such families can be understood as normatively secured rather than communicatively achieved action contexts, that is, as contexts where actions are (sometimes) mediated by consensus and shared values but where such consensus is suspect because it is prereflective or because it is achieved through dialogue vitiated by unfairness, coercion, or inequality.

To what extent does the distinction between normatively secured and communicatively achieved action contexts succeed in overcoming the problems discussed earlier? Only partially, I think. On the one hand, this distinction is a morally significant and empirically useful one. The notion of a normatively secured action context fits nicely with recent research on patterns of communication between husbands and wives. This research shows that men tend to control conversations, determining what topics are pursued, whereas women do more "interaction work" like asking questions and providing verbal support.[19] Research also reveals differences in men's and women's uses of the bodily and gestural dimensions of speech, differences that confirm men's dominance and women's subordination.[20] Thus, Habermas's distinction enables us to capture something important about intrafamilial dynamics. What is insufficiently stressed, however, is that actions coordinated by normatively secured consensus in the male-headed nuclear family are actions regulated by power. It seems to me a grave mistake to restrict the use of the term 'power' to bureaucratic contexts. Habermas would do better to distinguish different kinds of power, for example, domestic-patriarchal power, on the one hand, and bureaucratic-patriarchal power, on the other—not to mention various other kinds and combinations in between.

But even that distinction does not by itself suffice to make Habermas's framework fully adequate to all the empirical forms of male dominance in modern societies, for normative-domestic-patriarchal power is only one of the elements that enforce women's subordination in the domestic sphere. To capture the others would require a social-theoretical framework capable of analyzing families also as economic systems involving the appropriation of women's unpaid labor and interlocking in complex ways with other economic systems involving paid work. Because Habermas's framework draws its major categorial divide between system and lifeworld institutions, and hence between (among other things) the official economy and the family, it is not very well suited to that task.

Let me turn now from the question of the empirical adequacy of Habermas's model to the question of its normative political implications. What sorts of social arrangements and transformations does his conception of modernization tend to legitimate? And what sorts does it tend to rule out? Here, it will be necessary to reconstruct some implications of the model that are not explicitly thematized by Habermas.

Consider that the conception of modernization as the uncoupling of system and lifeworld institutions tends to legitimate the modern institutional separation of family and official economy, childrearing and paid work. For Habermas argues that with respect to system integration, symbolic reproduction and material reproduction are asymmetrical. Symbolic reproduction activities, he claims, are unlike material reproduction activities in that they cannot be turned over to specialized, system-integrated institutions set apart from the lifeworld; their inherently symbolic character requires that they be socially integrated.[21] It follows that women's unpaid childrearing work could not be incorporated into the (official) economic system without "pathological" results. Moreover, Habermas also holds that it is a mark of societal rationalization that system-integrated institutions be differentiated to handle material reproduction functions. The separation of a specialized (official) economic system enhances a society's capacity to deal with its natural and social environment. "System complexity," then, constitutes a "developmental advance."[22] It follows that the (official) economic system of paid work could not be dedifferentiated with respect to, say, childrearing, without societal "regression." But if childrearing could not be nonpathologically incorporated into the (official) economic system and if the (official) economic system could not be nonregressively dedifferentiated, then the continued separation of childrearing from paid work would be unavoidable.

This amounts to a defense of one aspect of what feminists call "the separation of public and private," namely, the separation of the official economic sphere from the domestic sphere and the enclaving of childrearing from the rest of social labor. It amounts, that is, to a defense of an institutional arrangement that is widely held to be one, if not the, linchpin of modern women's subordination. And it should be noted that the fact that Habermas is a socialist does not alter the matter, because the (undeniably desirable) elimination of private ownership, profit-orientation, and hierarchical command in paid work would not of itself affect the official economic/domestic separation.

Now I want to challenge several premises of the reasoning I have just reconstructed. First, this reasoning assumes the natural kinds interpretation of the symbolic versus material reproduction distinction. But since, as I have argued, childrearing is a dual aspect activity and since it is not categorially different in this respect from other work, there is no warrant for the claim of an asymmetry vis-à-vis system integration. That is, there is no warrant for assuming that the system-integrated organization of childrearing would be any more (or less) pathological than that of other work. Second, this reasoning assumes the absolute differences interpretation of the social versus system integration distinction. But since, as I have argued, the modern male-headed nuclear family is a mélange of (normatively secured) consensuality, normativity, and strategicality and since it is in this respect not categorially different from the paid workplace, then privatized childrearing is already, to a not insignificant extent, permeated by the media of money and power. Moreover, there is no empirical evidence that children raised in commercial day care centers (even profit-based or corporate ones) turn out any more pathological than those raised, say, in suburban homes by full-time mothers. Third, the reasoning just sketched elevates system complexity to the status of an overriding consideration with effective veto power over proposed social transformations aimed at overcoming women's subordination. But this is at odds with Habermas's professions that system complexity is only one measure of "progress" among others.[23] More importantly, it is at odds with any reasonable standard of justice.

What, then, should we conclude about the normative political implications of Habermas's model? If the conception of modernization as the uncoupling of system and lifeworld institutions does indeed have the implications I have just drawn from it, then it is in important respects androcentric and ideological.

2. Public and Private in Classical Capitalism: Thematizing the Gender Subtext

The foregoing difficulties notwithstanding, Habermas offers an account of the interinstitutional relations among various spheres of public and private life in classical capitalism that has some genuine critical potential. But in order to realize this potential fully, we need to reconstruct the unthematized gender subtext of his material.

Let me return to his conception of the way in which the (official) economic system and the state system are situated with respect to the lifeworld. Habermas holds that with modernization the (official) economic and state systems are not simply disengaged or detached from the lifeworld; they must also be related to and embedded in it. Concomitant with the beginnings of classical capitalism, then, is the development *within* the lifeworld of "institutional orders" that situate the systems in a context of everyday meanings and norms. The lifeworld, as we saw, gets differentiated into two spheres that provide appropriate complementary environments for the two systems. The "private sphere" — or modern restricted nuclear family — is linked to the (official) economic system. The "public sphere" — or space of political participation, debate, and opinion formation — is linked to the state administrative system. The family is linked to the (official) economy by means of a series of exchanges conducted in the medium of money: it supplies the (official) economy with appropriately socialized labor power in exchange for wages, and it provides appropriate, monetarily measured demand for commodified goods and services. Exchanges between family and (official) economy, then, are channeled through the "roles" of worker and consumer. Parallel exchange processes link the public sphere and the state system. These, however, are conducted chiefly in the medium of power: loyalty, obedience, and tax revenues are exchanged for "organizational results" and "political decisions." Exchanges between public sphere and state, then, are channeled through the "role" of citizen and, in late welfare state capitalism, that of client.[24]

This account of interinstitutional relations in classical capitalism offers a number of important advantages. First, it treats the modern restricted nuclear family as a historically emergent institution with its own positive, determinate features. It specifies that this type of family emerges concomitantly with, and in relation to, the emerging capitalist economy, administrative state, and (eventually) the political public sphere. Moreover, it charts some of the dynamics of exchange among these institutions and indicates some ways in which they are fitted to the needs of one another so as to accommodate those exchanges among them.

Finally, Habermas's account offers an important corrective to the standard dualistic approaches to the separation of public and private in capitalist societies. He conceptualizes the problem as a relation among four terms: family, (official) economy, state, and public sphere. His view suggests that in classical capitalism there are actually two distinct but interrelated public/private separations. One public/private separation operates at the level of "systems," namely, the separation of the state, or public system, from the (official) capitalist economy, or private system. The other public/private separation operates at the level of the "lifeworld," namely, the separation of the family, or private lifeworld sphere, from the space of political opinion formation and participation, or public lifeworld sphere. Moreover, each of these public/private separations is coordinated with the other. One axis of exchange runs between private system and private lifeworld sphere, that is, between (official) capitalist economy and modern restricted nuclear family. Another axis of exchange runs between public system and public lifeworld sphere, or between state administration and the organs of public opinion and will formation. In both cases, the exchanges can occur because of the institutionalization of specific roles that connect the domains in question. Hence, the roles of worker and consumer link the (official) private economy and the private family, while the roles of citizen and (later) client link the public state and the public opinion institutions.

Thus, Habermas provides an extremely sophisticated account of the relations between public and private institutions in classical capitalist societies. At the same time, however, his account evinces some weaknesses. Many of these stem from his failure to thematize the gender subtext of the relations and arrangements he describes.[25] Consider, first, the relations between (official) private economy and private family as mediated by the roles of worker and consumer. These roles, I submit, are gendered roles. And the links they forge between family and (official) economy are effected as much in the medium of gender identity as in the medium of money.

Take the role of the worker.[26] In male-dominated, classical capitalist societies, this role is a masculine role—and not just in the relatively superficial statistical sense. There is, rather, a very deep sense in which masculine identity in these societies is bound up with the breadwinner role. Masculinity is in large part a matter of leaving home each day for a place of paid work and returning with a wage that provides for one's dependents. It is this internal relation between being a man and being a provider that explains why in capitalist societies unemployment is often not just economically but also psychologically devastating for men. It also sheds light on the centrality of the struggle for a "family wage" in the history of the workers' and trade-union movements of the nineteenth and twentieth centuries. This was a struggle for a wage conceived not as a payment to a genderless individual for the use of labor power but rather as a payment to a man for the support of his economically dependent wife and children—a conception, of course, that legitimized the practice of paying women less for equal or comparable work.

The masculine subtext of the worker role is confirmed by the vexed and strained character of women's relation to paid work in male-dominated, classical capitalism. As Carole Pateman puts it, it is not that women are absent from the paid workplace; it's rather that they are present differently[27]—for example, as feminized and sometimes sexualized "service" workers (secretaries, domestic workers, salespersons, prostitutes, and, more recently, flight attendants); as members of the "helping professions," utilizing mothering skills (nurses, social workers, childcare workers, primary school teachers); as targets of sexual harassment; as low-waged, low-skilled, low-status workers in sex-segregated occupations; as part-time workers; as workers who work a double shift (both unpaid domestic labor and paid labor); as "working wives" and "working mothers," that is, as primarily wives and mothers, who happen, secondarily, also to "go out to work" as "supplemental earners." These differences in the quality of women's presence in the paid workplace testify to the conceptual dissonance between femininity and the worker role in classical capitalism. And this in turn confirms the masculine subtext of that role. It confirms that the role of the worker, which links the private (official) economy and the private family in male-dominated, capitalist societies, is a masculine role, and that, *pace* Habermas, the link it forges is elaborated as much in the medium of masculine gender identity as in the medium of seemingly gender-neutral money.

Conversely, the other role linking (official) economy and family in Habermas's scheme has a feminine subtext. The consumer, after all, is the worker's companion and helpmeet in classical capitalism. The sexual division of domestic labor assigns to women the work—and it is indeed work, though unpaid and usually unrecognized work—of purchasing and preparing goods and services for domestic consumption. You can confirm this even today by visiting any supermarket or department store or by looking at the history of consumer goods advertising. Such advertising has nearly always interpellated its subject, the consumer, as feminine.[28] In fact, it has elaborated an entire phantasmatics of desire premised on the femininity of the subject of consumption. It is only relatively recently, and with some difficulty, that advertisers have devised ways of interpellating a masculine subject of consumption. The trick was to find means of positioning a male consumer that did not feminize, emasculate, or sissify him. In *The Hearts of Men,* Barbara Ehrenreich—quite shrewdly, I think—credits *Playboy* magazine with pioneering such means.[29] But the difficulty and lateness of the project confirm the gendered character of the consumer role in classical capitalism. Men occupy it with conceptual strain and cognitive dissonance, much as women occupy the role of worker. Thus, the role of consumer that links official economy and family is manifestly a feminine role. *Pace* Habermas, it forges the link in the medium of feminine gender identity as much as in the apparently gender-neutral medium of money.

Moreover, Habermas's account of the roles linking family and (official) economy contains a significant omission: there is no mention in his schema of any childrearer role, although the material clearly requires one. For who other than the childrearer is performing the unpaid work of overseeing the production of the "appropriately socialized labor power" that the family exchanges for wages? Of course, the childrearer role in classical capitalism (as elsewhere) is patently a feminine role. Its omission here is a mark of androcentrism, and it has some significant consequences. A consideration of the childrearer role in this context might well have pointed to the central relevance of gender to the institutional structure of classical capitalism. And this, in turn, could have led to the disclosure of the gender subtext of the other roles and of the importance of gender identity as an "exchange medium."

What, then, of the other set of roles and linkages identified by Habermas? What of the citizen role, which he claims connects the public system of the administrative state with the public lifeworld sphere of political opinion and will formation? This role, too, is a gendered role in classical capitalism, indeed, a masculine role[30]—and not simply in the sense that women did not win the vote in the United States and Britain (for example) until the twentieth century. Rather, the lateness and difficulty of that victory are symptomatic of deeper strains. As Habermas understands it, the citizen is centrally a participant in political debate and public opinion formation. This means that citizenship, in his view, depends crucially on the capacities for consent and speech, the ability to participate on a par with others in dialogue. But these are capacities that are connected with masculinity in male-dominated, classical capitalism; they are capacities that are in myriad ways denied to women and deemed at odds with femininity. I have already cited studies about the effects of male dominance and female subordination on the dynamics of dialogue. Now consider that even today in most jurisdictions there is no such thing as marital rape. That is, a wife is legally subject to her husband; she is not an individual who can give or withhold consent to his demands for sexual access. Consider also that even outside of marriage the legal test of rape often boils down to whether a "reasonable man" would have assumed that the woman had consented. Consider what that means when both popular and legal opinion widely holds that when a woman says no she means yes. It means, says Carole Pateman, that "women find their speech . . . persistently and systematically invalidated in the crucial matter of consent, a matter that is fundamental to democracy. [But] if women's words about consent are consistently reinterpreted, how can they participate in the debate among citizens?"[31]

Thus, there is conceptual dissonance between femininity and the dialogical capacities central to Habermas's conception of citizenship. And another aspect of citizenship not discussed by him is even more obviously bound up with masculinity. This is the soldiering aspect of citizenship, the conception of the citizen as the defender of the polity and protector of those—women, children, the elderly—who allegedly cannot protect themselves. As Judith Stiehm has argued, this division between male protectors and female protected introduces further dissonance into women's relation to citizenship.[32] It confirms the gender subtext of the citizen role. The view of women as in need of men's protection "underlies access not just to the means of destruction, but also [to] the means of production—witness all the 'protective' legislation that has surrounded women's access to the workplace—and [to] the means of reproduction [—witness] women's status as wives and sexual partners."[33]

The citizen role in male-dominated, classical capitalism is therefore a manifestly masculine role. It links the state and the public sphere, as Habermas claims, but it also links these to the official economy and the family. And in every case the links are forged in the medium of masculine gender identity rather than, as Habermas has it, in the medium of a gender-neutral power. Or, if the medium of exchange here is power, then the power in question is masculine power: it is power as the expression of masculinity.

Thus, there are some major lacunae in Habermas's otherwise powerful and sophisticated model of the relations between public and private institutions in classical capitalism. Because his model is blind to the significance and operation of gender, it is bound to miss important features of the arrangements he wants to understand. By omitting any mention of the childrearer role and by failing to thematize the gender subtext underlying the roles of worker and consumer, Habermas fails to understand precisely how the capitalist workplace is linked to the modern restricted male-headed nuclear family. Similarly, by failing to thematize the masculine subtext of the citizen role, he misses the full meaning of the way the state is linked to the public sphere of political speech. Moreover, Habermas misses important cross-connections among the four elements of his two public/ private schemata. He misses, for example, the way the masculine citizen-soldier-protector role links the state and the public sphere not only to each other but also to the family and to the paid workplace—that is, the way the assumptions of man's capacity to protect and woman's need of man's protection run through all of them. He misses, too, the way the masculine citizen-speaker role links the state and the public sphere not only to each other but also to the family and the official economy—that is, the way the assumptions of man's capacity to speak and consent and woman's comparative incapacity run through all of them. He misses, also, the way the masculine worker-breadwinner role links the family and the official economy not only to each other but also to the state and the political public sphere—that is, the way the assumptions of man's provider status and of woman's dependent status run through all of them, so that even the coin in which classical capitalist wages and taxes are paid is not gender-neutral. And he misses, finally, the way the feminine childrearer role links all four institutions to one another by overseeing the construction of the masculine and feminine gendered subjects needed to fill *every* role in classical capitalism.

Once the gender-blindness of Habermas's model is overcome, however, all these connections come into view. It then becomes clear that feminine and masculine gender identity run like pink and blue threads through the areas of paid work, state administration, and citizenship as well as through the domain of familial and sexual relations. This is to say that gender identity is lived out in all arenas of life. It is one (if not the) "medium of exchange" among all of them, a basic element of the social glue that binds them to one another.

Moreover, a gender-sensitive reading of these connections discloses some important theoretical and conceptual implications. It reveals that male dominance is intrinsic rather than accidental to classical capitalism, for the institutional structure of this social formation is actualized by means of gendered roles. It follows that the forms of male dominance at issue here are not properly understood as lingering forms of premodern status inequality. They are, rather, intrinsically modern in Habermas's sense, since they are premised on the separation of waged labor and the state from childrearing and the household. It also follows that a critical social theory of capitalist societies needs gender-sensitive categories. The preceding analysis shows that, contrary to the usual androcentric understanding, the relevant concepts of worker, consumer, and wage are not, in fact, strictly economic concepts. Rather, they have an implicit gender subtext and thus are "gender-economic" concepts. Likewise, the relevant concept of citizenship is not strictly a political concept; it has an implicit gender subtext and so, rather, is a "gender-political" concept. Thus, this analysis reveals the inadequacy of those critical theories that treat gender as incidental to politics and political economy. It highlights the need for a critical theory with a categorial framework in which gender, politics, and political economy are internally integrated.[34]

In addition, a gender-sensitive reading of these arrangements reveals the thoroughly multidirectional character of social motion and causal influence in classical capitalism. It reveals, that is, the inadequacy of the orthodox Marxist assumption that all or most significant causal influence runs from the (official) economy to the family and not vice versa. It shows that gender identity structures paid work, state administration, and political participation. Thus, it vindicates Habermas's claim that in classical capitalism the (official) economy is not all-powerful but is, rather, in some significant measure inscribed within and subject to the norms and meanings of everyday life. Of course, Habermas assumed that in making this claim he was saying something more or less positive. The norms and meanings he had in mind were not the ones I have been discussing. Still, the point is a valid one. It remains to be seen, though, whether it holds also for late, welfare state capitalism, as I believe, or whether it ceases to hold, as Habermas claims.

Finally, this reconstruction of the gender subtext of Habermas's model has normative political implications. It suggests that an emancipatory transformation of male-dominated, capitalist societies, early and late, requires a transformation of these gendered roles and of the institutions they mediate. As long as the worker and childrearer roles are constituted as fundamentally incompatible with one another, it will not be possible to universalize either of them to include both genders. Thus, some form of dedifferentiation of unpaid childrearing and other work is required. Similarly, as long as the citizen role is defined to encompass death-dealing soldiering but not life-fostering childrearing, as long as it is tied to male-dominated modes of dialogue, then it, too, will remain incapable of including women fully. Thus, changes in the very concepts of citizenship, childrearing and paid work are necessary, as are changes in the relationships among the domestic, official economic, state, and political public spheres.

3. The Dynamics of Welfare State Capitalism: A Feminist Critique

Let me turn, then, to Habermas's account of late welfare state capitalism. I must acknowledge at the outset that its critical potential, unlike the critical potential of his account of classical capitalism, cannot be released simply by reconstructing the unthematized gender subtext. Here, the problematic features of his social-theoretical framework tend to inflect the analysis as a whole and diminish its capacity to illuminate the struggles and wishes of contemporary women. In order to show how this is the case, I shall present Habermas's view in the form of six theses.

First, welfare state capitalism emerges as a result of, and in response to, instabilities or crisis tendencies inherent in classical capitalism. It realigns the relations between the (official) economy and the state, that is, between the private and public systems. These become more deeply intertwined with one another as the state actively assumes the task of "crisis management." It tries to avert or manage economic crises by Keynesian "market-replacing" strategies, which create a "public sector." And it tries to avert or manage social and political crises by "market-compensating" measures, including welfare concessions to trade unions and social movements. Thus, welfare state capitalism partially overcomes the separation of public and private at the level of systems.[35]

Second, the realignment of (official) economy/state relations is accompanied by a change in the relations of those systems to the private and public spheres of the lifeworld. With respect to the private sphere, there is a major increase in the importance of the consumer role as dissatisfactions related to paid work are compensated by enhanced commodity consumption. With respect to the public sphere, there is a major decline in the importance of the citizen role as journalism becomes mass media, political parties are bureaucratized, and participation is reduced to occasional voting. Instead, the relation to the state is increasingly channeled through a new role, the social-welfare client.[36]

Third, these developments are "ambivalent." On the one hand, there are gains in freedom with the institution of new social rights limiting the heretofore unrestrained power of capital in the (paid) workplace and of the paterfamilias in the bourgeois family, and social insurance programs represent a clear advance over the paternalism of poor relief. On the other hand, the means employed to realize these new social rights tend perversely to endanger freedom. These means—bureaucratic procedure and the money form—structure the entitlements, benefits, and social services of the welfare system and, in so doing, disempower clients, rendering them dependent on bureaucracies and "therapeutocracies" and preempting their capacities to interpret their own needs, experiences, and life problems.[37]

Fourth, the most ambivalent welfare measures are those concerned with things like health care, care of the elderly, education, and family law, for when bureaucratic and monetary media structure these things, they intrude upon "core domains" of the lifeworld. They turn over symbolic reproduction functions like socialization and solidarity formation to system-integration mechanisms that position people as strategically acting, self-interested monads. But given the inherently symbolic character of these functions and given their internal relation to social integration, the results, necessarily, are "pathological." Thus, these measures are more ambivalent than, say, reforms of the paid workplace. The latter bear on a domain that is already system-integrated via money and power and that serves material, as opposed to symbolic, reproduction functions. So paid workplace reforms—unlike, say, family law reforms—do not necessarily generate "pathological" side effects.[38]

Fifth, welfare state capitalism thus gives rise to an "inner colonization of the lifeworld." Money and power cease to be mere media of exchange *between* system and lifeworld. Instead, they tend increasingly to penetrate the lifeworld's *internal* dynamics. The private and public spheres cease to subordinate (official) economic and administrative systems to the norms, values, and interpretations of everyday life. Rather, the latter are increasingly subordinated to the imperatives of the (official) economy and administration. The roles of worker and citizen cease to channel the influence of the lifeworld to the systems. Instead, the newly inflated roles of consumer and client channel the influence of the system to the lifeworld. Moreover, the intrusion of system-integration mechanisms into domains inherently requiring social integration gives rise to "reification phenomena." The affected domains are detached not merely from traditional, normatively secured consensus but from "value orientations per se." The result is the "desiccation of communicative contexts" and the "depletion of the nonrenewable cultural resources" needed to maintain personal and collective identity. Thus, symbolic reproduction is destabilized, identities are threatened, and social crisis tendencies develop.[39]

Sixth, the colonization of the lifeworld sparks new forms of social conflict specific to welfare state capitalism. "New social movements" emerge in a "new conflict zone" at the "seam of system and lifeworld." They respond to system-induced identity threats by contesting the roles that transmit these. They contest the instrumentalization of professional labor and of education transmitted via the worker role, the monetarization of relations and life-styles transmitted via the inflated consumer role, the bureaucratization of services and life problems transmitted via the client role, and the rules and routines of interest politics transmitted via the impoverished citizen role. Thus, the conflicts at the cutting edge of developments in welfare capitalism differ both from class struggles and from bourgeois liberation struggles. They respond to crisis tendencies in symbolic, as opposed to material, reproduction, and they contest reification and "the grammar of forms of life" as opposed to distribution or status inequality.[40]

The various new social movements can be classified with respect to their emancipatory potential. The criterion is the extent to which they advance a genuinely emancipatory resolution of welfare capitalist crisis, namely, the "decolonization of the lifeworld." Decolonization encompasses three things: (1) the removal of system-integration mechanisms from symbolic reproduction spheres, (2) the replacement of (some) normatively secured contexts by communicatively achieved ones, and (3) the development of new, democratic institutions capable of asserting lifeworld control over state and (official) economic systems. Thus, those movements, like religious fundamentalism, that seek to defend traditional lifeworld norms against system intrusions are not genuinely emancipatory; they actively oppose the second element of decolonization and do not take up the third. Movements advocating peace and ecology are better; they aim both to resist system intrusions and also to instate new, reformed, communicatively achieved zones of interaction. But even these are "ambiguous" inasmuch as they tend to "retreat" into alternative communities and "particularistic" identities, thereby effectively renouncing the third element of decolonization and leaving the (official) economic and state systems unchecked. In this respect, they are more symptomatic than emancipatory: they express the identity disturbances caused by colonization. The feminist movement, on the other hand, represents something of an anomaly. It alone is "offensive," aiming to "conquer new territory," and it alone retains links to historic liberation movements. In principle, then, feminism remains rooted in "universalist morality." Yet it is linked to resistance movements by an element of "particularism." And it tends, at times, to "retreat" into identities and communities organized around the natural category of biological sex.[41]

Now, what are the critical insights and blind spots of Habermas's account of the dynamics of welfare state capitalism? To what extent does it serve the self-clarification of the struggles and wishes of contemporary women? I shall take up the six theses one by one.

Habermas's first thesis is straightforward and unobjectionable. Clearly, the welfare state does engage in crisis management and does partially overcome the separation of public and private at the level of systems.

Habermas's second thesis contains some important insights. Clearly, welfare state capitalism does inflate the consumer role and deflate the citizen role, reducing the latter essentially to voting—and, I should add, also to soldiering. Moreover, the welfare state does indeed increasingly position its subjects as clients. On the other hand, Habermas again fails to see the gender subtext of these developments. He fails to see that the new client role has a gender, that it is a paradigmatically feminine role. He overlooks the fact that it is overwhelmingly women who are the clients of the welfare state, especially older women, poor women, single women with children. Nor does he notice that many welfare systems are internally dualized and gendered, that they include two basic kinds of programs — "masculine" social insurance programs tied to primary labor force participation and designed to benefit principal breadwinners, and "feminine" relief programs oriented to what are understood as domestic "failures," in short, to families without a male breadwinner. Not surprisingly, these two welfare subsystems are separate and unequal. Clients of feminine programs, virtually exclusively women and their children, are positioned in a distinctive, feminizing fashion as the "negatives of possessive individuals": they are largely excluded from the market both as workers and as consumers and are familialized, that is, made to claim benefits not as individuals but as members of "defective" households. They are also stigmatized, denied rights, subjected to surveillance and administrative harassment and generally made into abject dependents of state bureaucracies.[42] But this means that the rise of the client role in welfare state capitalism has a more complex meaning than Habermas allows. It is not only a change in the link between system and lifeworld institutions; it is also a change in the character of male dominance, a shift, in Carol Brown's phrase, "from private patriarchy to public patriarchy."[43]

This gives a rather different twist to the meaning of Habermas's third thesis. It suggests that he is right about the "ambivalence" of welfare state capitalism — but not quite and not only in the way he thought. It suggests that welfare measures do have a positive side insofar as they reduce women's dependence on an individual male breadwinner. However, they also have a negative side insofar as they substitute dependence on a patriarchal and androcentric state bureaucracy. The benefits provided are, as Habermas says, "system-conforming" ones. But the system they conform to is not adequately characterized as the system of the official, state-regulated capitalist economy. It is also the system of male dominance, which extends even to the sociocultural lifeworld. In other words, the ambivalence here does not stem only, as Habermas implies, from the fact that the role of client carries effects of "reification." It stems also from the fact that this role, qua feminine role, perpetuates in a new, let us say "modernized" and "rationalized" form, women's subordination. Or so Habermas's third thesis might be rewritten in a feminist critical theory — without, of course, abandoning his insights into the ways in which welfare bureaucracies and therapeutocracies disempower clients by preempting their capacities to interpret their own needs, experiences, and life problems.

Habermas's fourth thesis, by contrast, is not so easily rewritten. This thesis states that welfare reforms of, for example, the domestic sphere are more ambivalent than reforms of the paid workplace. This is true empirically in the sense I have just described—but it is due to the patriarchal character of welfare systems, not to the inherently symbolic character of lifeworld institutions, as Habermas claims. His claim depends on two assumptions I have already challenged. First, it depends on the natural kinds interpretation of the distinction between symbolic and material reproduction activities, that is, on the false assumption that child-rearing is inherently more symbolic and less material than other work. And, second, it depends upon the absolute differences interpretation of the system-integrated versus socially integrated action contexts distinction, that is, on the false assumption that money and power are not already entrenched in the internal dynamics of the family. Once we repudiate these assumptions, however, there is no categorial, as opposed to empirical, basis for differentially evaluating the two kinds of reforms. If it is basically progressive that paid workers acquire the means to confront their employers strategically and match power against power, right against right, then it must be just as basically progressive *in principle* that women acquire similar means to similar ends in the politics of familial and personal life. And if it is "pathological" that in the course of achieving a better balance of power in familial and personal life, women become clients of state bureaucracies, then it must be just as "pathological" *in principle* that in the course of achieving a similar end at paid work, paid workers, too, become clients—which does not alter the fact that *in actuality* unpaid mothers and paid workers become two different sorts of clients. But of course the real point is that the term 'pathological' is misused here insofar as it supposes the untenable assumption that childrearing and other work are asymmetrical with respect to system integration.

This sheds new light as well on Habermas's fifth thesis. This thesis states that welfare state capitalism inaugurates an inner colonization of the lifeworld by systems. It depends on three assumptions. The first two of these are the two just rejected, namely, the natural kinds interpretation of the distinction between symbolic and material reproduction activities and the assumed virginity of the domestic sphere with respect to money and power. The third assumption is that the basic vector of motion in late capitalist society is from state-regulated economy to lifeworld and not vice versa. The feminine gender subtext of the client role contradicts this assumption: it suggests that even in late capitalism the norms and meanings of gender identity continue to channel the influence of the lifeworld into systems. These norms continue to structure the state-regulated economy, as the persistence, indeed exacerbation, of labor force segmentation according to sex shows.[44] And these norms also structure state administration, as the gender segmentation of U.S. and European social-welfare systems shows.[45] Thus, it is not the case that in late capitalism "system intrusions" detach life contexts from "value-orientations per se." On the contrary, welfare capitalism simply uses other means to uphold the familiar "normatively secured consensus" concerning male dominance and female subordination. But Habermas's theory overlooks this countermotion from lifeworld to system. Thus, it posits the evil of welfare state capitalism as the evil of a general and indiscriminate reification. It fails, in consequence, to account for the fact that it is disproportionately women who suffer the effects of bureaucratization and monetarization and for the fact that, viewed structurally, bureaucratization and monetarization are, among other things, instruments of women's subordination.

This entails the revision, as well, of Habermas's sixth thesis. This thesis concerns the causes, character, and emancipatory potential of social movements, including feminism, in late capitalist societies. Since these issues are so central to the concerns of this paper, they warrant a more extended discussion.

Habermas explains the existence and character of new social movements, including feminism, in terms of colonization, that is, in terms of the intrusion of system-integration mechanisms into symbolic reproduction spheres and the consequent erosion and desiccation of contexts of interpretation and communication. But given the multidirectionality of causal influence in welfare capitalism, the terms 'colonization,' 'intrusion,' 'erosion,' and 'desiccation' are too negative and one-sided to account for the identity shifts manifested in social movements. Let me attempt an alternative explanation, at least for women, by returning to Habermas's important insight that much contemporary contestation surrounds the institution-mediating roles of worker, consumer, citizen, and client. Let me add to these the childrearer role and the fact that all of them are gendered roles. Now, consider in this light the meaning of the experience of millions of women, especially married women and women with children, who have in the postwar period become paid workers and/or social-welfare clients. I have already indicated that this has been an experience of new, acute forms of domination; it has also, however, been an experience in which women could, often for the first time, taste the possibilities of a measure of relative economic independence, an identity outside the domestic sphere, and expanded political participation. Above all, it has been an experience of conflict and contradiction as women try to do the impossible, namely, to juggle simultaneously the existing roles of childrearer and worker, client and citizen. The cross-pulls of these mutually incompatible roles have been painful and identity-threatening but not simply negative.[46] Interpellated simultaneously in contradictory ways, women have become split subjects; as a result, the roles themselves, previously shielded in their separate spheres, have suddenly been opened to contestation. Should we, like Habermas, speak here of a ''crisis in symbolic reproduction''? Surely not, if this means the desiccation of meaning and values wrought by the intrusion of money and organizational power into women's lives. Emphatically yes, if it means, rather, the emergence into visibility and contestability of problems and possibilities that cannot be solved or realized within the established framework of gendered roles and institutions.

If colonization is not an adequate explanation of contemporary feminism (and other new social movements), then decolonization cannot be an adequate conception of an emancipatory solution. From the perspective I have been sketching, the first element of decolonization—namely, the removal of system integration mechanisms from symbolic reproduction spheres—is conceptually and empirically askew of the real issues. If the real point is the moral superiority of cooperative and egalitarian interactions over strategic and hierarchical ones, then it mystifies matters to single out lifeworld institutions—the point should hold for paid work and political administration as well as for domestic life. Similarly, the third element of decolonization—namely, the reversal of the direction of influence and control from system to lifeworld—needs modification. Since the social meanings of gender still structure late capitalist official economic and state systems, the question is not *whether* lifeworld norms will be decisive but, rather, *which* lifeworld norms will.

This implies that the key to an emancipatory outcome lies in the second element of Habermas's conception of decolonization—namely, the replacement of normatively secured contexts of interaction by communicatively achieved ones. The centrality of this element is evident when we consider that this process occurs simultaneously on two fronts. First, it occurs in the struggles of social movements with the state and official economic system institutions; these struggles are not waged over systems media alone—they are also waged over the meanings and norms embedded and enacted in government and corporate policy. Second, this process occurs in a phenomenon not thematized by Habermas: in the struggles between opposing social movements with conflicting interpretations of social needs. Both kinds of struggles involve confrontations between normatively secured and communicatively achieved action. Both involve contestation for hegemony over what I call the "sociocultural means of interpretation and communication." For example, in many late capitalist societies, women's contradictory, self-dividing experience of trying to be both workers and mothers, clients and citizens has given rise to not one but two women's movements, a feminist one and an antifeminist one. These movements, along with their respective allies, are engaged in struggles with one another and with state and corporate institutions over the social meanings of "woman" and "man," "femininity" and "masculinity"; over the interpretation of women's needs; over the interpretation and social construction of women's bodies; and over the gender norms that shape the major institution-mediating social roles. Of course, the means of interpretation and communication in terms of which the social meanings of these things are elaborated have always been controlled by men. Thus, feminist women are struggling in effect to redistribute and democratize access to, and control over, discursive resources. We are, therefore, struggling for women's autonomy in the following special sense: a measure of collective control over the means of interpretation and communication sufficient to permit us to participate on a par with men in all types of social interaction, including political deliberation and decision making.[47]

The foregoing suggests that a caution is in order concerning the use of the terms 'particularism' and 'universalism'. Recall that Habermas's sixth thesis emphasized feminism's links to historic liberation movements and its roots in universalist morality. Recall that he was critical of those tendencies within feminism, and in resistance movements in general, that try to resolve the identity problematic by recourse to particularism, that is, by retreating from arenas of political struggle into alternative communities delimited on the basis of natural categories like biological sex. I want to suggest that there are really three issues here and that they need to be disengaged from one another. One is the issue of political engagement versus apolitical countercultural activity. Insofar as Habermas's point is a criticism of cultural feminism, it is well-taken in principle, but it needs to be qualified by two perceptions: cultural separatism, although inadequate as long-term political strategy, is in many cases a shorter-term necessity for women's physical, psychological, and moral survival; and separatist communities have, in fact, been the source of numerous reinterpretations of women's experience that have proved politically fruitful in contestation over the means of interpretation and communication. The second issue is the status of women's biology in the elaboration of new social identities. Insofar as Habermas's point is a criticism of reductive biologism, it is well-taken. But this does not mean that one can ignore the fact that women's biology has nearly always been interpreted by men and that women's struggle for autonomy necessarily and properly involves, among other things, the reinterpretation of the social meanings of our bodies. The third issue is the difficult and complex one of universalism versus particularism. Insofar as Habermas's endorsement of universalism pertains to the meta-level of access to, and control over, the means of interpretation and communication, it is well-taken. At this level, women's struggle for autonomy can be understood in terms of a universalist conception of distributive justice. But it does not follow that the substantive content that is the fruit of this struggle— namely, the new social meanings we give our needs and our bodies, our new social identities and conceptions of femininity—can be dismissed as particularistic lapses from universalism. These, certainly, are no more particular than the sexist and androcentric meanings and norms they are meant to replace. More generally, at the level of substantive content, as opposed to dialogical form, the contrast between universalism and particularism is out of place. Substantive social meanings and norms are always necessarily culturally and historically specific; they always express distinctive shared but nonuniversal forms of life. Feminist meanings and norms will be no exception—but they will not, on that account, be particularistic in any pejorative sense. Let us simply say that they will be different.

I have been arguing that struggles of social movements over the means of interpretation and communication are central to an emancipatory resolution of crisis tendencies in welfare state capitalism. Let me now clarify their relation to institutional change. Such struggles, I claim, are implicitly and explicitly raising a number of important questions: Should the roles of worker, childrearer, citizen, and client be fully degendered? Can they be? Or do we, rather, require arrangements that permit women to be workers and citizens *as women,* just as men have always been workers and citizens *as men?* And what might that mean? In any case, does not an emancipatory outcome require a profound transformation of the current gender roles at the base of contemporary social organization? And does not this, in turn, require a fundamental transformation of the content, character, boundaries, and relations of the spheres of life that these roles mediate? How should the character and position of paid work, childrearing, and citizenship be defined vis-à-vis one another? Should democratic-socialist-feminist, self-managed paid work encompass childrearing? Or should childrearing, rather, replace soldiering as a component of transformed, democratic-socialist-feminist, participatory citizenship? What other possibilities are conceivable?

Let me conclude this discussion of the six theses by restating the most important critical points. First, Habermas's account fails to theorize the patriarchal, norm-mediated character of late capitalist official economic and administrative systems. Likewise, it fails to theorize the systemic, money- and power-mediated character of male dominance in the domestic sphere of the late capitalist lifeworld. Consequently, his colonization thesis fails to grasp that the channels of influence between system and lifeworld institutions are multidirectional. And it tends to replicate, rather than to problematize, a major institutional support of women's subordination in late capitalism, namely, the gender-based separation of both the masculine public sphere and the state-regulated economy of sex-segmented paid work and social welfare from privatized female childrearing. Thus, although Habermas wants to be critical of male dominance, his diagnostic categories deflect attention elsewhere, to the allegedly overriding problem of gender-neutral reification. Consequently, his programmatic conception of decolonization bypasses key feminist questions; it fails to address the issue of how to restructure the relation of childrearing to paid work and citizenship. Finally, Habermas's categories tend to misrepresent the causes and underestimate the scope of the feminist challenge to welfare state capitalism. In short, the struggles and wishes of contemporary women are not adequately clarified by a theory that draws the basic battle line between system and lifeworld institutions. From a feminist perspective, there is a more basic battle line between the forms of male dominance linking "system" to "lifeworld" *and us.*

Conclusion

In general, then, the principal blind spots of Habermas's theory with respect to gender are traceable to his categorial opposition between system and lifeworld institutions and to the two more elementary oppositions from which it is compounded, the reproduction one and the action-contexts one. Or, rather, the blind spots are traceable to the way in which these oppositions, ideologically and androcentrically interpreted, tend to override and eclipse other, potentially more critical elements of Habermas's framework—elements like the distinction between normatively secured and communicatively achieved action contexts and like the four-term model of public/private relations.

Habermas's blind spots are instructive, I think. They permit us to conclude something about what the categorial framework of a socialist-feminist critical theory of welfare state capitalism should look like. One crucial requirement is that this framework not be such as to put the male-headed nuclear family and the state-regulated official economy on two opposite sides of the major categorial divide. We require, rather, a framework sensitive to the similarities between them, one that puts them on the same side of the line as institutions that, albeit in different ways, enforce women's subordination, since both family and official economy appropriate our labor, short-circuit our participation in the interpretation of our needs, and shield normatively secured need interpretations from political contestation. A second crucial requirement is that this framework contain no a priori assumptions about the unidirectionality of social motion and causal influence, that it be sensitive to the ways in which allegedly disappearing institutions and norms persist in structuring social reality. A third crucial requirement, the last I shall mention here, is that this framework not be such as to posit the evil of welfare state capitalism exclusively or primarily as the evil of reification. What we need instead is a framework capable of foregrounding the evil of dominance and subordination.[48]

Notes

1. Karl Marx, "Letter to A. Ruge, September 1843," in *Karl Marx: Early Writings*. ed. L. Colletti, trans. Rodney Livingstone and Gregor Benton (New York, 1975), 209.

2. Jürgen Habermas, *The Theory of Communicative Action*, vol. 1, *Reason and the Rationalization of Society*, trans. Thomas McCarthy (Boston, 1984), hereafter cited as *Theory*, and *Theorie des kommunikativen Handelns*, vol. 2, *Zur Kritik der funktionalistischen Vernunft* (Frankfurt am Main, 1981), hereafter cited as *Theorie*. *Theorie* is now available in English as *The Theory of Communicative Action*, vol. 2, *Lifeworld and System: A Critique of Functionalist Reason*, trans. Thomas McCarthy (Boston, 1987).

See also Habermas, *Legitimation Crisis*, trans. Thomas McCarthy (Boston, 1975); Introduction to *Observations on "The Spiritual Situation of the Age": Contemporary German Perspectives*, ed. Jürgen Habermas, trans. Andrew Buchwalter (Cambridge, Mass., 1984); and "A Reply to My Critics," in *Habermas: Critical Debates*, ed. David Held and John B. Thompson (Cambridge, Mass., 1982).

I have also consulted two helpful overviews of this material in English: Thomas McCarthy, Translator's Introduction to vol. 1 of *The Theory of Communicative Action*, by Habermas, v–xxxvii.; and John B. Thompson, "Rationality and Social Rationalisation: An Assessment of Habermas's Theory of Communicative Action," *Sociology* 17, no. 2 (1983), 278–94.

3. I shall not take up such widely debated issues as Habermas's theories of universal pragmatics

and social evolution. For helpful discussions of these issues, see the essays in *Habermas: Critical Debates.*

4. Habermas, *Theorie,* 214, 217, 348–49; *Legitimation Crisis,* 8–9; and "A Reply to My Critics," 268, 278–79. See also McCarthy, Translator's Introduction xxv–xxvii; and Thompson, "Rationality," 285.

5. Habermas, *Theorie,* 208, and "A Reply to My Critics," 223–25; McCarthy, Translator's Introduction, xxiv–xxv.

6. I am indebted to Martin Schwab for the expression "dual aspect activity."

7. It might be argued that Habermas's categorial distinction between "social labor" and "socialization" helps overcome the androcentrism of orthodox Marxism. Orthodox Marxism allowed for only one kind of historically significant activity, namely, "production," or "social labor." Moreover, it understood that category androcentrically and thereby excluded women's unpaid childrearing activity from history. By contrast, Habermas allows for two kinds of historically significant activity, "social labor" and the "symbolic" activities that comprise, among other things, childrearing. Thus, he manages to include women's unpaid activity in history. Although this is an improvement, it does not suffice to remedy matters. At best, it leads to what has come to be known as "dual systems theory," an approach that posits two distinct "systems" of human activity and, correspondingly, two distinct "systems" of oppression: capitalism and male dominance. But this is misleading. These are not, in fact, two distinct systems but, rather, two thoroughly interfused dimensions of a single social formation. In order to understand that social formation, a critical theory requires a single set of categories and concepts that integrate *internally* both gender and political economy (perhaps also race). For a classic statement of dual systems theory, see Heidi Hartmann, "The Unhappy Marriage of Marxism and Feminism: Towards a More Progressive Union," in *Women and Revolution: A Discussion of the Unhappy Marriage of Marxism and Feminism,* ed. Lydia Sargent (Boston, 1981). For a critique of dual systems theory, see Iris Young, "Beyond the Unhappy Marriage: A Critique of Dual Systems Theory," in *Women and Revolution;* and "Socialist Feminism and the Limits of Dual Systems Theory," *Socialist Review,* 50–51 (Summer, 1980) 169–80.

In sections 2 and 3 of this essay, I am developing arguments and lines of analysis that rely on concepts and categories that internally integrate gender and political economy (see n. 34 below). This might be considered a "single system" approach, by contrast to dual systems theory. However, I find that label misleading, because I do not consider my approach primarily or exclusively a "systems" approach in the first place. Rather, like Habermas, I am trying to link structural (in the sense of objectivating) and interpretive approaches to the study of societies. Unlike him, however, I do not do this by dividing society into two components, "system" and "lifeworld"; see the rest of this section, especially n. 16 below.

8. Habermas, *Theory,* 85, 87–88, 101, 342, 357–60; *Theorie,* 179; *Legitimation Crisis,* 4–5; "A Reply to My Critics," 234, 237, 264–65. See also McCarthy, Translator's Introduction, ix, xvix–xxx. In presenting the distinction between system-integrated and socially-integrated action contexts, I am relying on the terminology of *Legitimation Crisis* and modifying the terminology of *Theory of Communicative Action.* Or, rather, I am selecting one of the several different usages deployed in the latter work. There, Habermas often speaks of what I have called "socially integrated action" as "communicative action." But this gives rise to confusion. For Habermas also uses this latter expression in another, stronger sense, namely, for actions in which coordination occurs by explicit, dialogically achieved consensus only (discussed further later in this section). In order to avoid repeating Habermas's equivocation on 'communicative action,' I adopt the following terminology: I reserve the term 'communicatively achieved action' for actions coordinated by explicit, reflective, dialogically achieved consensus. I contrast such action, in the first instance, with 'normatively secured action' or actions coordinated by tacit, prereflective, pregiven consensus. I take 'communicatively achieved' and 'normatively secured' actions, so defined, to be subspecies of what I here call 'socially integrated action' or actions coordinated by any form of normed consensus whatever. This last category, in turn,

contrasts with 'system-integrated action', or actions coordinated by the functional interlacing of un-intended consequences, determined by egocentric calculations in the media of money and power, and involving little or no normed consensus of any sort. These terminological commitments do not so much represent a departure from Habermas's usage—he does, in fact, frequently use these terms in the senses I have specified—as a stabilization or regularization of his usage.

9. Habermas, *Theory,* 341, 357–59; and *Theorie,* 256, 266. See also McCarthy, Translator's Introduction, xxx.

10. In "Complexity and Democracy, or the Seducements of Systems Theory," (*New German Critique* 35 [Spring/Summer 1985], 27–55), McCarthy argues that state administrative bureaucracies cannot be distinguished from participatory democratic political associations on the bases of function-ality, intentionality, and linguisticality, since all three of these features are found in both contexts. Thus, McCarthy argues that functionality, intentionality, and linguisticality are not mutually exclu-sive. I find these arguments persuasive. I see no reason why they do not hold also for the capitalist workplace and the modern restricted nuclear family.

11. Here, again, I follow McCarthy, "Complexity and Democracy." He argues that in modern state administrative bureaucracies, managers must often deal consensually with their subordinates. This seems to be equally the case for corporate organizations.

12. I have in mind especially the brilliant and influential discussion of gifting by Pierre Bourdieu in *Outline of a Theory of Practice,* trans. Richard Nice (New York, 1977). By recovering the dimen-sion of time, Bourdieu substantially revises the classical account by Marcel Mauss in *The Gift: Forms and Functions of Exchange in Archaic Societies,* trans. Ian Cunnison (New York, 1967). For a dis-cussion of some recent revisionist work in cultural economic anthropology, see Arjun Appadurai, "Commodities and the Politics of Value," in *The Social Life of Things: Commodities in Cultural Perspective,* ed. Appadurai, (New York, 1986).

13. Hereafter I shall use the expression 'the official economy' to designate the institutions and relations in male-dominated capitalist societies that are officially recognized as economic. The point is to call attention to the androcentrism of the standard usage of 'the economy', which is premised on the ideological assumption that domestic institutions and relations are not also economic. I shall use 'offical economic' as the adjectival form of this expression, and I shall use 'the (official) economy' when explicating the views of someone—like Habermas—who follows androcentric usage.

14. Habermas, *Theorie,* 348–49. See also McCarthy, Translator's Introduction, xxvi–xxvii. The terms 'pragmatic-contextual' and 'natural kinds' are mine, not Habermas's.

15. Habermas, *Theory* 94–95, 101; *Theorie,* 348–49; "A Reply to My Critics," 227, 237, 266–68; and *Legitimation Crisis,* 10. See also McCarthy, Translator's Introduction, xxvi–xxvii. Again, the terms 'absolute differences' and 'difference of degree' are mine, not Habermas's.

16. Habermas, *Theory,* 341–42, 359–60; *Theorie,* 179; "A Reply to My Critics," 268, 279–80; and *Legitimation Crisis,* 20–21. See also McCarthy, Translator's Introduction, xxviii–xxix; and Thompson, "Rationality," 285, 287. It should be noted that in *Theory of Communicative Action* Ha-bermas draws the contrast between system and lifeworld in two distinct senses. On the one hand, he contrasts them as two different methodological perspectives on the study of societies. The system perspective is objectivating and "externalist," whereas the lifeworld perspective is hermeneutical and "internalist." Although in principle either can be applied to the study of any given set of societal phenomena, Habermas argues that neither alone is adequate and, consequently, seeks to develop a methodology combining both. On the other hand, Habermas also contrasts system and lifeworld in another way, namely, as two different kinds of institutions. It is this second system/lifeworld contrast that I am concerned with here; I do not explicitly treat the first one in this essay. I am sympathetic to Habermas's general methodological intention of combining or linking structural (in the sense of ob-jectivating) and interpretive approaches to the study of societies. I do not, however, believe that this can be done by assigning structural properties to one set of institutions (the official economy and the state) and interpretive properties to another set (the family and the public sphere). I maintain, rather,

that all these institutions have both structural and interpretive dimensions and that all should be studied both structurally and hermeneutically. I have tried to develop an approach that meets these desiderata in "Women, Welfare, and the Politics of Need Interpretation" (Chapter 7 of this volume) and in "Struggle over Needs: Outline of a Socialist-Feminist Critical Theory of Late Captialist Political Culture" (Chapter 8 of this volume). I have discussed the general methodological problem in "On the Political and the Symbolic: Against the Metaphysics of Textuality," *Enclitic* 9, nos. 1–2 (Spring/Fall 1987): 100–114.

17. See, for example, the essays in *Rethinking the Family: Some Feminist Questions,* ed. Barrie Thorne and Marilyn Yalom (New York and London, 1982). See also, Michele Barrett and Mary McIntosh, *The Anti-Social Family* (London, 1982).

18. Habermas, *Theory,* 85–86, 88–90, 101, 104–5; and *Theorie,* 179. See also McCarthy, Translator's Introduction, ix, xxx. In presenting the distinction between normatively secured action and comunicatively achieved action, I am again modifying, or rather stabilizing, the variable usage of *Theory of Communicative Action* (see n. 8 above).

19. Pamela Fishman, "Interaction: The Work Women Do," *Social Problems* 25, no. 4 (1978) 397–406.

20. Nancy Henley, *Body Politics* (Englewood Cliffs, NJ, 1977).

21. Habermas, *Theorie,* 523–24, 547; and "A Reply to My Critics," 237. See also Thompson, "Rationality," 288, 292.

22. McCarthy pursues some of the normative implications of this for the differentiation of the administrative state system from the public sphere in "Complexity and Democracy" (see n. 10 above).

23. McCarthy makes this point with respect to the dedifferentiation of the state administrative system and the public sphere; see "Complexity and Democracy."

24. Habermas, *Theory,* 341–42, 359–60; *Theorie,* 256, 473; and "A Reply to My Critics," 280. See also McCarthy, Translator's Introduction, xxxii; and Thompson, "Rationality," 286–88.

25. I borrow the phrase "gender subtext" from Dorothy Smith, "The Gender Subtext of Power" (Ontario Institute for Studies in Education, Toronto, 1984).

26. The following account of the masculine gender subtext of the worker role draws heavily on Carole Pateman, "The Personal and the Political: Can Citizenship Be Democratic?" (Lecture 3 of her "Women and Democratic Citizenship" series), The Jefferson Memorial Lectures, University of California, Berkeley, February 1985.

27. Ibid., 5.

28. I am here adapting Althusser's notion of the interpellation of a subject to a context in which he, of course, never used it; for the general notion, see Louis Althusser, "Ideology and Ideological State Apparatuses (Notes toward an Investigation)," in *"Lenin and Philosophy" and Other Essays,* trans. Ben Brewster (New York, 1971).

29. Barbara Ehrenreich, *The Hearts of Men: American Dreams and the Flight from Commitment* (Garden City, N.Y., 1984).

30. The following discussion of the masculine gender subtext of the citizen role draws heavily on Carole Pateman, "The Personal and the Political."

31. Ibid., 8.

32. Judith Hicks Stiehm, "The Protected, the Protector, the Defender," in *Women and Men's Wars,* ed. Stiehm (New York, 1983). This is not to say, however, that I accept Stiehm's conclusions about the desirability of integrating women fully into the U.S. military as it is presently structured and deployed.

33. Pateman, "The Personal and the Political," 10.

34. Insofar as the preceding analysis of the gender subtext of Habermas's role theory deploys categories in which gender and political economy are internally integrated, it represents a contribution to the overcoming of "dual systems theory" (see n. 7 above). It is also a contribution to the

development of a more satisfactory way of linking structural (in the sense of objectivating) and interpretive approaches to the study of societies than that proposed by Habermas. In other words, I am suggesting here that the domestic sphere has a structural as well as an interpretive dimension and that the official economic and the state spheres have an interpretive as well as a structural dimension.

35. Habermas, *Theorie*, 505–9; and *Legitimation Crisis*, 33–36, 53–55. See also McCarthy, Translator's Introduction, xxxiii.

36. Habermas, *Theorie* 522–24, and *Legitimation Crisis*, 36–37. See also McCarthy, Translator's Introduction, xxxiii.

37. Habermas, *Theorie*, 530–40. See also McCarthy, Translator's Introduction, xxxiii–xxxiv.

38. Habermas, *Theorie*, 540–47. See also McCarthy, Translator's Introduction, xxxi.

39. Habermas, *Theorie*, 275–77, 452, 480, 522–24; "A Reply to My Critics," 226, 280–1; and Introduction to *Observations*, 11–12, 16–20. See also McCarthy, Translator's Introduction, xxxi–xxxii, and Thompson, "Rationality," 286, 288.

40. Habermas, *Theorie*, 581–83, and Introducton to *Observations*, 18–19, 27–8.

41. Habermas, *Theorie*, 581–83; and Introducton to *Observations*,16–17, 27–28.

42. For the U.S. social-welfare system, see the analysis of male versus female participation rates, and the account of the gendered character of the two subsystems in my "Women, Welfare and the Politics of Need Interpretation" (Chapter 7 of this volume). See also Barbara J. Nelson, "Women's Poverty and Women's Citizenship: Some Political Consequences of Economic Marginality," *Signs: Journal of Women in Culture and Society* 10, no. 2 (Winter 1984): Steven P. Erie, Martin Rein, and Barbara Wiget, "Women and the Reagan Revolution: Thermidor for the Social Welfare Economy," in *Families, Politics and Public Policies: A Feminist Dialogue on Women and the State*, ed. Irene Diamond, (New York, 1983); Diana Pearce, "Women, Work and Welfare: The Feminization of Poverty," in *Working Women and Families*, Karen Wolk Feinstein, ed., (Beverly Hills, Calif., 1979), and "Toil and Trouble: Women Workers and Unemployment Compensation," *Signs: Journal of Women in Culture and Society*, 10, no. 3 (Spring, 1985), 439–59; and Barbara Ehrenreich and Frances Fox Piven, "The Feminization of Poverty," *Dissent* (Spring 1984): 162–70. For an analysis of the gendered character of the British social-welfare system, see Hilary Land, "Who Cares for the Family?" *Journal of Social Policy* 7, no. 3 (July 1978): 257–84. For Norway, see the essays in *Patriarchy in a Welfare Society*, ed. Harriet Holter (Oslo, 1984). See also two comparative studies: Mary Ruggie, *The State and Working Women: A Comparative Study of Britain and Sweden* (Princeton, NJ, 1984); and Birte Siim, "Women and the Welfare State: Between Private and Public Dependence" (Stanford University, 1985).

43. Carol Brown, "Mothers, Fathers, and Children: From Private to Public Patriarchy," in *Women and Revolution* (see n. 7 above). Actually, I believe Brown's formulation is theoretically inadequate, since it presupposes a simple, dualistic conception of public and private. Nonetheless, the phrase "from private to public patriarchy" evokes in a rough but suggestive way the phenomena for which a socialist-feminist critical theory of the welfare state would need to account.

44. The most recent available data for the U.S. indicate that sex segmentation in paid work is increasing, not decreasing. And this is so despite the entry of small but significant numbers of women into professions like law and medicine. Even when the gains won by those women are taken into account, there is no overall improvement in the aggregated comparative economic position of paid women workers vis-à-vis male workers. Women's wages remain less than 60 percent of men's wages—which means, of course, that the mass of women are losing ground. Nor is there any overall improvement in occupational distribution by sex. The ghettoization of women in low-paying, low-status "pink collar" occupations is increasing. For example, in the U.S. in 1973, women held 96 percent of all paid childcare jobs, 81 percent of all primary school teaching jobs, 72 percent of all health technician jobs, 98 percent of all registered nurse jobs, 83 percent of all librarian jobs, 99 percent of all secretarial jobs and 92 percent of all waitperson jobs. The figures for 1983 were, respectively, 97 percent, 83 percent, 84 percent, 96 percent, 87 percent, 99 percent and 88 percent,

(Bureau of Labor Statistics figures cited by Drew Christie, "Comparable Worth and Distributive Justice" [Paper read at meetings of the American Philosophical Association, Western Division, April 1985]). The U.S. data are consistent with data for the Scandinavian countries and Britain; see Siim, "Women and the Welfare State."

45. See n. 42, above.

46. This account draws on some elements of Zillah R. Eisenstein's analysis in *The Radical Future of Liberal Feminism* (Boston, 1981), chap. 9. What follows has some affinities with the perspective of Ernesto Laclau and Chantal Mouffe in *Hegemony and Socialist Strategy* (New York, 1985).

47. I develop this notion of the "socio–cultural means of interpretation and communication" and the associated conception of autonomy in "Toward a Discourse Ethic of Solidarity," *Praxis International* 5, no. 4 (January 1986): 425–29, and in Chapter 8 of this volume. Both notions are extensions and modifications of Habermas's conception of "communicative ethics."

48. My own recent work attempts to construct a conceptual framework for a socialist-feminist critical theory of the welfare state that meets these requirements. See "Women, Welfare and the Politics of Need Interpretation" (Chapter 7 of this volume),"Toward a Discourse Ethic of Solidarity" (see n. 47 above), and "Struggle Over Needs" (Chapter 8 of this volume). Each of these essays draws heavily on those aspects of Habermas's thought that I take to be unambiguously positive and useful, especially his conception of the irreducibly sociocultural, interpretive character of human needs and his contrast between dialogical and monological processes of need interpretation. The present paper, on the other hand, focuses mainly on those aspects of Habermas's thought that I find problematical or unhelpful and so does not convey the full range either of his work or of my views about it. Readers are warned, therefore, against drawing the conclusion that Habermas has little or nothing positive to contribute to a socialist-feminist critical theory of the welfare state. They are urged, rather, to consult the essays cited above for the other side of the story.

Chapter 7
Women, Welfare, and the Politics of Need Interpretation

What some writers are calling "the coming welfare wars" will be largely wars about, even against, women. Because women constitute the overwhelming majority of social-welfare program recipients and employees, women and women's needs will be the principal stakes in the battles over social spending likely to dominate national politics in the coming period. Moreover, the welfare wars will not be limited to the tenure of Reagan or even of Reaganism. On the contrary, they will be protracted, both in time and in space. What James O'Connor theorized over fifteen years ago as "the fiscal crisis of the state" is a long-term, structural phenomenon of international proportions.[1] Not just the United States but every late capitalist welfare state in Western Europe and North America is facing some version of it. And the fiscal crisis of the welfare state coincides everywhere with a second long-term, structural tendency: the feminization of poverty. This is Diana Pearce's term for the rapidly increasing proportion of women in the adult poverty population, an increase tied to, among other things, the rise in "female-headed households."[2] In the U.S. this increase is so pronounced and so steep that

I am grateful for the helpful comments, suggestions, and criticisms of Sandra Bartky, John Brenkman, Jane Collier, Ann Garry, Virginia Held, Thomas McCarthy, Carole Pateman, Birte Siim, Howard Winant, Terry Winant, Iris Young, and the members of the Midwest Society for Women in Philosophy. I also thank Drucilla Cornell and Betty Safford for the invitations that provided occasions for developing the essay, The Stanford Humanities Center for a congenial working environment and financial support, and Dee Marquez and Marina Rosiene for crackerjack word processing.

analysts project that should it continue, the poverty population will consist entirely of women and their children before the year 2000.[3]

This conjunction of the fiscal crisis of the state and the feminization of poverty suggests that struggles around social welfare will and should become increasingly focal for feminists. But such struggles raise a great many problems, some of which can be thought of as structural. To take one example, increasing numbers of women depend directly for their livelihoods on social-welfare programs; and many other women benefit indirectly, since the existence of even a minimal and inadequate "safety net" increases the leverage of women who are economically dependent on individual men. Thus, feminists have no choice but to oppose social-welfare cuts. However, economists like Pearce, Nancy Barrett, and Steven Erie, Martin Rein, and Barbara Wiget have shown that programs like Aid to Families with Dependent Children actually institutionalize the feminization of poverty.[4] The benefits they provide are system-conforming ones that reinforce rather than challenge basic structural inequalities. Thus, feminists cannot simply support existing social-welfare programs. To use the suggestive but ultimately too simple terms popularized by Carol Brown: If to eliminate or to reduce welfare is to bolster "private patriarchy," then simply to defend it is to consolidate "public patriarchy."[5]

Feminists also face a second set of problems in the coming welfare wars. These problems, seemingly more ideological and less structural than the first set, arise from the typical way in which issues get framed, given the institutional dynamics of the political system.[6] Typically, social-welfare issues are posed like this: Shall the state undertake to satisfy the social needs of a given constituency, and if so, to what degree? Now, this way of framing issues permits only a relatively small number of answers, and it tends to cast debates in quantitative terms. More importantly, it takes for granted the definition of the needs in question, as if that were self-evident and beyond dispute. It therefore occludes the fact that the interpretation of people's needs is itself a political stake, indeed sometimes *the* political stake. Clearly, this way of framing issues poses obstacles for feminist politics, since at the heart of such politics lie questions about what various groups of women really need and whose interpretations of women's needs should be authoritative. Only in terms of a discourse oriented to the *politics of need interpretation*[7] can feminists meaningfully intervene in the coming welfare wars. But this requires a challenge to the dominant policy framework.

Both sets of problems, the structural and the ideological, are extremely important and difficult. In what follows, I shall not offer solutions to either of them. Rather, I want to attempt the much more modest and preliminary task of exploring how they might be thought about in relation to one another. Specifically, I want to propose a framework for inquiry that can shed light on both of them simultaneously.

Consider that in order to address the structural problem it will be necessary to clarify the phenomenon of "public patriarchy." One type of inquiry that is useful here is the familiar sort of economic analysis alluded to earlier, analysis that shows, for example, that "workfare" programs function to subsidize employers of low-wage "women's work" in the service sector and thus to reproduce the sex-segmented, dual labor market. Now, important as such inquiry is, it does not tell the whole story, since it leaves out of focus the discursive or ideological dimension of social-welfare programs. By the discursive or ideological dimension, I do not mean anything distinct from, or epiphenomenal to, welfare practices; I mean, rather, the tacit norms and implicit assumptions that are constitutive of those practices. To get at this dimension requires a meaning-oriented sort of inquiry, one that considers welfare programs as, among other things, institutionalized patterns of interpretation.[8] Such inquiry would make explicit the social meanings embedded within welfare programs, meanings that tend otherwise simply to go without saying.

In spelling out such meanings, the inquiry I am proposing could do two things simultaneously. First, it could tell us something important about the structure of the U.S. welfare system, since it might identify some underlying norms and assumptions that lend a measure of coherence to diverse programs and practices. Second, it could illuminate what I called "the politics of need interpretation," since it could expose the processes by which welfare practices construct women and women's needs according to certain specific — and, in principle, contestable — interpretations, even as they lend those interpretations an aura of facticity that discourages contestation. Thus, this inquiry could shed light on both the structural and ideological problems identified earlier.

The principal aim of this paper is to provide an account of this sort for the present U.S. social-welfare system. The account is intended to help clarify some key structural aspects of male dominance in late capitalist welfare state societies. At the same time, it is meant to point the way to a broader, discourse-oriented focus that can address political conflicts over the interpretation of women's needs.

The paper proceeds from some relatively "hard," uncontroversial facts about the U.S. social-welfare system (section 1) through a series of increasingly interpreted accounts of that system (sections 2 and 3). These culminate (in section 4) in a highly theorized characterization of the welfare system as a "juridical-administrative-therapeutic state apparatus." Finally, (in section 5) the paper situates that apparatus as one force among others in a larger and highly contested political field of discourse about needs that also includes the feminist movement.

1

Long before the emergence of welfare states, governments have defined legally secured arenas of societal action. In so doing, they have at the same time codified corresponding patterns of agency or social roles. Thus, early modern states defined an economic arena and the corresponding role of an economic person capable of entering into contracts. More or less at the same time, they codified the "private sphere" of the household and the role of head of the household. Somewhat later, governments were led to secure a sphere of political participation and the corresponding role of citizen with (limited) political rights. In each of these cases, the original and paradigmatic subject of the newly codified social role was male. Only secondarily, and much later, was it conceded that women, too, could occupy these subject-positions, without, however, entirely dispelling the association with masculinity.

Matters are different, however, with the contemporary welfare state. When this type of government defined a new arena of activity—call it "the social"—and a new societal role—the welfare client—it included women among its original and paradigmatic subjects. Today, in fact, women have become the principal subjects of the welfare state. On the one hand, they make up the overwhelming majority both of program recipients and of paid social-service workers. On the other hand, they are the wives, mothers, and daughters whose unpaid activities and obligations are redefined as the welfare state increasingly oversees forms of caregiving. Since this beneficiary/social worker/caregiver nexus of roles is constitutive of the social-welfare arena, one might even call this arena a feminized terrain.

A brief statistical overview confirms women's greater involvement with and dependence on the U.S. social-welfare system. Consider, first, women's greater dependence as program clients and beneficiaries. In each of the major "means-tested" programs in the U.S., women and the children for whom they are responsible now comprise the overwhelming majority of clients. For example, more than 81 percent of households receiving Aid to Families with Dependent Children (AFDC) are headed by women, more than 60 percent of families receiving food stamps or Medicaid are headed by women, and 70 percent of all households in publicly owned or subsidized housing are headed by women.[9] High as they are, these figures actually underestimate the representation of women. As Barbara Nelson notes, in the androcentric reporting system, households counted as female-headed contain by definition no healthy adult men.[10] But healthy adult women live in most households counted as male-headed. Such women may directly or indirectly receive benefits going to "male-headed" households, but they are invisible in the statistics, even though they usually do the work of securing and maintaining program eligibility.

Women also predominate in the major U.S. "age-tested" programs. For example, 61.6 percent of all adult beneficiaries of Social Security are women, and 64 percent of those covered by Medicare are women.[11] In sum, because women as a group are significantly poorer than men—indeed, women now compose nearly two-thirds of all U.S. adults below the official poverty line—and because women tend to live longer than men, women depend more on the social-welfare system as clients and beneficiaries.

But this is not the whole story. Women also depend more on the social-welfare system as paid human-service workers—a category of employment that includes education and health as well as social work and services administration. In 1980, 70 percent of the 17.3 million paid jobs in this sector in the U.S. were held by women. This accounts for one-third of U.S. women's total paid employment and a full 80 percent of all professional jobs held by women. The figures for women of color are even higher than this average, since 37 percent of their total paid employment and 82.4 percent of their professional employment is in this sector.[12] It is a distinctive feature of the U.S. social-welfare system—as opposed to, say, the British and Scandinavian systems—that only 3 percent of these jobs are in the form of direct federal government employment. The rest are in state and local government, in the "private non-profit" sector, and in the "private" sector. However, the more decentralized and privatized character of the U.S. system does not make paid welfare workers any less vulnerable in the face of federal program cuts. On the contrary, the level of federal social-welfare spending affects the level of human-service employment in *all* sectors. State and local government jobs depend on federal and federally financed state and local government contracts, and private profit and nonprofit jobs depend on federally financed transfer payments to individuals and households for the purchase in the market of services like health care.[13] Thus, reductions in social spending mean the loss of jobs for women. Moreover, as Barbara Ehrenreich and Frances Fox Piven note, this loss is not compensated when spending is shifted to the military, since only one-half of 1 percent of the entire female paid workforce is employed in work on military contracts. In fact, one study they cite estimates that with each one-billion-dollar increase in military spending, ninety-five hundred jobs are lost to women.[14]

Finally, women are subjects of and subject to the social-welfare system in their traditional capacity as unpaid caregivers. It is well known that the sexual division of labor assigns women primary responsibility for the care of those who cannot care for themselves. (I leave aside women's traditional obligations to provide personal services to adult males—husbands, fathers, grown sons, lovers—who can very well care for themselves.) Such responsibility includes child care, of course, but also care for sick and/or elderly relatives, often parents. For example, a British study conducted in 1975 and cited by Hilary Land found that three times as many elderly people live with married daughters as with married sons and that those without a close female relative were more likely to be institutionalized, irrespective of degree of infirmity.[15] Thus, as unpaid caregivers, women are more directly affected than men by the level and character of government social services for children, the sick, and the elderly.

As clients, paid human-service workers and unpaid caregivers, then, women are the principal subjects of the social-welfare system. It is as if this branch of the state were in effect a Bureau of Women's Affairs.

2

Of course, the welfare system does not deal with women on women's terms. On the contrary, it has its own characteristic ways of interpreting women's needs and positioning women as subjects. In order to understand these, we need to examine how gender norms and meanings are encoded in the structure of the U.S. social-welfare system.

This issue is quite complicated. On the one hand, nearly all U.S. social-welfare programs are officially gender-neutral. Nevertheless, the system as a whole is a dual or two-tiered one, and it has an unmistakable gender subtext.[16] One set of programs is oriented to *individuals* and tied to participation in the paid work force—for example, unemployment insurance and Social Security. This set of programs is designed to supplement and compensate for the primary market in paid labor power. A second set of programs is oriented to *households* and tied to combined household income—for example, AFDC, food stamps, and Medicaid. This set of programs is designed to compensate for what are considered to be family failures, in particular the absence of a male breadwinner.

What integrates the two sets of programs is a common core of assumptions concerning the sexual division of labor, domestic and nondomestic. It is assumed that families do or should contain one primary breadwinner who is male and one unpaid domestic worker (homemaker and mother) who is female. It is further assumed that when a woman undertakes paid work outside the home, this is or should be in order to supplement the male breadwinner's wage and neither does nor should override her primary housewifely and maternal responsibilities. It is assumed, in other words, that society is divided into two separate spheres of home and outside work and that these are women's and men's spheres, respectively.[17]

These assumptions are increasingly counterfactual. At present, fewer than 15 percent of U.S. families conform to the normative ideal of a domicile shared by a husband who is the sole breadwinner, a wife who is a full-time homemaker, and their offspring. Nonetheless, the "separate spheres" norms determine the structure of the social-welfare system. They determine that it contain one subsystem related to the primary labor market and another subsystem related to the family or household. Moreover, they determine that these subsystems be gender-linked, that the primary-labor-market-related system be implicitly "masculine" and the family-related system be implicitly "feminine." Consequently, the normative, ideal-typical recipient of primary-labor-market-oriented programs is a (white) male, whereas the normative, ideal-typical adult client of household-based programs is a female.

This gender subtext of the U.S. welfare system is confirmed when we take a second look at participation figures. Consider again the figures just cited for the "feminine" or family-based programs, which I referred to earlier as "means-tested" programs: more than 81 percent of households receiving AFDC are female-headed, as are more than 70 percent of those receiving housing assistance and more than 60 percent of those receiving Medicaid and food stamps. Now recall that these figures do not compare female *individuals* with male *individuals* but, rather, female-headed *households* with male-headed *households*. They therefore confirm four things: (1) these programs have a distinctive administrative identity in that their recipients are not individualized but *familialized;* (2) they serve what are considered to be defective families, overwhelmingly families without a male breadwinner; (3) the ideal-typical (adult) client is female; and (4) she makes her claim for benefits on the basis of her status as an unpaid domestic worker, a homemaker, and mother, not as a paid worker based in the labor market.

Now, contrast this with the case of a typical labor-market-based and thus "masculine" program, namely, unemployment insurance. Here the percentage of female claimants drops to 38 percent, a figure that contrasts female and male *individuals,* as opposed to female-headed and male-headed households. As Diana Pearce notes, this drop reflects at least two different circumstances.[18] First, and most straightforwardly, it reflects women's lower rate of participation in the paid work force. Second, it reflects the fact that many women wageworkers are not eligible to participate in this program, for example, paid household service workers, part-time workers, pregnant workers, and workers in the "irregular economy" such as prostitutes, baby-sitters, and home typists. The exclusion of these female wageworkers testifies to the existence of a gender-segmented labor market, divided into "primary" and "secondary" employment. It reflects the more general assumption that women's earnings are "merely supplementary," not on a par with those of the primary (male) breadwinner. Altogether, then, the figures tell us four things about programs like unemployment insurance: (1) they are administered in a way that *individualizes* rather than familializes recipients; (2) they are designed to compensate primary-labor-market effects, such as the temporary displacement of a primary breadwinner; (3) the ideal-typical recipient is male; and (4) he makes his claim on the basis of his identity as a paid worker, not as an unpaid domestic worker or parent.

One final example will round out the picture. The Social Security system of retirement insurance presents the interesting case of a hermaphrodite or androgyne. I shall soon show that this system has a number of characteristics of "masculine" programs in virtue of its link to participation in the paid work force. However, it is also internally dualized and gendered, and thus stands as a microcosm of the entire dual benefit welfare system. Consider that whereas a majority — 61.6 percent — of adult beneficiaries are female, only somewhat more than half of these — or 33.3 percent of all recipients — claim benefits on the basis of their own paid work records.[19] The remaining female recipients claim benefits on the basis of their husbands' records, that is, as wives or unpaid domestic workers. By contrast, virtually no male recipients claim benefits as husbands. On the contrary, they claim benefits as paid workers, a labor-market-located as opposed to family-located identity. So the Social Security system is hermaphroditic or androgynous; it is internally divided between family-based, "feminine" benefits, on the one hand, and labor-market-based, "masculine" benefits, on the other hand. Thus, it too gets its structure from gender norms and assumptions.

3

So far, I have established the dualistic structure of the U.S. social-welfare system and the gender subtext of that dualism. Now I can better tease out the system's implicit norms and tacit assumptions by examining its mode of operation. To see how welfare programs interpret women's needs, we must consider what benefits consist in. To see how programs position women as subjects, we need to examine administrative practices. In general, we shall see that the "masculine" and "feminine" subsystems are not only separate but also unequal.

Consider that the "masculine" social-welfare programs are social insurance schemes. They include unemployment insurance, Social Security (retirement insurance), Medicare (age-tested health insurance), and Supplemental Social Security Insurance (disability insurance for those with paid work records). These programs are contributory (wageworkers and their employers pay into trust funds), they are administered on a national basis, and benefit levels are uniform across the country. Though bureaucratically organized and administered, they require less, and less demeaning, effort on the part of beneficiaries in qualifying and maintaining eligibility than do "feminine" programs. They are far less subject to intrusive controls and in most cases lack the dimension of surveillance. They also tend to require less of beneficiaries in the way of actual efforts to collect their benefits, with the notable exception of unemployment insurance.

In sum, "masculine" social insurance schemes position recipients primarily as *rights-bearers*. The beneficiaries of these programs are in the main not stigmatized. Neither administrative practice nor popular discourse constitutes them as "on the dole." They are constituted rather as receiving what they deserve; what they, in "partnership" with their employers, have already "paid in" for; what they, therefore, have a *right* to. Moreover, these beneficiaries are also positioned as *purchasing consumers*. They often receive cash as opposed to "in kind" benefits and so are positioned as having "the liberty to strike the best bargain they can in purchasing services of their choice on the open market." In sum, these beneficiaries are what C. B. MacPherson calls "possessive individuals."[20] Proprietors of their own persons who have freely contracted to sell their labor power, they become participants in social insurance schemes and, thence, paying consumers of human services. They therefore qualify as *social citizens* in virtually the fullest sense that term can acquire within the framework of a male-dominated, capitalist society.

All this stands in stark contrast to the "feminine" sector of the U.S. social-welfare system. This sector consists in relief programs, such as AFDC, food stamps, Medicaid, and public-housing assistance. These programs are not contributory but are financed out of general tax revenues (usually with one-third of the funds coming from the federal government and two-thirds coming from the states); and they are not administered federally but rather by the states. As a result, benefit levels vary dramatically, though they are everywhere inadequate, deliberately pegged below the official poverty line. The relief programs are notorious for the varieties of administrative humiliation they inflict upon clients. They require considerable work in qualifying and maintaining eligibility, and they have a heavy component of surveillance.

These programs do not in any meaningful sense position their subjects as rights-bearers. Far from being considered as having a right to what they receive, recipients are defined as "beneficiaries of governmental largess" or "clients of public charity."[21] Moreover, their actual treatment fails to live up to even that definition, since they are treated as "chiselers," "deviants," and "human failures." In the androcentric administrative framework, "welfare mothers" are considered not to work and so are sometimes required—that is to say, coerced— to "work off" their benefits via "workfare." They thus become inmates of what Diana Pearce calls a "workhouse without walls."[22] Indeed, the only sense in which the category of rights is relevant to these clients' situation is the somewhat dubious one according to which they are entitled to treatment governed by the standards of formal bureaucratic procedural rationality. But if that right is construed as protection from administrative caprice, then even it is widely and routinely disregarded.

Moreover, recipients of public relief are generally not positioned as purchasing consumers. A significant portion of their benefits is "in kind," and what cash they receive comes already carved up and earmarked for specific, administratively designated purposes. These recipients are therefore essentially *clients,* a subject-position that carries far less power and dignity in capitalist societies than does the alternative position of purchaser. In these societies, to be a client (in the sense relevant to relief recipients) is to be an abject dependent. Indeed, this sense of the term carries connotations of a fall from autonomy, as when we speak, for example, of "the client states of empires or superpowers." As clients, then, recipients of relief are *the negatives of possessive individuals*. Largely excluded from the market both as workers and as consumers, claiming benefits not as individuals but as members of "failed" families, these recipients are effectively denied the trappings of social citizenship as it is defined within male-dominated, capitalist societies.[23]

Clearly, this system creates a double bind for women raising children without a male breadwinner. By failing to offer these women day care for their children, job training, a job that pays a "family wage;" or some combination of these, it constructs them exclusively as mothers. As a consequence, it interprets their needs as maternal needs and their sphere of activity as that of "the family." Now, according to the ideology of separate spheres, this should be an honored social identity. Yet the system does not honor these women. On the contrary, instead of providing them a guaranteed income equivalent to a family wage as a matter of right, it stigmatizes, humiliates, and harasses them. In effect, it decrees simultaneously that these women must be and yet cannot be normative mothers.

Moreover, the way in which the U.S. social-welfare system interprets "maternity" and "the family" is both race-specific and culture-specific. The bias is made plain in Carol Stack's study, *All Our Kin*.[24] Stack analyzes domestic arrangements of very poor black welfare recipients in a midwestern city. Where conservative ideologues see the "disorganization of *the* black family," she finds complex, highly organized kinship structures. These include kin-based networks of resource pooling and exchange, which enable those in direst poverty to survive economically and communally. The networks organize delayed exchanges or "gifts," in Mauss's sense,[25] of prepared meals, food stamps, cooking, shopping, groceries, furniture, sleeping space, cash (including wages and AFDC allowances), transportation, clothing, child care, even children. They span several physically distinct households and so transcend the principal administrative category that organizes relief programs. It is significant that Stack took great pains to conceal the identities of her subjects, even going so far as to disguise the identity of their city. The reason, though unstated, is obvious: these people would lose their benefits if program administrators learned that they did not utilize them within the confines and boundaries of a "household."

We can summarize the separate and unequal character of the two-tiered, gender-linked, race- and culture-biased U.S. social-welfare system in the following formulas: Participants in the "masculine" subsystem are positioned as *rights-bearing beneficiaries* and *purchasing consumers of services*, thus as *possessive individuals*. Participants in the "feminine" subsystem, on the other hand, are positioned as *dependent clients,* or *the negatives of possessive individuals.*

4

Clearly, the identities and needs that the social-welfare system fashions for its recipients are *interpreted* identities and needs. Moreover, they are highly political interpretations and, as such, are in principle subject to dispute. Yet these needs and identities are not always recognized as interpretations. Too often, they simply go without saying and are rendered immune from analysis and critique. Doubtless one reason for this "reification effect" is the depth at which gender meanings and norms are embedded in our general culture. But there may also be another reason more specific to the welfare system.

Let me suggest yet another way of analyzing the U.S. social-welfare system, this time as a "juridical-administrative-therapeutic state apparatus" (JAT).[26] The point is to emphasize a distinctive style of operation. Qua JAT, the welfare system works by linking together a series of juridical, administrative, and therapeutic procedures. As a consequence, it tends to translate political issues concerning the interpretation of people's needs into legal, administrative, and/or therapeutic matters. Thus, the system executes political policy in a way that appears nonpolitical and tends to be depoliticizing.

Considered abstractly, the subject-positions constructed for beneficiaries of *both* the "masculine" and the "feminine" components of the system can be analyzed as combinations of three distinct elements. The first element is a *juridical* one, which positions recipients vis-à-vis the legal system by according or denying them various *rights*. Thus, the subject of the "masculine" subsystem has a right to benefits and is protected from some legally sanctioned forms of administrative caprice, whereas the subject of the "feminine" subsystem largely lacks rights.

This juridical element is then linked with a second one, an *administrative* element. In order to qualify to receive benefits, subjects must assume the stance of petitioners with respect to an administrative body; they must petition a bureaucratic institution empowered to decide their claims on the basis of administratively defined criteria. In the "masculine" subsystem, for example, claimants must prove their "cases" meet administratively defined criteria of entitlement; in the "feminine" subsystem, on the other hand, claimants must prove conformity to administratively defined criteria of need. The enormous qualitative differences between the two sets of procedures notwithstanding, both are variations on the same administrative moment. Both require claimants to translate their experienced situations and life problems into administrable needs, to present their predicaments as bona fide instances of specified generalized states of affairs that could in principle befall anyone.[27]

If and when they qualify, social-welfare claimants get positioned either as purchasing consumers or dependent clients. In either case, their needs are redefined as correlates of bureaucratically administered satisfactions. This means they are quantified, rendered as equivalents of a sum of money.[28] Thus, in the "feminine" subsystem, clients are positioned passively to receive monetarily measured, predefined, and prepackaged services; in the "masculine" subsystem, on the other hand, beneficiaries receive a specified, predetermined amount of cash.

In both subsystems, then, people's needs are subject to a sort of rewriting operation. Experienced situations and life problems are translated into administrable needs; and since the latter are not necessarily isomorphic to the former, the possibility of a gap between them arises. This possibility is especially likely in the "feminine" subsystem, for there, as we saw, clients are constructed as deviant, and service provision has the character of normalization—albeit normalization designed more to stigmatize than to "reform."

Here, then, is the opening for the third, *therapeutic*, moment of the JAT's modus operandi. Especially in the "feminine" subsystem, service provision often includes an implicit or explicit therapeutic or quasi-therapeutic dimension. In AFDC, for example, social workers concern themselves with the "mental health" aspects of their clients' lives, often construing these in terms of "character problems." More explicitly and less moralistically, municipal programs for poor unmarried pregnant teenage women include not only prenatal care, mothering instruction, and tutoring or schooling but also counseling sessions with psychiatric social workers. As observed by Prudence Rains, such sessions are intended to bring girls to acknowledge what are considered to be their true, deep, latent, emotional problems, on the assumption that this will enable them to avoid future pregnancies.[29] Ludicrous as this sounds, it is only an extreme example of a more pervasive phenomenon, namely, the tendency of especially "feminine" social-welfare programs to construct gender-political and political-economic problems as individual, psychological problems. In fact, some therapeutic or quasi-therapeutic welfare services can be regarded as second-order services to compensate for the debilitating effects of first-order services. In any case, the therapeutic dimension of the U.S. social-welfare system encourages clients to close gaps between their culturally shaped lived experience and their administratively defined situation by bringing the former into line with the latter.

Clearly, this analysis of the U.S. welfare system as a "juridical-administrative-therapeutic state apparatus" lets us see both "feminine" and "masculine" subsystems more critically. It suggests that the problem is not only that women are disempowered by the *denial* of social citizenship in the "feminine" subsystem—although they are—but also that women and men are disempowered by the *realization* of an androcentric, possessive individualist form of social citizenship in the "masculine" subsystem. In both subsystems, even the "masculine" one, the JAT positions its subjects in ways that do not empower them. It personalizes them as "cases" and so militates against their collective identification. It imposes monological, administrative definitions of situation and need and so preempts dialogically achieved self-definition and self-determination. It positions its subjects as passive client or consumer recipients and not as active co-participants involved in shaping their life conditions. Lastly, it construes experienced discontent with these arrangements as material for adjustment-oriented, usually sexist therapy and not as material for empowering processes of consciousness-raising.

All told, then, the form of social citizenship constructed even in the *best* part of the U.S. social-welfare system is a degraded and depoliticized one. It is a form of passive citizenship in which the state preempts the power to define and satisfy people's needs. This form of passive citizenship arises in part as a result of the JAT's distinctive style of operation. The JAT treats the interpretation of people's needs as pregiven and unproblematic, while itself redefining them as amenable to system-conforming satisfactions. Thus, the JAT shifts attention away from the question, Who interprets social needs and how? It tends to substitute the *juridical, administrative, and therapeutic management of need satisfaction* for the *politics of need interpretation*. That is, it tends to substitute *monological, administrative processes of need definition* for *dialogical, participatory processes of need interpretation.*[30]

5

Usually, analyses of social complexes as "institutionalized patterns of interpretation" are implicitly or explicitly functionalist. They purport to show how culturally hegemonic systems of meaning are stabilized and reproduced over time. As a result, such analyses often screen out "dysfunctional" events like micro- and macro-political resistances and conflicts. More generally, they tend to obscure the active side of social processes, the ways in which even the most routinized practice of social agents involves the active construction, deconstruction, and reconstruction of social meanings. It is no wonder, then, that many feminist scholars have become suspicious of functionalist methodologies, for when applied to gender issues, these methods occult female agency and construe women as mere passive victims of male dominance.

In order to avoid any such suggestion here, I want to conclude by situating the foregoing analysis in a broader, nonfunctionalist perspective. I want to sketch a picture according to which the social-welfare apparatus is one force among others in a larger and highly contested political arena.

Consider that the ideological (as opposed to economic) effects of the JAT's mode of need interpretation operate within a specific and relatively new societal arena. I call this arena "the social" in order to mark its noncoincidence with the familiar institutionalized spaces of family and official economy. As I conceive it, the social is not exactly equivalent to the traditional public sphere of political discourse defined by Jürgen Habermas,[31] nor is it coextensive with the state. Rather, the social is a site of discourse about people's needs, specifically about those needs that have broken out of the domestic and/or official economic spheres that earlier contained them as "private matters." Thus, the social is a site of discourse about problematic needs, needs that have come to exceed the apparently (but not really) self-regulating domestic and official economic institutions of male-dominated, capitalist societies.[32]

As the site of this excess, the social is by definition a terrain of contestation. It is a space in which conflicts among rival interpretations of people's needs are played out. "In" the social, then, one would expect to find a plurality of competing ways of talking about needs. And, in fact, what we do find here are at least three major kinds: (1) "expert" needs discourses of, for example, social workers and therapists, on the one hand, and welfare administrators, planners, and policy makers, on the other, (2) oppositional movement needs discourses of, for example, feminists, lesbians and gays, people of color, workers, and welfare clients, and (3) "reprivatization" discourses of constituencies seeking to repatriate newly problematized needs to their former domestic or official economic enclaves. Such discourses, and others, compete with one another in addressing the fractured social identities of potential adherents.[33]

Seen from this vantage point, the social has a twofold character. It is simultaneously a new arena of state activity and, equally important, a new terrain of wider political contestation. It is both the home turf of the JAT and a field of struggle on which the JAT acts as simply one contestant among others. It would be a mistake, then, to treat the JAT as the undisputed master of the terrain of the social. In fact, much of the growth and activity of the social branch of the state has come in response to the activities of social movements, especially the labor, black, feminist, and Progressive movements. Moreover, as Theda Skocpol has shown, the social state is not simply a unified, self-possessed political agent.[34] It is, rather, in significant respects a resultant, a complex and polyvalent nexus of compromise formations in which are sedimented the outcomes of past struggles as well as the conditions for present and future ones. In fact, even when the JAT does act as an agent, the results are often unintended. When it takes responsibility for matters previously left to the family and/or the official economy, it tends to denaturalize those matters and thus risks fostering their further politicization.

In any case, social movements, too, act on the terrain of the social (as do, on a smaller scale, clients who engage the JAT in micropolitical resistances and negotiations). In fact, the JAT's monological, administrative approach to need definition can also be seen as a strategy to contain social movements. Such movements tend by their very nature to be dialogic and participatory. They represent the emergent capacities of newly politicized groups to cast off the apparently natural and prepolitical interpretations that enveloped their needs in the official economy and/or family. In social movements, people come to articulate alternative, politicized interpretations of their needs as they engage in processes of dialogue and collective struggle. Thus, the confrontation of such movements with the JAT on the terrain of the social is a confrontation between conflicting logics of need definition.

Feminists too, then, are actors on the terrain of the social. Indeed, from this perspective, we can distinguish several analytically distinct but practically intermingled kinds of feminist struggles worth engaging in the coming welfare wars.

First, there are struggles to secure the political status of women's needs, that is, to legitimate women's needs as genuine political issues as opposed to "private" domestic or market matters. Here, feminists would engage especially antiwelfarist defenders of privatization. Second, there are struggles over the interpreted content of women's needs, struggles to challenge the apparently natural, traditional interpretations still enveloping needs only recently sprung from domestic and official economic enclaves of privacy. Here, feminists would engage all those forces in the culture that perpetuate androcentric and sexist interpretations of women's needs, including, but not only, the social state. Third, there are struggles over the who and how of need interpretation, struggles to empower women to interpret their own needs and to challenge the antiparticipatory, monological practices of the welfare system qua JAT. Fourth, there are struggles to elaborate and win support for policies based on feminist interpretations of women's needs, policies that avoid both the Scylla of private patriarchy and the Charybdis of public patriarchy.

In all these cases, the focus would be as much on need interpretation as on need satisfaction. This is as it should be, since any satisfactions we are able to win will be problematic to the degree we fail to fight and win the battle of interpretation.

Notes

1. James O'Connor, *The Fiscal Crisis of the State* (New York, 1973).

2. Diana Pearce, "Women, Work, and Welfare: The Feminization of Poverty," in *Working Women and Families,* ed. Karen Wolk Feinstein (Beverly Hills, Calif., 1979).

3. Barbara Ehrenreich and Frances Fox Piven, "The Feminization of Poverty," *Dissent* 31, no. 2 (Spring 1984): 162–70.

4. Pearce, "Women, Work, and Welfare"; Nancy S. Barrett, "The Welfare Trap" (American Economic Association, Dallas, Texas, 1984); and Steven P. Erie, Martin Rein, and Barbara Wiget, "Women and the Reagan Revolution: Thermidor for the Social Welfare Economy," in *Families, Politics, and Public Policies: A Feminist Dialogue on Women and the State,* ed. Irene Diamond (New York, 1983).

5. Carol Brown, "Mothers, Fathers, and Children: From Private to Public Patriarchy," in *Women and Revolution: A Discussion of the Unhappy Marriage of Marxism and Feminism,* ed. Lydia Sargent (Boston, 1981). I believe that Brown's terms are too simple on two counts. First, for reasons elaborated by Gayle Rubin ("The Traffic in Women: Notes on the 'Political Economy' of Sex," in *Towards an Anthropology of Women,* ed. Rayna R. Reiter [New York, 1975]), I prefer not to use 'patriarchy' as a generic term for male dominance but rather as the designation of a specific historical social formation. Second, Brown's public/private contrast oversimplifies the structure of both laissez-faire and welfare state capitalism, since it posits two major societal zones where there are actually four (family, official economy, state, and sphere of public political discourse) and conflates two distinct public/private divisions. (For a discussion of this second problem, see "What's Critical about Critical Theory? The Case of Habermas and Gender," Chapter 6 of this volume.) These problems notwithstanding, it remains the case that Brown's terms are immensely suggestive and that we currently have no better terminology. Thus, in what follows I occasionally use 'public patriarchy' for want of an alternative.

6. For an analysis of the dynamics whereby late capitalist political systems tend to select certain types of interests while excluding others, see Claus Offe, "Political Authority and Class Structure: An Analysis of Late Capitalist Societies," *International Journal of Sociology* 2, no. 1 (Spring 1982): 73–108; Structural Problems of the Capitalist State: Class Rule and the Political System—On the Selectiveness of Political Institutions," in *German Political Studies,* ed. Klaus von Beyme (London, 1974); and "The Separation of Form and Content in Liberal Democratic Politics," *Studies in Political Economy* 3 (Spring 1980): 5–16. For a feminist application of Offe's approach, see Drude Dahlerup, "Overcoming the Barriers: An Approach to the Study of How Women's Issues are kept from the Political Agenda," in *Women's Views of the Political World of Men,* ed. Judith H. Stiehm (Dobbs Ferry, N.Y., 1984).

7. This phrase owes its inspiration to Jürgen Habermas, *Legitimation Crisis,* trans. Thomas McCarthy (Boston, 1975).

8. I owe this phrase to Thomas McCarthy (personal communication).

9. Erie, Rein, and Wiget, "Women and the Reagan Revolution"; and Barbara J. Nelson, "Women's Poverty and Women's Citizenship: Some Political Consequences of Economic Marginality," *Signs: Journal of Women in Culture and Society* 10, no. 2 (Winter 1984): 209–31.

10. Nelson, "Women's Poverty and Women's Citizenship."

11. Erie, Rein, and Wiget, "Women and the Reagan Revolution"; and Nelson, "Women's Poverty and Women's Citizenship."

12. Erie, Rein, and Wiget, "Women and the Reagan Revolution."

13. Ibid.

14. Ehrenreich and Piven, "The Feminization of Poverty."

15. Hilary Land, "Who Cares for the Family?" *Journal of Social Policy* 7, no. 3 (July 1978): 257–84.

16. I owe the phrase "gender subtext" to Dorothy Smith "The Gender Subtext of Power" (Ontario Institute for Studies in Education, Toronto, 1984). A number of writers have noticed the two-tiered character of the U.S. social-welfare system. Andrew Hacker ("'Welfare': The Future of an Illusion," *New York Review of Books,* 28 February 1985, 37–43) correlates the dualism with class but not with gender. Diana Pearce ("Women, Work, and Welfare") and Erie, Rein, and Wiget ("Women and the Reagan Revolution") correlate the dualism with gender and with the dual labor market, itself gender-correlated. Barbara Nelson ("Women's Poverty and Women's Citizenship") correlates the dualism with gender, the dual labor market, and the sexual division of paid *and unpaid* labor. My account owes a great deal to all of these writers, especially to Barbara Nelson.

17. Hilary Land ("Who Cares for the Family?") identifies similar assumptions at work in the British social-welfare system. My formulation of them is much indebted to her.

18. Pearce, "Women, Work, and Welfare."

19. Nelson, "Women's Poverty and Women's Citizenship"; and Erie, Rein, and Wiget, "Women and the Reagan Revolution."

20. C. B. MacPherson, *The Political Theory of Possessive Individualism: Hobbes to Locke* (New York, 1964).

21. I owe these formulations to Virginia Held (personal communication).

22. Pearce, "Women, Work, and Welfare."

23. It should be noted that I am here taking issue with the view of some left theorists that "decommodification" in the form of in kind social-welfare benefits represents an emancipatory or progressive development. In the context of a two-tiered welfare system like the one described here, this assumption is clearly false, since in kind benefits are qualitatively and quantitatively inferior to the corresponding commodities and since they function to stigmatize those who receive them.

24. Carol B. Stack, *All Our Kin: Strategies for Survival in a Black Community* (New York, 1974).

25. Marcel Mauss, *The Gift: Forms and Functions of Exchange in Archaic Societies,* trans. Ian Cunnison (New York, 1967).

26. This term echoes Louis Althusser's term, "ideological state apparatus." ("Ideology and Ideological State Apparatuses: Notes towards an Investigation," in *Essays on Ideology,* trans. Ben Brewster [London, 1984]). Certainly, the U.S. social-welfare system as described in the present section of this paper counts as an "ISA" in Althusser's sense. However, I prefer the term 'juridical-administrative-therapeutic state apparatus' as more concrete and descriptive of the specific ways in which welfare programs produce and reproduce ideology. In general, then, a JAT can be understood as a subclass of an ISA. On the other hand, Althusserian-like terminology aside, readers will find that the account in this section owes more to Michel Foucault (*Discipline and Punish: The Birth of the Prison,* trans. Alan Sheridan [New York, 1979]) and Jürgen Habermas (*Theorie des kommunikativen Handelns,* vol. 2, *Zur Kritik der funktionalistischen Vernunft* [Frankfurt on Main, 1981]) than to Althusser. Of course, neither Habermas nor Foucault is sensitive to the gendered character of social-welfare programs. For a critique of Habermas in this respect, see Chapter 6 of this volume. For my views about Foucault, see Chapters 1, 2, and 3.

27. Habermas, *Theorie des kommunikativen Handelns,* vol. 2.

28. Ibid.

29. Prudence Mors Rains, *Becoming an Unwed Mother: A Sociological Account* (Chicago, 1971).

30. These formulations owe much to Jürgen Habermas, *Legitmation Crisis,* and *Theorie des Kommunikativen Handelns,* vol. 2.

31. Habermas, *Legitimation Crisis,* and *Theorie des Kommunikativen Handelns,* vol. 2.

32. I borrow the term 'social' from Hannah Arendt (*The Human Condition* [Chicago, 1958]). However, my use of it differs from hers in several important ways. First, Arendt and I both understand the social as a historically emergent societal space specific to modernity. And we both understand the emergence of the social as tending to undercut or blur an earlier, more distinct separation of public and private spheres. But she treats the emergence of the social as a fall or lapse, and she valorizes the earlier separation of public and private as a preferred state of affairs appropriate to "the human condition." I, on the other hand, make no assumptions about the human condition; nor do I regret the passing of the private/public separation; nor do I consider the emergence of the social a fall or lapse. Second, Arendt and I agree that one salient, defining feature of the social is the emergence of heretofore "private" needs into public view. Arendt, however, treats this as a violation of the proper order of things: she assumes that needs are wholly natural and are forever doomed to be things of brute compulsion. Thus, she supposes that needs can have no genuinely political dimension and that their emergence from the private sphere into the social spells the death of authentic politics. I, on the other hand, assume that needs are irreducibly interpretive and that need interpretations are in principle contestable. It follows from my view that the emergence of needs from the "private" into the social is a generally positive development, since such needs thereby lose their illusory aura of naturalness as their interpretations become subject to critique and contestation. I, therefore, suppose that this represents the (possible) flourishing of politics, rather than the (necessary) death of politics. Finally, Arendt assumes that the emergence of the social and of public concern with needs necessarily means the triumph of administration and instrumental reason. I, on the other hand, assume that instrumental reason represents only one possible way of defining and addressing social needs and that administration represents only one possible way of institutionalizing the social. Thus, I would argue for the existence of another possibility: an alternative socialist-feminist, dialogical mode of need interpretation and a participatory-democratic institutionalization of the social.

33. See Chapter 8 of this volume for a fuller development of these ideas.

34. Theda Skocpol, "Political Response to Capitalist Crisis: Neo-Marxist Theories of the State and the Case of the New Deal," *Politics and Society* 10 (1980): 155–201.

Chapter 8
Struggle over Needs: Outline of a Socialist-Feminist Critical Theory of Late Captialist Political Culture

*Need is also a political instrument, meticulously prepared,
calculated, and used.*
—Michel Foucault, *Discipline and Punish*[1]

In late capitalist welfare state societies, talk about people's needs is an important species of political discourse. We argue, in the United States, for example, about whether the government should provide for citizens' needs. Thus, feminists claim there should be state provision of parents' day-care needs, while social conservatives insists on *children's* needs for their mothers' care, and economic conservatives claim that the market, not the government, is the best institution for meeting needs. Likewise, Americans also argue about whether existing social-welfare programs really do meet the needs they purport to satisfy or whether, instead, they misconstrue those needs. For example, right-wing critics claim that Aid to Families with Dependent Children destroys the incentive to work and undermines the family. Left critics, in contrast, oppose workfare proposals as coercive and punitive, while many poor women with young children say they want to work at good-paying jobs. All these cases involve disputes about what exactly various groups of people really do need and about who should have the last word in such matters. In all these cases, moreover, needs talk functions as a medium for the making and contesting of political claims: it is an idiom in which political

Many of the ideas in this paper were first developed in my "Social Movements versus Disciplinary Bureaucracies" (CHS Occasional Paper, no. 8, Center for Humanistic Studies, University of Minnesota, 1987). I am grateful for helpful comments from Sandra Bartky, Linda Gordon, Paul Mattick, Frank Michelman, Martha Minow, Linda Nicholson, and Iris Young. The Mary Ingraham Bunting Institute of Radcliffe College provided crucial financial support and a utopian working situation.

conflict is played out and through which inequalities are symbolically elaborated and challenged.

Talk about needs has not always been central to Western political culture; it has often been considered antithetical to politics and relegated to the margins of political life. However, in welfare state societies needs talk has been institutionalized as a major vocabulary of political discourse.[2] It coexists, albeit often uneasily, with talk about rights and interests at the very center of political life. Indeed, this peculiar juxtaposition of a discourse about needs with discourses about rights and interests is one of the distinctive marks of late capitalist political culture.

Feminists (and others) who aim to intervene in this culture could benefit from considering the following questions: Why has needs talk become so prominent in the political culture of welfare state societies? What is the relation between this development and changes in late capitalist social structure? What does the emergence of the needs idiom imply about shifts in the boundaries between "political," "economic," and "domestic" spheres of life? Does it betoken an extension of the political sphere or, rather, a colonization of that domain by newer modes of power and social control? What are the major varieties of needs talk and how do they interact polemically with one another? What opportunities and/or obstacles does the needs idiom pose for movements, like feminism, that seek far-reaching social transformation?

In what follows, I outline an approach for thinking about such questions rather than proposing definitive answers to them. What I have to say falls into five parts. In section 1, I suggest a break with standard theoretical approaches by shifting the focus of inquiry from needs to discourses about needs, from the distribution of need satisfactions to "the politics of need interpretation." Accordingly, I propose a model of social discourse designed to bring into relief the contested character of needs talk in welfare state societies. Then, in section 2, I relate this discourse model to social-structural considerations, especially to shifts in the boundaries between "political," "economic," and "domestic" or "personal" spheres of life. In section 3, I identify three major strands of needs talk in late capitalist political culture, and I map some of the ways in which they compete for potential adherents. In section 4, I apply the model to some concrete cases of contemporary needs politics in the United States. Finally, in a brief conclusion, I consider some moral and epistemological issues raised by the phenomenon of needs talk.

1

Let me begin by explaining some of the peculiarities of the approach I am proposing. In my approach, the focus of inquiry is not needs but rather *discourses* about needs. The point is to shift our angle of vision on the politics of needs.

Usually the politics of needs is understood as pertaining to the distribution of satisfactions. In my approach, by contrast, the focus is *the politics of need interpretation*.

My reason for focusing on discourses and interpretation is to bring into view the contextual and contested character of needs claims. As many theorists have noted, needs claims have a relational structure; implicitly or explicitly, they have the form "A needs *x* in order to *y*." Now, this structure poses no problems when we are considering very general, or "thin," needs such as food or shelter *simpliciter*. Thus, we can uncontroversially say that homeless people, like all people who live in nontropical climates, need shelter in order to live. And most people will infer that governments, as guarantors of life and liberty, have a responsibility to provide for this need. However, as soon as we descend to a lesser level of generality, needs claims become far more controversial. What, more "thickly," do homeless people need in order to be sheltered from the cold? What specific forms of provision are entailed once we acknowledge their very general, thin need? Do homeless people need forbearance, so that they may sleep undisturbed next to a hot-air vent on a street corner? A space in a subway tunnel or a bus terminal? A bed in a temporary shelter? A permanent home? Suppose we say the latter. What kind of permanent housing do homeless people need? Rental units in high-rises in central city areas remote from good schools, discount shopping, and job opportunities? Single-family homes designed for single-earner, two-parent families? And what else do homeless people need in order to have permanent homes? Rent subsidies? Income supports? Jobs? Job training and education? Day care? Finally, what is needed, at the level of housing policy, in order to insure an adequate stock of affordable housing? Tax incentives to encourage private investment in low income housing? Concentrated or scatter-site public housing projects within a generally commodified housing environment? Rent control? Decommodification of urban housing?

We could continue proliferating such questions indefinitely. And we would, at the same time, be proliferating controversy. That is precisely the point about needs claims. These claims tend to be nested, connected to one another in ramified chains of "in-order-to" relations. Moreover, when these chains are unraveled in the course of political disputes, disagreements usually deepen rather than abate. Precisely how such chains are unraveled depends on what the interlocutors share in the way of background assumptions. Does it go without saying that policy designed to deal with homelessness must not challenge the basic ownership and investment structure of urban real estate? Or is that a point at which people's assumptions and commitments diverge?

It is the implication of needs claims in contested networks of in-order-to relations to which I call attention when I speak of the politics of need interpretation. Thin theories of needs that do not undertake to explore such networks cannot shed much light on the politics of needs. Such theories assume that the politics of needs concerns only whether various predefined needs will or will not be provided for. As a result, they deflect attention from a number of important political questions.[3] First, they take the *interpretation* of people's needs as simply given and unproblematic; they thus occlude the interpretive dimension of needs politics, the fact that not just satisfactions but *need interpretations* are politically contested. Second, they assume that it doesn't matter who interprets the needs in question and from what perspective and in the light of what interests; they thus overlook the fact that *who* gets to establish authoritative thick definitions of people's needs is itself a political stake. Third, they take for granted that the socially authorized forms of public discourse available for interpreting people's needs are adequate and fair; they thus neglect the question of whether these forms of public discourse are skewed in favor of the self-interpretations and interests of dominant social groups and, so, work to the disadvantage of subordinate or oppositional groups — they occlude, in other words, the fact that the means of public discourse themselves may be at issue in needs politics.[4] Fourth, such theories fail to problematize the social and institutional logic of processes of need interpretation; they thus neglect such important political questions as, Where in society, in what institutions, are authoritative need interpretations developed? and What sorts of social relations are in force among the interlocutors or co-interpreters?

In order to remedy these blind spots, I propose a more politically critical, discourse-oriented alternative. I take the politics of needs to comprise three moments that are analytically distinct but interrelated in practice. The first is the struggle to establish or deny the political status of a given need, the struggle to validate the need as a matter of legitimate political concern or to enclave it as a nonpolitical matter. The second is the struggle over the interpretation of the need, the struggle for the power to define it and, so, to determine what would satisfy it. The third moment is the struggle over the satisfaction of the need, the struggle to secure or withhold provision.

Now, a focus on the politics of need interpretation requires a model of social discourse. The model I have developed foregrounds the multivalent and contested character of needs talk, the fact that in welfare state societies we encounter a plurality of competing ways of talking about people's needs. The model theorizes what I call "the sociocultural means of interpretation and communication" (MIC). By this I mean the historically and culturally specific ensemble of discursive resources available to members of a given social collectivity in pressing claims against one another. Included among these resources are the following:

1. The officially recognized idioms in which one can press claims; for example, needs talk, rights talk, interests talk
2. The vocabularies available for instantiating claims in these recognized idioms; thus, with respect to needs talk, What are the vocabularies available for interpreting and communicating one's needs? For example, therapeutic vocab-

ularies, administrative vocabularies, religious vocabularies, feminist vocabularies, socialist vocabularies

3. The paradigms of argumentation accepted as authoritative in adjudicating conflicting claims; thus, with respect to needs talk, How are conflicts over the interpretation of needs resolved? By appeals to scientific experts? By brokered compromises? By voting according to majority rule? By privileging the interpretations of those whose needs are in question?

4. The narrative conventions available for constructing the individual and collective stories that are constitutive of people's social identities

5. Modes of subjectification; the ways in which various discourses position the people to whom they are addressed as specific sorts of subjects endowed with specific sorts of capacities for action; for example, as "normal" or "deviant," as causally conditioned or freely self-determining, as victims or as potential activists, as unique individuals or as members of social groups[5]

Now, in welfare state societies, there are a plurality of forms of association, roles, groups, institutions, and discourses. Thus, the means of interpretation and communication are not all of a piece. They do not constitute a coherent, monolithic web but rather a heterogeneous, polyglot field of diverse possibilities and alternatives. In fact, in welfare state societies, discourses about needs typically make at least implicit reference to alternative interpretations. Particular claims about needs are "internally dialogized"; implicitly or explicitly they evoke resonances of competing need interpretations.[6] They therefore allude to a conflict of need interpretations. For example, groups seeking to restrict or outlaw abortion counterpose "the sanctity of life" to the "mere convenience" of "career women"; thus, they cast their claims in terms that refer, however disparagingly, to feminist interpretations of reproductive needs.[7]

Of course, late capitalist societies are not simply pluralist. Rather, they are stratified, differentiated into social groups with unequal status, power, and access to resources, traversed by pervasive axes of inequality along lines of class, gender, race, ethnicity, and age. The MIC in these societies are also stratified, organized in ways that are congruent with societal patterns of dominance and subordination.

It follows that we must distinguish those elements of the MIC that are hegemonic, authorized, and officially sanctioned, on the one hand, from those that are nonhegemonic, disqualified, and discounted, on the other hand. Some ways of talking about needs are institutionalized in the central discursive arenas of late capitalist societies: parliaments, academies, courts, and the mass circulation media. Other ways of talking about needs are enclaved as subcultural sociolects and normally excluded from the central discursive arenas.[8] For example, moralistic and scientific discourses about the needs of people with AIDS, and of people at risk with respect to AIDS, are well represented on government commissions; in contrast, gay and lesbian rights activists' interpretations of those needs are largely excluded.

From this perspective, needs talk appears as a site of struggle where groups with unequal discursive (and nondiscursive) resources compete to establish as hegemonic their respective interpretations of legitimate social needs. Dominant groups articulate need interpretations intended to exclude, defuse, and/or co-opt counterinterpretations. Subordinate or oppositional groups, on the other hand, articulate need interpretations intended to challenge, displace, and/or modify dominant ones. In neither case are the interpretations simply "representations." In both cases, rather, they are acts and interventions.[9]

2

Now I should like to situate the discourse model I have just sketched with respect to some social-structural features of late capitalist societies. Here, I seek to relate the rise of politicized needs talk to shifts in the boundaries separating "political," "economic," and "domestic" dimensions of life. However, unlike many social theorists, I shall treat the terms 'political,' 'economic', and 'domestic' as cultural classifications and ideological labels rather than as designations of structures, spheres, or things.[10]

Let me begin by noting that the terms 'politics' and 'political' are highly contested and have a number of different senses.[11] In the present context, two senses in particular are the most important. First, there is the institutional sense, in which a matter is deemed "political" if it is handled directly in the institutions of the official governmental system, including parliaments, administrative apparatuses, and the like. In this sense, what is "political" — call it "official political" — contrasts with what is handled in institutions like "the family" and "the economy," which are defined as being outside the official political system even though they are in actuality underpinned and regulated by it. Second, there is the discourse sense, in which something is "political" if it is contested across a range of different discursive arenas and among a range of different publics. In this sense, what is "political" — call it "discursive-political" or "politicized" — contrasts both with what is not contested in public at all and with what is contested only in relatively specialized, enclaved, and/or segmented publics. These two senses are not unrelated. In democratic theory, if not always in practice, a matter does not usually become subject to legitimate state intervention until it has been debated across a wide range of discourse publics.

In general, there are no a priori constraints dictating that some matters simply are intrinsically political and others simply are intrinsically not. As a matter of fact, these boundaries are drawn differently from culture to culture and from historical period to historical period. For example, reproduction became an intensely political matter in the 1890s in the United States amid a panic about "race suicide.'' By the 1940s, however, there was a consensus that birth control was a ''private'' matter. Finally, with the emergence of the women's movement in the 1960s, reproduction was repoliticized.[12]

However, it would be misleading to suggest that for any society in any period the boundary between what is political and what is not is simply fixed or given. On the contrary, this boundary may itself be an object of conflict. For example, struggles over Poor Law ''reform'' in nineteenth-century England were also conflicts about the scope of the political. And as I shall argue shortly, one of the primary stakes of social conflict in late capitalist societies is precisely where the limits of the political will be drawn.

Let me spell out some of the presuppositions and implications of the discourse sense of 'politics'. This sense stipulates that a matter is ''political'' if it is contested across a range of different discursive arenas and among a range of different discourse publics. Note, therefore, that it depends upon the ideal of discursive publicity. However, in this conception publicity is not understood in a simple unitary way as the undifferentiated opposite of discursive privacy. Rather, publicity is understood to be differentiated, on the assumption that it is possible to identify a plurality of distinct discourse publics and to theorize the relations among them.

Clearly, publics can be distinguished along a number of different axes, for example, by ideology (the readership of the *Nation* versus the readership of the *Public Interest*), by stratification principles like gender (the viewers of ''Cagney and Lacey'' versus the viewers of ''Monday Night Football'') and class (the readership of the *New York Times* versus that of the *New York Post*), by profession (the membership of the American Economic Association versus that of the American Bar Association), by central mobilizing issue (the nuclear freeze movement versus the ''pro-life'' movement).

Publics can also be distinguished in terms of relative power. Some are large, authoritative, and able to set the terms of debate for many of the rest. Others, by contrast, are small, self-enclosed, and enclaved, unable to make much of a mark beyond their own borders. Publics of the former sort are often able to take the lead in the formation of hegemonic blocs: concatenations of different publics that together construct the ''common sense'' of the day. As a result, such leading publics usually have a heavy hand in defining what is ''political'' in the discourse sense. They can politicize an issue simply by entertaining constestation about it, since such contestation will be transmitted as a matter of course to and through other allied and opposing publics. Smaller, counterhegemonic publics, by contrast, generally lack the power to politicize issues in this way. When they succeed in fomenting widespread contestation over what previously was not ''political,'' it is usually by far slower and more laborious means. In general, it is the relative power of various publics that determines the outcome of struggles over the boundaries of the political.

Now, how should we conceptualize the politicization of needs in late capitalist societies? Clearly, this involves processes whereby some matters break out of zones of discursive privacy and out of specialized or enclaved publics so as to become focuses of generalized contestation. When this happens, previously taken-for-granted interpretations of these matters are called into question, and heretofore reified chains of in-order-to relations become subject to dispute.

What are the zones of privacy and the specialized publics that previously enveloped newly politicized needs in late capitalist societies? What are the institutions in which these needs were enclaved and depoliticized, where their interpretations were reified by being embedded in taken-for-granted networks of in-order-to relations?

In male-dominated, capitalist societies, what is "political" is normally defined contrastively over against what is "economic" and what is "domestic" or "personal." Here, then, we can identify two principal sets of institutions that depoliticize social discourses: they are, first, domestic institutions, especially the normative domestic form, namely, the modern restricted male-headed nuclear family; and, second, official economic capitalist system institutions, especially paid workplaces, markets, credit mechanisms and "private" enterprises and corporations.[13] Domestic institutions depoliticize certain matters by personalizing and/or familializing them; they cast these as private-domestic or personal-familial matters in contradistinction to public, political matters. Official economic capitalist system institutions, on the other hand, depoliticize certain matters by economizing them; the issues in question here are cast as impersonal market imperatives, or as "private" ownership prerogatives, or as technical problems for managers and planners, all in contradistinction to political matters. In both cases, the result is a foreshortening of chains of in-order-to relations for interpreting people's needs; interpretive chains are truncated and prevented from spilling across the boundaries separating "the domestic" and "the economic" from "the political."

Clearly, domestic institutions and official economic system institutions differ in many important respects. However, in *these* respects they are exactly on a par with one another: both enclave certain matters into specialized discursive arenas; both thereby shield such matters from generalized contestation and from widely disseminated conflicts of interpretation; and, as a result, both entrench as authoritative certain specific interpretations of needs by embedding them in certain specific, but largely unquestioned, chains of in-order-to relations.

Since both domestic and official economic system institutions support relations of dominance and subordination, the specific interpretations they naturalize usually tend, on the whole, to advantage dominant groups and individuals and to disadvantage their subordinates. If wife battering, for example, is enclaved as a "personal" or "domestic" matter within male-headed restricted families and if public discourse about this phenomenon is canalized into specialized publics associated with, say, family law, social work, and the sociology and psychology of "deviancy," then this serves to reproduce gender dominance and subordination.

Similarly, if questions of workplace democracy are enclaved as "economic" or "managerial" problems in profit-oriented, hierarchically managed paid workplaces and if discourse about these questions is shunted into specialized publics associated with, say, "industrial relations" sociology, labor law, and "management science," then this serves to perpetuate class (and usually also gender and race) dominance and subordination.

As a result of these processes, members of subordinated groups commonly internalize need interpretations that work to their own disadvantage. However, sometimes culturally dominant need interpretations are superimposed upon latent or embryonic oppositional interpretations. This is most likely where there persist, however fragmentedly, subculturally transmitted traditions of resistance, as in some sections of the U.S. labor movement and in the historical memory of many African-Americans. Moreover, under special circumstances, hard to specify theoretically, processes of depoliticization are disrupted. At that point dominant classifications of needs as "economic" or "domestic" — as opposed to "political" — come to lose their "self-evidence," and alternative, oppositional, and *politicized* interpretations emerge in their stead.[14]

In any case, family and official economy are the principal depoliticizing enclaves that needs must exceed in order to become "political" in the discourse sense in male-dominated, capitalist societies. Thus, the emergence of needs talk as a political idiom in these societies is the other side of the increased permeability of domestic and official economic institutions, their growing inability fully to depoliticize certain matters. The politicized needs at issue in late capitalist societies, then, are "leaky" or "runaway" needs: they are needs that have broken out of the discursive enclaves constructed in and around domestic and official economic institutions.

Runaway needs are a species of *excess* with respect to the normative modern domestic and economic institutions. Initially, at least, they bear the stamp of those institutions, remaining embedded in conventional chains of in-order-to relations. For example, many runaway needs are colored by the assumption that "the domestic" is supposed to be separated from "the economic" in male-dominated, capitalist societies. Thus, throughout most of U.S. history, child care has been cast as a "domestic" rather than an "economic" need, it has been interpreted as the need of children for the full-time care of their mothers rather than as the need of workers for time away from their children, and its satisfaction has been construed along the lines of "mothers' pensions" rather than of day care.[15] Here, the assumption of separate spheres truncates possible chains of in-order-to relations that would yield alternative interpretations of social needs.

Now, where do runaway needs run to when they break out of domestic or official economic enclaves? I propose that runaway needs enter a historically specific and relatively new societal arena. Following Hannah Arendt, I call this arena "the social" in order to mark its noncoincidence with the family, the official economy, and the state.[16] As a site of contested discourse about runaway needs, "the social" cuts across these traditional divisions. It is an arena of conflict among rival interpretations of needs embedded in rival chains of in-order-to relations.[17]

As I conceive it, the social is a switch point for the meeting of heterogeneous contestants associated with a wide range of different discourse publics. These contestants range from proponents of politicization to defenders of (re)depoliticization, from loosely organized social movements to members of specialized, expert publics in and around the social state. Moreover, they vary greatly in relative power. Some are associated with leading publics capable of setting the terms of political debate; others, by contrast, are linked to enclaved publics and must oscillate between marginalization and co-optation.

The social is also the site where successfully politicized runaway needs get translated into claims for government provision. Here, rival need interpretations are transformed into rival programmatic conceptions, rival alliances are forged around rival policy proposals, and unequally endowed groups compete to shape the formal policy agenda. For example, in the United States today, various interest groups, movements, professional associations, and parties are scrambling for formulations around which to build alliances sufficiently powerful to dictate the shape of impending welfare "reform."

Eventually, if and when such contests are (at least temporarily) resolved, runaway needs may become objects of state intervention. Then, they become targets and levers for various strategies of crisis management. They also become the *raisons d'être* for the proliferation of the various agencies constituting the social state.[18] These agencies are engaged in regulating, and/or funding, and/or providing the satisfaction of social needs—and in so doing, they are in the business of interpreting, as well as of satisfying, the needs in question. For example, the U.S. social-welfare system is currently divided into two gender-linked and unequal subsystems: an implicitly "masculine" social insurance subsystem tied to "primary" labor force participation and geared to (white male) "breadwinners"; and an implicitly "feminine" relief subsystem tied to household income and geared to homemaker-mothers and their "defective" (that is, female-headed) families. With the underlying (but counterfactual) assumption of "separate spheres," the two subsystems differ markedly in the degree of autonomy, rights, and presumption of desert they accord beneficiaries, as well as in their funding base, mode of administration, and character and level of benefits.[19] Thus, the various agencies comprising the social-welfare system provide more than material aid. They also provide clients, and the public at large, with a tacit but powerful interpretive map of normative, differentially valued gender roles and gendered needs. Consequently, the different branches of the social state, too, are players in the politics of need interpretation.[20]

To summarize: in late capitalist societies, runaway needs that have broken out of domestic or official economic enclaves enter that hybrid discursive space that Arendt aptly dubbed "the social." They may then become focuses of state intervention geared to crisis management. These needs are thus markers of major social-structural shifts in the boundaries separating what are classified as "political," "economic," and "domestic" or "personal" spheres of life.

3

Now I would like to propose a scheme for classifying the many varieties of needs talk in late capitalist societies. The point is to identify some distinct types of discourse and to map the lines along which they compete. This, in turn, will permit us to theorize some basic axes of needs politics in welfare state societies.

I suggest there are three major kinds of needs discourses in late capitalist societies. First, there are what I call "oppositional" forms of needs talk, which arise when needs are politicized "from below." These contribute to the crystallization of new social identities on the part of subordinated social groups. Second, there are what I call "reprivatization" discourses, which emerge in response to the first. These articulate entrenched need interpretations that could previously go without saying. Finally, there are what I call "expert" need discourses, which link popular movements to the state. These can best be understood in the context of "social problem solving," institution building, and professional class formation. In general, it is the polemical interaction of these three kinds of needs talk that structures the politics of needs in late capitalist societies.[21]

Let us look first at the politicization of runaway needs via oppositional discourses. Here, needs become politicized when, for example, women, workers, and/or peoples of color come to contest the subordinate identities and roles, the traditional, reified, and disadvantageous need interpretations previously assigned to and/or embraced by them. By insisting on speaking publicly of heretofore depoliticized needs, by claiming for these needs the status of legitimate political issues, such persons and groups do several things simultaneously. First, they contest the established boundaries separating "politics" from "economics" and "domestics." Second, they offer alternative interpretations of their needs embedded in alternative chains of in-order-to relations. Third, they create new discourse publics from which they try to disseminate their interpretations of their needs throughout a wide range of different discourse publics. Finally, they challenge, modify, and/or displace hegemonic elements of the means of interpretation and communication; they invent new forms of discourse for interpreting their needs.

In oppositional discourses, needs talk is a moment in the self-constitution of new collective agents or social movements. For example, in the current wave of feminist ferment, groups of women have politicized and reinterpreted various needs, have instituted new vocabularies and forms of address, and, so, have become "women" in a different, though not uncontested or univocal, sense. By speaking publicly the heretofore unspeakable, by coining terms like 'sexism', 'sexual harassment', 'marital, date, and acquaintance rape', 'labor force sex-segregation', 'the double shift', 'wife battering', and so on, feminist women have become "women" in the sense of a discursively self-constituted political collectivity, albeit a very heterogeneous and fractured one.[22]

Of course, the politicization of needs in oppositional discourses does not go uncontested. One type of resistance involves defense of the established boundaries separating "political," "economic," and "domestic" spheres by means of "reprivatization" discourses. Institutionally, 'reprivatization' designates initiatives aimed at dismantling or cutting back social-welfare services, selling off nationalized assets, and/or deregulating "private" enterprise; discursively, it means depoliticization. Thus, in reprivatization discourses, speakers oppose state provision of runaway needs, and they seek to contain forms of needs talk that threaten to spill across a wide range of discourse publics. Reprivatizers may insist, for example, that domestic battery is not a legitimate subject of political discourse but a familial or religious matter, or, to take a different example, that a factory closing is not a political question but an unimpeachable prerogative of "private" ownership or an unassailable imperative of an impersonal market mechanism. In both cases, the speakers are contesting the breakout of runaway needs and are trying to (re)depoliticize them.

Interestingly, reprivatization discourses blend the old and the new. On the one hand, they seem merely to render explicit those need interpretations that could earlier go without saying. But, on the other hand, by the very act of articulating such interpretations, they simultaneously modify them. Because reprivatization discourses respond to competing, oppositional interpretations, they are internally dialogized, incorporating references to the alternatives they resist, even while rejecting them. For example, although "pro-family" discourses of the social New Right are explicitly antifeminist, some of them incorporate in a depoliticized form feminist-inspired motifs implying women's right to sexual pleasure and to emotional support from their husbands.[23]

In defending the established social division of discourses, reprivatization discourses deny the claims of oppositional movements for the legitimate political status of runaway needs. However, in so doing, they tend further to politicize those needs in the sense of increasing their cathectedness as focuses of contestation. Moreover, in some cases reprivatization discourses, too, become vehicles for mobilizing social movements and for reshaping social identities. Doubtless the most stunning example is Thatcherism in Britain, where a set of reprivatization discourses articulated in the accents of authoritarian populism has refashioned the subjectivities of a wide range of disaffected constituencies and united them in a powerful coalition.[24]

Together, oppositional discourses and reprivatization discourses define one axis of needs struggle in late capitalist societies. But there is also a second, rather different line of conflict. Here, the focal issue is no longer politicization versus depoliticization but, rather, the interpreted *content* of contested needs once their political status has been successfully secured. And the principal contestants are oppositional social movements and organized interests, like business, that seek to influence public policy.

For example, today in the United States, day care is gaining increasing legitimacy as a political issue. As a result, we are seeing the proliferation of competing interpretations and programmatic conceptions. In one view, day care would serve poor children's needs for "enrichment" and/or moral supervision. In a second, it would serve the middle-class taxpayer's need to get AFDC recipients off the welfare rolls. A third interpretation would shape day care as a measure for increasing the productivity and competitiveness of American business, while yet a fourth would treat it as part of a package of policies aimed at redistributing income and resources to women. Each of these interpretations carries a distinct programmatic orientation with respect to funding, institutional siting and control, service design, and eligibility. As they collide, we see a struggle to shape the hegemonic understanding of day care, which may eventually make its way onto the formal political agenda. Clearly, not just feminist groups but also business interests, trade unions, children's rights advocates, and educators are contestants in this struggle, and they bring to it vast differentials in power.[25]

The struggle for hegemonic need interpretations usually points toward the future involvement of the state. Thus, it anticipates yet a third axis of needs struggle in late capitalist societies. Here, the focal issues concern politics versus administration and the principal contestants are oppositional social movements and the experts and agencies in the orbit of the social state.

Recall that "the social" is a site where needs that have become politicized in the discourse sense become candidates for state-organized provision. Consequently, these needs become the object of yet another group of discourses: the complex of "expert" "public policy" discourses based in various "private," "semi-public," and state institutions.

Expert needs discourses are the vehicles for translating sufficiently politicized runaway needs into objects of potential state intervention. They are closely connected with institutions of knowledge production and utilization,[26] and they include qualitative and especially quantitative social science discourses generated in universities and "think tanks"; legal discourses generated in judicial institutions and their satellite schools, journals, and professional associations; administrative discourses circulated in various agencies of the social state; and therapeutic discourses circulated in public and private medical and social service agencies.

As the term suggests, expert discourses tend to be restricted to specialized publics. Thus, they are associated with professional class formation, institution building, and social "problem solving." But in some cases, such as law and psychotherapy, expert vocabularies and rhetorics are disseminated to a wider spectrum of educated laypersons, some of whom are participants in social movements. Moreover, social movements sometimes manage to co-opt or create critical, oppositional segments of expert discourse publics. For all these reasons, expert discourse publics sometimes acquire a certain porousness. And expert discourses become the *bridge* discourses linking loosely organized social movements with the social state.

Because of this bridge role, the rhetoric of expert needs discourses tends to be administrative. These discourses consist in a series of rewriting operations, procedures for translating politicized needs into administrable needs. Typically, the politicized need is redefined as the correlate of a bureaucratically administrable satisfaction, a "social service." It is specified in terms of an ostensibly general state of affairs that could, in principle, befall anyone—for example, unemployment, disability, death or desertion of a spouse.[27] As a result, the need is decontextualized and recontextualized: on the one hand, it is represented in abstraction from its class, race, and gender specificity and from whatever oppositional meanings it may have acquired in the course of its politicization; on the other hand, it is cast in terms that tacitly presuppose such entrenched, specific background institutions as ("primary" versus "secondary") wage labor, privatized childrearing, and their gender-based separation.

As a result of these expert redefinitions, the people whose needs are in question are repositioned. They become individual "cases" rather than members of social groups or participants in political movements. In addition, they are rendered passive, positioned as potential recipients of predefined services rather than as agents involved in interpreting their needs and shaping their life conditions.

By virtue of this administrative rhetoric, expert needs discourses, too, tend to be depoliticizing. They construe persons simultaneously as rational utility maximizers and as causally conditioned, predictable, and manipulable objects, thereby screening out those dimensions of human agency that involve the construction and deconstruction of social meanings.

Moreover, when expert needs discourses are institutionalized in state apparatuses, they tend to become normalizing, aimed at "reforming," or more often stigmatizing, "deviancy."[28] This sometimes becomes explicit when services incorporate a therapeutic dimension designed to close the gap between clients' recalcitrant self-interpretations and the interpretations embedded in administrative policy.[29] Now the rational-utility-maximizer-cum-causally-conditioned-object becomes, in addition, a deep self to be unraveled therapeutically.[30]

To summarize: when social movements succeed in politicizing previously depoliticized needs, they enter the terrain of the social, where two other kinds of struggles await them. First, they have to contest powerful organized interests bent on shaping hegemonic need interpretations to their own ends. Second, they encounter expert needs discourses in and around the social state. These encounters define two additional axes of needs struggle in late capitalist societies. They are highly complex struggles, since social movements typically seek state provision of their runaway needs even while they tend to oppose administrative and therapeutic need interpretations. Thus, these axes, too, involve conflicts among rival interpretations of social needs and among rival constructions of social identity.

4

Now I would like to apply the model I have been developing to some concrete cases of conflicts of need interpretation. The first example is designed to identify a tendency in welfare state societies whereby the politics of need interpretation devolves into the management of need satisfactions. A second group of examples, by contrast, charts the countertendency that runs from administration to resistance and potentially back to politics.[31]

First, consider the example of the politics of needs surrounding wife battering. Until about fifteen years ago, the term 'wife battering' did not exist. When spoken of publicly at all, this phenomenon was called 'wife beating' and was often treated comically, as in "Have you stopped beating your wife?" Linguistically, it was classed with the disciplining of children and servants as a "domestic" — as opposed to a "political" — matter. Then, feminist activists renamed the practice with a term drawn from criminal law and created a new kind of public discourse. They claimed that battery was not a personal, domestic problem but a systemic, political one; its etiology was not to be traced to individual women's or men's emotional problems but, rather, to the ways these problems refracted pervasive social relations of male dominance and female subordination.

Thus, feminist activists contested established discursive boundaries and politicized a heretofore depoliticized phenomenon. In addition, they reinterpreted the experience of battery and posited a set of associated needs. Here, they situated battered women's needs in a long chain of in-order-to relations that spilled across conventional separations of "spheres"; they claimed that in order to be free from dependence on batterers, battered women needed not just temporary shelter but also jobs paying a "family wage," day care, and affordable permanent housing. Further, feminists created new discourse publics, new spaces and institutions in which such oppositional need interpretations could be developed and from which they could be spread to wider publics. Finally, feminists modified elements of the authorized means of interpretation and communication; they coined new terms of description and analysis and devised new ways of addressing female subjects. In their discourse, battered women were not addressed as individualized victims but as potential feminist activists, members of a politically constituted collectivity.

This discursive intervention was accompanied by feminist efforts to provide for some of the needs they had politicized and reinterpreted. Activists organized battered women's shelters, places of refuge and of consciousness-raising. The organization of these shelters was nonhierarchical; there were no clear lines between staff and users. Many of the counselors and organizers had themselves been battered, and a high percentage of the women who used the shelters went on to counsel other battered women and to become movement activists. Concomitantly, these women came to adopt new self-descriptions. Whereas most had originally blamed themselves and defended their batterers, many came to reject that interpretation in favor of a politicized view that offered them new models of human agency. In addition, these women modified their affiliations and social identifications. Whereas many had originally felt deeply identified with their batterers, they came to affiliate with other women.

This organizing eventually had an impact on wider discursive publics. By the late 1970s, feminists had largely succeeded in establishing domestic violence against women as a legitimate political issue. They managed in some cases to change the attitudes and policies of police and the courts, and they won for this issue a place on the informal political agenda. Now the needs of battered women were sufficiently politicized to become candidates for publicly organized satisfaction. Finally, in several municipalities and localities, movement shelters began receiving local government funding.

From the feminist perspective, this represented a significant victory, but it was not without cost. Municipal funding brought with it a variety of new, administrative constraints ranging from accounting procedures to regulation, accreditation, and professionalization requirements. As a consequence, publicly funded shelters underwent a transformation. Increasingly, they came to be staffed by professional social workers, many of whom had not themselves experienced battery. Thus, a division between professional and client supplanted the more fluid continuum of relations that had characterized the earlier shelters. Moreover, since many social work staffs have been trained to frame problems in a quasi-psychiatric perspective, this perspective structures the practices of many publicly funded shelters even despite the intentions of individual staff members, many of whom are politically committed feminists. Consequently, the practices of such shelters have become more individualizing and less politicized. Battered women tend now to be positioned as clients. They are increasingly psychiatrized, addressed as victims with deep, complicated selves. They are only rarely addressed as potential feminist activists. Increasingly, the language game of therapy has supplanted that of consciousness-raising. And the neutral scientific language of 'spouse abuse' has supplanted more political talk of 'male violence against women'. Finally, the needs of battered women have been substantially reinterpreted. The far-reaching earlier claims for the social and economic prerequisites of independence have tended to give way to a narrower focus on the individual woman's problems of "low self-esteem."[32]

The battered women's shelter case exemplifies one tendency of needs politics in late capitalist societies: the tendency for the politics of need interpretation to devolve into the administration of need satisfaction. However, there is also a countertendency that runs from administration to client resistance and potentially back to politics. I would like now to document this countertendency by discussing four examples of client resistance, examples ranging from the individual, cultural, and informal to the collective, political, and formally organized.

First, individuals may locate some space for maneuver within the administrative framework of a government agency. They may displace and/or modify an agency's official interpretations of their needs, even without mounting an overt challenge. Historian Linda Gordon has uncovered examples of this sort of resistance in the records of child-protection agencies during the Progressive Era.[33] Gordon cites cases in which women who had been beaten by their husbands filed complaints alleging child abuse. Having involved case workers in their situations by invoking an interpreted need that *was* recognized as legitimate and as falling within the agency's jurisdiction, they managed to interest the case workers in a need that was *not* so recognized. In some cases, these women succeeded in securing intervention under the child abuse rubric that provided them some measure of relief from domestic battery. Thus, they informally broadened the agency's jurisdiction to include, indirectly, a hitherto excluded need. While citing the social state's official definition of their need, they simultaneously displaced that definition and brought it closer in line with their own interpretations.

Second, informally organized groups may develop practices and affiliations that are at odds with the social state's way of positioning them as clients. In so doing, they may alter the uses and meanings of benefits provided by government agencies, even without explicitly calling these into question. Anthropologist Carol Stack has documented examples of this sort of resistance in her study of "domestic kin networks" among poor black AFDC recipients in a midwestern city in the late 1960s.[34] Stack describes elaborate kinship arrangements that organize delayed exchanges, or "gifts," of prepared meals, food stamps, cooking, shopping, groceries, sleeping space, cash (including wages and AFDC allowances), transportation, clothing, child care, even children. It is significant that these domestic kin networks span several physically distinct households. This means that AFDC recipients use their benefits beyond the confines of the principal administrative category of government relief programs, namely, "the household." Consequently, these clients circumvent the nuclear-familializing procedures of welfare administration. By utilizing benefits beyond the confines of a "household," they alter the state-defined meanings of those benefits and, thus, of the needs those benefits purport to satisfy. At the same time, they indirectly contest the state's way of positioning them as subjects. Whereas AFDC addressed them as biological mothers who belong to deviant nuclear families that lack male breadwinners, they double that subject-position with another one, namely, members of socially, as opposed to biologically, constituted kin networks who cooperate in coping with dire poverty.

Third, individuals and/or groups may resist therapeutic initiatives of the social state while accepting material aid. They may reject state-sponsored therapeutic constructions of their life stories and capacities for agency and insist instead on alternative narratives and conceptions of identity. Sociologist Prudence Rains has documented an example of this kind of resistance in her comparative study of the "moral careers" of black and white pregnant teenagers in the late 1960s.[35]

Rains contrasts the ways the two groups of young women responded to therapeutic constructions of their experience in two different institutional settings. The young middle-class white women were in an expensive private residential facility. This facility combined traditional services, such as seclusion and a cover for "good girls who had made a mistake," with newer therapeutic services, including required individual and group counseling sessions with psychiatric social workers. In these sessions, the young women were addressed as deep, complicated selves. They were encouraged to regard their pregnancies not as simple "mistakes" but, rather, as unconsciously motivated, meaningful acts expressive of latent emotional problems. This meant that a girl was to interpret her pregnancy—and the sex that was its superficial cause—as a form of acting out, say, a refusal of parental authority or a demand for parental love. She was warned that unless she came to understand and acknowledge these deep, hidden motives, she would likely not succeed in avoiding future "mistakes."

Rains documents the process by which most of the young white women at this facility came to internalize this perspective and to rewrite themselves in the psychiatric idiom. She records the narratives they devised in the course of rewriting their "moral careers." For example:

> "When I first came here I had it all figured out in my mind that Tom . . . had kind of talked me into it and I gave in. I kind of put it all on him. I didn't really accept my own part in it. . . . [H]ere they stressed a lot that if you don't realize why you're here or why you ended up here and the emotional reasons behind it, that it will happen again. . . . I feel now that I have a pretty full understanding of why I did end up here and that there was an emotional reason for it. And I accept my part in it more. It wasn't just him."(93)

This narrative is interesting in several respects. As Rains notes, the exchange of a "mistake" view of the past for a psychiatric view provided certain comforts: the new interpretation "did not merely set aside the past but accounted for it, and accounted for it in ways which allowed girls to believe they would act differently in the future"(94). Thus, the psychiatric view offers the pregnant teenager a model of agency that seems to enhance her capacity for individual self-determination. On the other hand, the narrative is highly selective, avowing some aspects of the past while disavowing others. It plays down the narrator's sexuality, treating her sexual behavior and desires as epiphenomenal "manifestation[s] of other, deeper, and nonsexual emotional needs and problems"(93). In addition, it defuses the potentially explosive issue of consent versus coercion in the teenage heterosexual milieu by excusing Tom and by revising the girl's earlier sense that their intercourse was not consensual. Moreover, the narrative forecloses any question as to the legitimacy of "premarital sex," assuming that for a woman, at least, such sex is morally wrong. Finally, in light of the girls' declarations that they will not need contraceptives when they return home and resume dating, the narrative has yet another meaning. Encapsulating a new awareness of deep emotional problems, it becomes a shield against future pregnancies, a prophylactic. Given these elisions in the story, a skeptic might well conclude that the psychiatric promise of enhanced self-determination is largely illusory.

The relative ease with which Rains's white teenagers internalized the therapeutic interpretation of their situation stands in stark contrast with the resistance offered by her black subjects. The young black women were clients in a nonresidential municipal facility providing prenatal care, schooling, and counseling sessions with a psychiatric social worker. The counseling sessions were similar in intent and design to those at the private residential facility; the young women were encouraged to talk about their feelings and to probe the putative deep, emotional causes of their pregnancies. However, this therapeutic approach was much less successful at the public facility. The young black women resisted the terms of the psychiatric discourse and the language game of question-and-answer employed in the counseling sessions. They disliked the social worker's stance of nondirectiveness and moral neutrality—her unwillingness to say what *she* thought—and they resented what they considered her intrusive, overly personal questions. These girls did not acknowledge her right to question them in this fashion, given that they could not ask "personal" questions of her in turn. Rather, they construed "personal questioning" as a privilege reserved to close friends and intimates under conditions of reciprocity.

Rains documents several dimensions of the young black women's resistance to the "mental health" aspects of the program. In some instances, they openly challenged the rules of the therapeutic language game. In others, they resisted indirectly by humor, quasi-deliberately misunderstanding the social worker's vague, nondirective, yet "personal" questions. For example, one girl construed "How did you get pregnant?'' as a ''stupid'' question and replied, ''Shouldn't you know?''(136).

Some others subjected the constant therapeutic ''How did it feel?'' to an operation that can only be called ''carnivalesque.'' The occasion was a group counseling session for which the case worker was late. The young women assembled for the meeting began speculating as to her whereabouts. One mentioned that Mrs. Eckerd had gone to see a doctor. The conversation continued:

> ''To see if she's pregnant.''
> ''She probably thinks that's where you get babies.''
> ''Maybe the doctor's going to give her a baby.'' . . .
> Bernice then started doing an imitation interview pretending she was a social worker asking questions of a pretend-pregnant Mrs. Eckerd, ''Tell me, how did it feel? Did you like it?''
> This brought a storm of laughter, and everybody started mimicking questions they supposedly had had put to them. Someone said, ''She asked me did I want to put my baby for adoption, and how did it feel?''
> When Mrs. Eckerd finally arrived, May said, ''Why do social workers ask so many questions?''
> Mrs. Eckerd said, ''What kind of questions do you mean, May?''
> Bernice . . . said, ''Like 'How did it feel?''''
> There was an uproar over this.(137)

Thus, Rains's black subjects devised a varied repertoire of strategies for resisting expert, therapeutic constructions of their life stories and capacities for agency. They were keenly aware of the power subtext underlying their interactions with the social worker and of the normalization dimension of the therapeutic initiative. In effect, these young black women blocked efforts to inculcate in them white, middle-class norms of individuality and affectivity. They refused the case worker's inducements to rewrite themselves as psychologized selves, while availing themselves of the health services at the facility. Thus, they made use of those aspects of the agency's program that they considered appropriate to their self-interpreted needs and ignored or sidestepped the others.

Fourth, in addition to informal, ad hoc, strategic and/or cultural forms of resistance, there are also more formally organized, explicitly political, organized kinds. Clients of social-welfare programs may join together *as clients* to challenge administrative interpretations of their needs. They may take hold of the passive, normalized, and individualized or familialized identities fashioned for them in expert discourses and transform them into a basis for collective political action. Frances Fox Piven and Richard A. Cloward have documented an example of this kind of resistance in their account of the process by which AFDC recipients organized the welfare-rights movement of the 1960s.[36] Notwithstanding the atomizing and depoliticizing dimensions of AFDC administration, these women were brought together in welfare waiting rooms. It was as a result of their participation as clients, then, that they came to articulate common grievances and to act together. Thus, the same welfare practices that gave rise to these grievances created the enabling conditions for collective organizing to combat them. As Piven put it, "the structure of the welfare state itself has helped to create new solidarities and generate the political issues that continue to cement and galvanize them."[37]

Conclusion

Let me conclude by flagging some issues that are central to this project but that I have not yet discussed here. In this essay, I have concentrated on social-theoretical issues at the expense of moral and epistemological issues. However, the latter are very important for a project, like mine, that aspires to be a *critical* social theory.

My analysis of needs talk raises two very obvious and pressing philosophical issues. One is the question of whether and how it is possible to distinguish better from worse interpretations of people's needs. The other is the question of the relationship between needs claims and rights. Although I cannot offer full answers to these questions here, I would like to indicate something about how I would approach them. I want also to situate my views in relation to contemporary debates among feminist theorists.

Feminist scholars have demonstrated again and again that authoritative views purporting to be neutral and disinterested actually express the partial and interested perspectives of dominant social groups. In addition, many feminist theorists have made use of poststructuralist approaches that deny the possibility of distinguishing warranted claims from power plays. As a result, there is now a significant strand of relativist sentiment within feminist ranks. At the same time, many other feminists worry that relativism undermines the possibility of political commitment. How, after all, can one argue against the possibility of warranted claims while oneself making such claims as that sexism exists and is unjust?[38]

This issue about relativism surfaces in the present context in the form of the question, Can we distinguish better from worse interpretations of people's needs? Or, since all need interpretations emanate from specific, interested locations in society, are all of them equally compromised?

I claim that we *can* distinguish better from worse interpretations of people's needs. To say that needs are culturally constructed and discursively interpreted is not to say that any need interpretation is as good as any other. On the contrary, it is to underline the importance of an account of interpretive justification. However, I do not think that justification can be understood in traditional objectivist terms as correspondence, as if it were a matter of finding the interpretation that matches the true nature of the need as it really is in itself, independent of any interpretation.[39] Nor do I think that justification can be premised on a preestablished point of epistemic superiority, as if it were a matter of finding the one group in society with the privileged "standpoint."[40]

Then what *should* an account of interpretive justification consist in? In my view, there are at least two distinct kinds of considerations that such an account would have to encompass and to balance. First, there are procedural considerations concerning the social processes by which various competing need interpretations are generated. For example, how exclusive or inclusive are various rival needs discourses? How hierarchical or egalitarian are the relations among the interlocutors? In general, procedural considerations dictate that, all other things being equal, the best need interpretations are those reached by means of communicative processes that most closely approximate ideals of democracy, equality, and fairness.[41]

In addition, considerations of consequences are relevant in justifying need interpretations. This means comparing alternative distributive outcomes of rival interpretations. For example, would widespread acceptance of some given interpretation of a social need disadvantage some groups of people vis-à-vis others? Does the interpretation conform to, rather than challenge, societal patterns of dominance and subordination? Are the rival chains of in-order-to relations to which competing need interpretations belong more or less respectful, as opposed to transgressive, of ideological boundaries that delimit "separate spheres" and thereby rationalize inequality? In general, consequentialist considerations dictate that, all other things being equal, the best need interpretations are those that do not disadvantage some groups of people vis-à-vis others.

In sum, justifying some interpretations of social needs as better than others involves balancing procedural and consequentialist considerations. More simply, it involves balancing democracy and equality.

What, then, of the relationship between needs and rights? This, too, is a controversial issue in contemporary theory. Critical legal theorists have argued that rights claims work against radical social transformation by enshrining tenets of bourgeois individualism. Meanwhile, some feminist moral theorists suggest that an orientation toward responsibilities is preferable to an orientation toward rights.[42] Together, these views might lead some to want to think of needs talk as an alternative to rights talk. On the other hand, many feminists worry that left-wing critiques of rights play into the hands of our political opponents. After all, conservatives traditionally prefer to distribute aid as a matter of need *instead* of right precisely in order to avoid assumptions of entitlement that could carry egalitarian implications. For these reasons, some feminist activists and legal scholars have sought to develop and defend alternative understandings of rights.[43] Their approach might imply that suitably reconstructed rights claims and needs claims could be mutually compatible, even intertranslatable.[44]

Very briefly, I align myself with those who favor translating justified needs claims into social rights. Like many radical critics of existing social-welfare programs, I am committed to opposing the forms of paternalism that arise when needs claims are divorced from rights claims. And unlike some communitarian, socialist, and feminist critics, I do not believe that rights talk is inherently individualistic, bourgeois-liberal, and androcentric — rights talk takes on those properties only when societies establish the *wrong* rights, for example, when the (putative) right to private property is permitted to trump other, social rights.

Moreover, to treat justified needs claims as the bases for new social rights is to begin to overcome obstacles to the effective exercise of some existing rights. It is true, as Marxists and others have claimed, that classical liberal rights to free expression, assembly, and the like are "merely formal." But this says more about the social context in which they are currently embedded than about their "intrinsic" character, for, in a context devoid of poverty, inequality, and oppression, formal liberal rights could be broadened and transformed into substantive rights, say, to collective self-determination.

Finally, I should stress that this work is motivated by the conviction that, for the time being, needs talk is with us for better or worse. For the foreseeable future, political agents, including feminists, will have to operate on a terrain where needs talk is the discursive coin of the realm. But, as I have tried to show, this idiom is neither inherently emancipatory nor inherently repressive. Rather, it is multivalent and contested. The larger aim of my project is to help clarify the prospects for democratic and egalitarian social change by sorting out the emancipatory from the repressive possibilities of needs talk.

Notes

1. Michel Foucault, *Discipline and Punish: The Birth of the Prison,* trans. Alan Sheridan (New York, 1979), 26.

2. In this paper, I shall use the terms 'welfare state societies' and 'late capitalist societies' interchangeably to refer to the industrialized countries of Western Europe and North America in the present period. Of course, the process of welfare state formation begins at different times, proceeds at different rates, and takes different forms in these countries. Still, I assume that it is possible in principle to identify and characterize some features of these societies that transcend such differences. On the other hand, most of the examples invoked here are from the U.S. context, and it is possible that this skews the account. Further comparative work would be needed to determine the precise scope of applicability of the model presented here.

3. For a recent example of the kind of theory I have in mind, see David Braybrooke, *Meeting Needs* (Princeton, 1987). Braybrooke claims that a thin concept of need "can make a substantial contribution to settling upon policies without having to descend into the melee" (68). Thus, he does not take up any of the issues I am about to enumerate.

4. For a fuller discussion of this issue, see my essay "Toward a Discourse Ethic of Solidarity," *Praxis International* 5, no. 4 (January 1986): 425–29.

5. The expression 'mode of subjectification' is inspired by Michel Foucault, although his term is 'mode of subjection' and his usage differs somewhat from mine; see Foucault, "On the Genealogy

of Ethics: An Overview of Work in Progress," *The Foucault Reader,* ed. Paul Rabinow (New York, 1984), 340–73. For another account of this idea of the sociocultural means of interpretation and communication, see my "Toward a Discourse Ethic of Solidarity."

6. The expression 'internally dialogized' comes from Mikhail Bakhtin. By invoking it here, I mean to suggest that the Bakhtinian notion of a "dialogic heteroglossia" (or a cross-referential, multi-voiced field of significations) is more apt as a description of the MIC in complex societies than is the more monolithic Lacanian idea of the Symbolic or the Saussurean idea of a seamless code. However, in claiming that the Bakhtinian conceptions of heteroglossia and dialogization are especially apt with respect to complex, differentiated socieities, including late capitalist welfare state societies, I am intentionally breaking with Bakhtin's own view. He assumed, on the contrary, that these conceptions found their most robust expression in the "carnivalesque" culture of late Medieval Europe and that the subsequent history of Western societies brought a flattening of language and a restriction of dialogic heteroglossia to the specialized, esoteric domain of "the literary." This seems patently false—especially when we recognize that the dialogic, contestatory character of speech is related to the availability in a culture of a plurality of competing discourses and of subject-positions from which to articulate them. Thus, conceptually, one would expect what, I take it, is in fact the case: that speech in complex, differentiated societies would be especially suitable for analysis in terms of these Bakhtinian categories. For the Bakhtinian conceptions of heteroglossia and internal dialogization, see Bakhtin, "Discourse in the Novel," in *The Dialogic Imagination: Four Essays,* ed. Michael Holquist, trans. Caryl Emerson and Holquist (Austin, Tex., 1981), 259–422. For a helpful secondary account, see Dominick LaCapra, "Bakhtin, Marxism, and the Carnivalesque," in *Rethinking Intellectual History* (Ithaca, N.Y., 1983), 294–324. For a critique of the Romantic, antimodernist bias in both Bakhtin and LaCapra, see my "On the Political and the Symbolic: Against the Metaphysics of Textuality," *Enclitic* 9, nos. 1–2 (Spring/Fall 1987): 100–114.

7. See Kristin Luker, *Abortion and the Politics of Motherhood* (Berkeley, 1984).

8. If the previous point was Bakhtinian, this one could be considered Bourdieuian. There is probably no contemporary social theorist who has worked more fruitfully than Pierre Bourdieu at understanding cultural contestation in relation to societal inequality; see Bourdieu, *Outline of a Theory of Practice,* trans. Richard Nice (Cambridge, 1977). See also Bourdieu, *Distinction: A Social Critique of the Judgment of Pure Taste* (Cambridge, Mass., 1979).

9. Here the model aims to marry Bakhtin with Bourdieu.

10. I owe this formulation to Paul Mattick, Jr. For a thoughtful discussion of the advantages of this sort of approach, see his "On *Feminism as Critique*" (Paper read at the Socialist Scholars Conference, New York, 1988).

11. Included among the senses I shall not discuss are: (1) the pejorative colloquial sense according to which a decision is "political" when personal jockeying for power overrides germane substantive considerations; and (2) the radical political-theoretical sense according to which all interactions traversed by relations of power and inequality are "political."

12. Linda Gordon, *Woman's Body, Woman's Right* (New York, 1976).

13. Throughout this paper, I refer to paid workplaces, markets credit systems, and so forth as "*official* economic system institutions" so as to avoid the androcentric implication that domestic institutions are not also "economic." For a discussion of this issue, see my "What's Critical about Critical Theory? The Case of Habermas and Gender," Chapter 6 of this volume.

14. The difficulty in specifying theoretically the conditions under which processes of depoliticization are disrupted stems from the difficulty of relating what are usually, and doubtless misleadingly, considered "economic" and "cultural" "factors." Thus, rational choice models seem to me to err in overweighting "economic" at the expense of "cultural" determinants, as in the (not always accurate) prediction that culturally dominant but ultimately disadvantageous need interpretations lose their hold when economic prosperity heralds reduced inequality and promotes "rising expectations"; see Jon Elster, "Sour Grapes," in *Utilitarianism and Beyond,* ed. Amartya Sen and Bernard Wil-

liams (Cambridge, 1982). An alternative model developed by Jane Jenson emphasizes the cultural-ideological lens through which "economic" effects are filtered. Jenson relates "crises in the mode of regulation" to shifts in cultural "paradigms" that cast into relief previously present but nonemphasized elements of people's social identities; see her "Paradigms and Political Discourse: Labor and Social Policy in the USA and France before 1914" (Working Paper Series, Center for European Studies, Harvard University, Winter 1989).

15. See Sonya Michel, "American Women and the Discourse of the Democratic Family in World War II," in *Behind the Lines: Gender and the Two World Wars*, ed. Margaret Higonnet, Jane Jenson, and Sonya Michel (New Haven, Conn., 1987), and "Women to Women: The Nineteenth-Century Origins of American Child Care Policy" (Paper presented to the Department of History, University of California, Los Angeles, 28 January 1988). For an account of the current U.S. social-welfare system as a two-track, gendered system based on the assumption of separate economic and domestic spheres, see my "Women, Welfare, and the Politics of Need Interpretation," Chapter 7 of this volume.

16. See Hannah Arendt, *The Human Condition* (Chicago, 1958), especially Chap. 2, 22–78. However, it should be noted that my view of "the social" differs signficiantly from Arendt's. Whereas she sees the social as a one-dimensional space wholly under the sway of administration and instrumental reason, I see it as multivalent and contested. Thus, my view incorporates some features of the Gramscian conception of "civil society."

17. It is significant that, in some times and places, the idea of "the social" has been elaborated explicitly as an alternative to "the political." For example, in nineteenth-century England, "the social" was understood as the sphere in which (middle-class) women's supposed distinctive domestic virtues could be diffused for the sake of the larger collective good without suffering the "degradation" of participation in the competitive world of "politics." Thus, "social" work, figured as "municipal motherhood," was heralded as an alternative to suffrage; see Denise Riley, *'Am I That Name?' Feminism and the Category of 'Women' in History* (Minneapolis, 1988). Similarly, the invention of sociology required the conceptualization of an order of "social" interaction distinct from "politics"; see Jacques Donzelot, *The Policing of Families* (New York, 1979).

18. Of course, the social state is not a unitary entity but a multiform, differentiated complex of agencies and apparatuses. In the United States, the social state comprises the welter of agencies that make up, especially, the Department of Labor and the Department of Health and Human Services—or what currently remains of them.

19. For an analysis of the gendered structure of the U.S. social-welfare system, see my "Women, Welfare, and the Politics of Need Interpretation," Chapter 7 of this volume. See also Barbara J. Nelson, "Women's Poverty and Women's Citizenship: Some Political Consequences of Economic Marginality," *Signs: Journal of Women in Culture and Society* 10, no. 2 (1984): 209–31; and Diana Pearce, "Women, Work, and Welfare: The Feminization of Poverty," in *Working Women and Families*, ed. Karen Wolk Feinstein (Beverly Hills, Calif., 1979).

20. For an analysis of U.S. social-welfare agencies as purveyors and enforcers of need interpretations, see "Women, Welfare, and the Politics of Need Interpretation," Chapter 7 of this volume.

21. This picture is at odds with the one implicit in the writings of Foucault. From my perspective, Foucault focuses too single-mindedly on expert, institution-building discourses at the expense of oppositional and reprivatization discourses. Thus, he misses the dimension of constestation among competing discourses and the fact that the outcome is a result of such contestation. For all his theoretical talk about power without a subject, then, Foucault's practice as a social historian is surprisingly traditional in that it treats expert institution builders as in effect the only historical subjects.

22. The point could be reformulated more skeptically as follows: feminists have shaped discourses embodying a claim to speak for "women." In fact, this question of "speaking for 'women'" is currently a burning issue within the feminist movement. For an interesting take on it, see Riley, *'Am I That Name?'* For a thoughtful discussion of the general problem of the constitution and representation (in both senses) of social groups as sociological classes and as collective agents, see Bour-

dieu, "The Social Space and the Genesis of Groups," *Social Science Information* 24, no. 2 (1985): 195–220.

23. See the chapter "Fundamentalist Sex: Hitting below the Bible Belt," in *Re-making Love: The Feminization of Sex,* by Barbara Ehrenreich, Elizabeth Hess, and Gloria Jacobs (New York, 1987). For a fascinating account of "postfeminist" women incorporating feminist motifs into born-again Christianity, see Judith Stacey, "Sexism by a Subtler Name? Postindustrial Conditions and Postfeminist Consciousness in the Silicon Valley," *Socialist Review,* no. 96 (November/December 1987): 7–28.

24. See Stuart Hall, "Moving Right," *Socialist Review,* no. 55 (January–February 1981): 113–37. For an account of New Right reprivatization discourses in the United States, see Barbara Ehrenreich, "The New Right Attack on Social Welfare" in *The Mean Season: The Attack on the Welfare State,* ed. Fred Block, Richard A. Cloward, Barbara Ehrenreich, and Frances Fox Piven (New York, 1987), 161–95.

25. I am indebted to Teresa Ghilarducci for this point (personal communication).

26. In *Discipline and Punish,* Michel Foucault provides a useful account of some elements of the knowledge production apparatuses that contribute to administrative redefinitions of politicized needs. However, Foucault overlooks the role of social movements in politicizing needs and the conflicts of interpretation that arise between such movements and the social state. His account suggests, incorrectly, that policy discourses emanate unidirectionally from specialized, governmental or quasi-governmental, institutions; thus, it misses the contestatory interplay among hegemonic and nonhegemonic, institutionally bound and institutionally unbound, interpretations.

27. Cf. the discussion of the administrative logic of need definition in Jürgen Habermas, *Theorie des kommunikativen Handelns,* vol. 2, *Zur Kritik der funktionalistischen Vernunft* (Frankfurt am Main, 1981), 522–47.

28. See Foucault, *Discipline and Punish,* for an account of the normalizing dimensions of social science and of institutionalized social services.

29. Habermas discusses the therapeutic dimension of welfare state social services in *Theorie des kommunikativen Handelns,* vol. 2, 522–47.

30. In *Discipline and Punish,* Michel Foucault discusses the tendency of social-scientifically informed administrative procedures to posit a deep self. In *The History of Sexuality, Volume I: An Introduction* (trans. Robert Hurley [New York, 1978]), he discusses the positing of a deep self by therapeutic psychiatric discourses.

31. For the sake of simplicity, I shall restrict the examples treated to cases of contestation between two forces only, where one of the contestants is an agency of the social state. Thus, I shall not consider examples of three-sided contestation nor examples of two-sided contestation between competing social movements.

32. For an account of the history of battered women's shelters, see Susan Schechter, *Women and Male Violence: The Visions and Struggles of the Battered Women's Movement* (Boston, 1982).

33. Linda Gordon, "Feminism and Social Control: The Case of Child Abuse and Neglect," in *What Is Feminism? A Re-Examination,* ed. Juliet Mitchell and Ann Oakley (New York, 1986), 63–85, and *Heroes of Their Own Lives: The Politics and History of Family Violence — Boston, 1880–1960* (New York, 1988).

34. Carol B. Stack, *All Our Kin: Strategies for Survival in a Black Community* (New York, 1974).

35. Prudence Mors Rains, *Becoming an Unwed Mother: A Sociological Account* (Chicago, 1971); hereafter cited parenthetically, by page number, in my text. I am indebted to Kathryn Pyne Addelson for bringing Rains's work to my attention.

36. Frances Fox Piven and Richard A. Cloward, *Regulating the Poor: The Functions of Public Welfare* (New York, 1971), 285–340, and *Poor People's Movements* (New York, 1979). Unfortunately, Piven and Cloward's account is gender-blind and, as a consequence, androcentric. For a fem-

inist critique, see Linda Gordon, "What Does Welfare Regulate?" *Social Research* 55, no. 4 (Winter 1988): 610–30. For a more gender-sensitive account of the history of the NWRO, see Guida West, *The National Welfare Rights Movement: The Social Protest of Poor Women* (New York, 1981).

37. Piven, "Women and the State: Ideology, Power, and the Welfare State," *Socialist Review,* no. 74 (March–April 1984): 11–19.

38. For the view that objectivity is just the mask of domination, see Catharine A. MacKinnon, "Feminism, Marxism, Method, and the State: An Agenda for Theory," *Signs: Journal of Women in Culture and Society* 7, no. 3 (Spring 1982): 515–44. For the view that relativism undermines feminism, see Nancy Hartsock, "Rethinking Modernism: Minority vs. Majority Theories," *Cultural Critique* 7 (Fall 1987): 187–206. For a good discussion of the tensions among feminist theorists on this issue (which does not, however, in my view, offer a persuasive resolution), see Sandra Harding, "The Instability of the Analytical Categories of Feminist Theory," *Signs: Journal of Women in Culture and Society* 11, no. 4 (1986): 645–64. For a discussion of related issues raised by the phenomenon of postmoderism, see Nancy Fraser and Linda Nicholson, "Social Criticism without Philosophy: An Encounter between Feminism and Postmodernism," *Theory, Culture, and Society* 5, nos. 2–3 (June 1988): 373–94.

39. For a critique of the correspondence model of truth, see Richard Rorty, *Philosophy and the Mirror of Nature* (Princeton, N.J., 1979).

40. The "standpoint" approach has been developed by Nancy Hartsock. See her *Money, Sex, and Power: Toward a Feminist Historical Materialism* (New York, 1983). For a critique of Hartsock's position, see Harding, "The Instability of the Analytical Categories of Feminist Theory."

41. In its first-order normative content, this formulation is Habermassian. However, I do not wish to follow Habermas in giving it a transcendental or quasi-transcendental metainterpretation. Thus, whereas Habermas purports to ground "communicative ethics" in the conditions of possibility of speech understood universalistically and ahistorically, I consider it a contingently evolved, historically specific possibility; see Habermas, *The Theory of Communicative Action,* vol. 1, *Reason and the Rationalization of Society,* trans. Thomas McCarthy (Boston, 1984); *Communication and the Evolution of Society,* trans. Thomas McCarthy (Boston, 1979); and *Moralbewusstsein und kommunikatives Handeln* (Frankfurt am Main, 1983).

42. For arguments for and against this view, see the essays in *Women and Moral Theory,* ed. E. F. Kittay and Diana T. Meyers (Totowa, N.J., 1987).

43. For an interesting discussion of the uses and abuses of rights discourse, see Elizabeth M. Schneider, "The Dialectic of Rights and Politics: Perspectives from the Women's Movement," *New York University Law Review* 61, no. 4 (October 1986): 589–652. See also Martha Minow, "Interpreting Rights: An Essay for Robert Cover," *Yale Law Journal* 96 no. 8 (July 1987): 1860–1915; and Patricia J. Williams, "Alchemical Notes: Reconstructed Ideals from Deconstructed Rights," *Harvard Civil Rights-Civil Liberties Law Review* 22, no. 2 (Spring 1987): 401–33.

44. I owe this formulation to Martha Minow (personal communication).

Index

Index

Nancy Fraser is an associate professor of philosophy, comparative literature and theory, and women's studies at Northwestern University. She received her M.A. and Ph.D. in philosophy from the City University of New York. Fraser was guest editor, with Sandra Bartky, of a special issue of *Hypatia* (Vol. 3 No. 3, Winter 1989), devoted to French feminist philosophy. Her articles have been published in *Ethics*, *Hypatia*, *New German Critique*, *Praxis International*, *Salmagundi*, *Theory, Culture and Society*, and *Thesis Eleven.*